The Criminal Justice Dictionary

Second edition, revised

compiled by
Erik Beckman
Assistant Professor
School of Criminal Justice
Michigan State University

The
Criminal
Justice
Dictionary

Second edition, revised

1983
pierian press

Library of Congress Card No. 78-72049
ISBN 0-87650-152-8 (pa)
ISBN 0-87650-153-6 (cl)

The Pierian Press
5000 Washtenaw Ave.
Ann Arbor, MI 48104

TABLE OF CONTENTS

INTRODUCTION

Criminal justice has emerged in recent years as more of a dis--cipline in its own right than used to be the case. Practitioners are attempting to upgrade and professionalize the field, and academi--cians and students are studying, analyzing and critiquing the system of criminal justice and its components. Governmental commissions, agencies and funding programs are -- often spurred on by public concern -- scrutinizing, prodding and aiding the criminal justice field on federal, state and local levels.

Such increased attention to criminal justice has made it not only appropriate but indeed necessary for persons wishing to be know--ledgeable about the system to have an understanding of all its com--ponents and their special terminology. No longer is it possible to function professionally with knowledge restricted to only one seg--ment of the system.

It is with these thoughts in mind that this dictionary has been published. Terms from law, police administration, corrections, and criminology have been brought together in one volume. Some of the terms are common, others encountered infrequently. No pre--tense is made that the work is complete; the editor welcomes ad--ditions and suggestions.

It is hoped that this dictionary will make a contribution toward increased understanding of criminal justice, a field full of challenges now and in the years to come.

E.B.
East Lansing, Michigan

KEY TO
ABBREVIATIONS

Parenthetical abbreviations following each term denote the area of criminal justice from which the term is derived.

Cor:	Corrections
Cr's:	Criminalistics
Cr'y:	Criminology
L:	Law
PA:	Police Administration

ABANDON (L)

To give up one's interest in property.

ABANDUN (ABANDUM) (L)

Any thing abandoned, surrendered, or confiscated.

ABATE (L)

To put an end to.

ABANDONMENT (L)

Relinquishment of a claim or privilege.

ABDUCTION (L)

The crime or forcibly, fraudulently or by criminal persuasion, taking away a person; kidnapping.

See also: Kidnapping.

ABET (L)

To aid, encourage, or incite another to commit a criminal offense.

ABEYANCE (L)

In expectation; the condition of a right when there is no person presently entitled to it; a legal delay or holding period.

ABIDE (L)

To submit to or conform to something, i.e., an order of court or a legal decision.

ABJUDICATE (L)

To give away or transfer by force of law.

ABJURE (L)

To renounce.

ABNORMAL BEHAVIOR (Cr'y)

Deviation from socially accepted patterns of behavior, in dif–ferent historical periods, and in different social situations.

ABORTICIDE (Cr'y, L)

The removal of the fetus from the uterus.

ABORTION (Cr'y, L)

The termination of pregnancy before the fetus reaches a point viability or capability of life outside the womb. May be a miscarriage or a premature expulsion of the fetus.

ABORTIVE TRIAL (L)

A trial terminated without reaching a verdict, a mistrial.

ABROGATE (L)

To annul or repeal a former law by the passage of a new one.

ABSCOND (L)

To leave one's usual residence; to conceal oneself in order to avoid legal proceedings; to disappear, sometimes with the prop–erty of others.

ABSENCE (L)

Nonappearance; being away from one's domicile. When con–tinued for seven years, without the person being heard from, a presumption of death may be established.

ABSOLUTE LAW (L)

The law of nature, absolute in the abstract and in theory.

ABSOLUTION (L)

The dismissal of a charge, declaration of innocence, remission of penalties.

ABUSE (Cr'y, L)

Ill--use, improper treatment, words or acts contrary to appro-- priate behavior.

ACCESSORY (L)

One not the actual perpetrator of a felony, but in some way concerned with the commission of it. May be an accessory before the fact by inciting or counseling, or after the fact, by assisting the felon.

ACCESSORY AFTER THE FACT (L)

One who, having full knowledge that a feloney has been com- mitted, conceals it, harbors, assists, or protects the person sought for or convicted of the crime.

ACCESSORY BEFORE THE FACT (L)

One who, being absent at the time a crime is committed, assists, counsels, cites, encourages, engages, or commands another to commit it.

ACCESSORY DURING THE FACT (L)

One who fails to interfere or give such help as may be in his power to prevent the commission of a criminal offense.

ACCIDENT (L, PA)

An unforseen event, misfortune, act, or omission, not the result of negligence or misconduct, something which happens without any willful human intent.

ACCIDENTAL POISONING (Cr's)

Poisoning which is unintended and which is not associated with any illegal act, commonly caused by contaminated food, toxic substances mislabeled at home or otherwise mistaken, or by a medicine taken in overdose.

ACCIDENTALS (Cr's)

Fingerprint patterns for which no rules can be made. They are very rare and often have more than two deltas.

ACCOMMODATION (Cr'y)

A state occurring when two ethnically or racially distinct groups live side by side without hostility.

ACCOMPLICE (L)

One involved with others in the commission of a crime.

ACCORD (L)

Agreement.

ACCUMULATIVE SENTENCE (Cor)

A sentence passed before the first has expired, to commence upon its expiration.

ACCUSATION (L)

The legal charge that a person is guilty of a criminal offense, subject to later adjudication.

ACID (Cr'y)

A compound capable of donating a hydrogen ion (H+) to another compound.

ACIDOSIS (Cr's)

Abnormal condition in which there is reduced alkalinity of the blood and body tissues.

ACKNOWLEDGEMENT (L)

The act of going before a court and declaring the execution of a deed or other instrument; the certificate issued by the court.

ACQUIESCENCE (L)

Silent assent, or neglect to speak when one wishing to object or stand on his rights would naturally speak or act. Conduct from which consent may be implied.

ACQUIT (L)

To set free, release or discharge as from an obligation or accusation.

ACQUITTAL (L)

The dismissal by a jury or a court decision of criminal charges formally brought against an accused person, absolving him from further prosecution for the same offense.

ACT (L)

Something done or established. Laws passed by legislatures.

ACT IN PAIS (L)

A thing done out of court, and not a matter of record.

ACTIO AD EXHIBENDUM (L)

An action instituted for the purpose of compelling production of documents or testimony.

ACTIO FURTI (L)

An action of theft.

ACTION (Cr's)

The mechanism of a firearm.

ACTION (L)

A lawsuit; a proceeding taken in a court of law. May be civil or criminal.

ACTUAL (L)

That which is real or actually existing, as opposed to something which is only possible.

ACTUAL AUTHORITY (L)

Authority conferred by an individual upon his agent to act in his behalf.

ACTUAL BIAS (L)

An attitude on the part of a juror which leads to the belief that he will not act with impartiality.

ACTUAL BREAKING (Cr's, L)

The application of physical force to effect entry.

ACTUAL COMPULSION (L)

Forcibly compelling a person to do a certain act.

ACTUAL FORCE (L)

Personal violence, any force inflicted during a robbery directly upon the person robbed sufficient to compel that person to surrender his property.

ACTUAL FRAUD (L)

Any intentional false representation which misleads another.

ACTUAL KNOWLEDGE (L)

Facts which are within one's own knowledge.

ACTUAL MALICE (L)

Ill will or enmity toward an individual.

ACTUAL RESIDENCE (L)

The place where one actually lives or resides.

ACTUAL SERVICE (L)

Service of process made either by reading the process to the defendant or by delivering to him a copy.

ACUTE POISONING (Cr's)

The taking of an excessive single dose of poison.

ADDICT (Cr's, L)

Any person who regularly uses any habit--forming narcotic drug so as to endanger the public morals, health, safety, or welfare, or who is or has been so far addicted to the use of such habit--forming drugs as to have lost the power of self--control with reference to his addiction.

ADDICTION (Cr's, L)

A state of utter dependence on a drug for a sense of physical and mental sell--being. Addiction includes habituation. The test of true addiction is the abstinence syndrome (the charac--teristic symptoms of severe physical and mental distress follow—ing withdrawal).

ADENOMA (Cr's)

A benign tumor of glandular structure.

ADEQUATE PROVOCATION (L)

Provocation sufficient to affect the average, reasonable man.

ADJACENT (L)

Next to or near.

ADJECTIVE LAW (L)

The aggregate of rules or procedure or practice. The rules ac--cording to which the substantive law is administered.

4

ADJOURNMENT   (L)
    A postponing of a hearing or a session until another time or
    place.
ADJUDICATE   (L)
    To settle by judicial authority.
ADJUDICATION   (L)
    A judgement or decision.
ADJURATION   (L)
    A swearing or binding by oath.
ADMINISTRATIVE CONTROL   (PA)
    Control by management of all facets of a department's opera--
    tion. Provision built into the organization of the department
    by the creation of staff inspection elements.
ADMINISTRATIVE FUNCTIONS   (PA)
    The aggregate of functions including the task of management,
    facilitating the effective accomplishment of line or field opera--
    tions (primary functions) and services (auxiliary functions).
ADMINISTRATIVE LAW   (L)
    That branch of the law which determines the organization,
    powers, and duties of administrative authorities, the legal
    requirements governing their operation, and the remedies avail--
    able to those adversely affected by administrative action.
ADMINISTRATIVE PROCESSES   (PA)
    Interrelated means employed on a continuing basis by which an
    administrator achieves his organizational goals and objectives.
ADMISSIBLE EVIDENCE   (L)
    Evidence which may be received by a trial court.
ADMISSION   (L)
    A self--incriminatory statement by the subject falling short of
    an acknowledgement of guilt.
ADMONITION   (L)
    A caution given by a court to jurors concerning the rules for
    their conduct while they are participating in a lawsuit.
ADOLESCENCE   (Cr'y)
    The period between childhood and maturity.
ADRENAL GLAND
    An endocrine gland situated near the kidney.
ADULT   (L)
    Of majority age. In common law, a person who has attained the a
    age of 21. By law in some states, a person who has attained the
    age of 18.
ADULTERATION   (Cr's)
    The act of mixing cheap or inferior substances with another
    substance.
ADULTERY   (L)

Extramarital intercourse between a married person and some--
one other than the spouse.

ADVENTITIA (Cr's)

Outer layer of a blood vessel.

ADVERSARY (L)

Opponent or litigant in a legal controversy.

ADVISORY (L)

Informative; not legally binding.

ADVISORY OPINION (L)

An opinion rendered by a court as to the constitutional or legal
effect of a bill or a statute when no actual case is before it. The
Supreme Court has always refused to render such opinions on
the ground that it would be engaging in nonjudicial activity. A
few states authorize the governor or legislature to ask State
courts for advisory opinions but, when rendered, they have no
binding force except in Colorado.

AD VITAM (L)

For life.

AD VITAM AUT CULPAM (L)

For life or until bad behavior.

ADVOCATE (L)

An attorney who speaks or writes on behalf of his client.

AFFIDAVIT (L)

A written statement of fact, signed and sworn to before a person
having authority to administer an oath.

AFFRAY (L)

An altercation involving two or more persons engaged in mutual
combat or in an attack upon a third person. The place must be
public and the manner in which the participants conduct them--
selves must be such as to create or threaten a serious disturbance
to those in the vicinity or otherwise to terrorize them.

AFORESAID (L)

Contained in an earlier part of the same document.

AFORETHOUGHT (L)

Planned beforehand, premeditated, deliberate.

AGENT (L)

One authorized by a party to act in that party's behalf.

AGGLUTINATION (Cr's)

The clumping together of red blood cells by the action of an
antibody.

AGGRAVATED RAPE (L)

The violation of a female under 12 years of age.

AGGRESSION (Cr'y)

A hostile act intended to harm a person or object, often the
result of frustration. The term also refers to the desire or

tendency to perform hostile acts.

AGGRESSOR (L)

A person who initiates a quarrel, dispute or fight.

AGGRIEVED PARTY (L)

One who has been injured or who has suffered a loss.

AID AND ABET (L)

To knowingly assist, encourage or urge on someone to commit a crime.

AIDER BY VERDICT (L)

The presumption which arises after verdict, whether in a civil or criminal case, that those facts, without proof of which the verdict could not have been found, were proved though they were not distinctly alleged.

ALARM SYSTEM (PA)

An assembly of equipment and devices designated and arranged to signal the presence of an alarm condition requiring urgent attention.

ALIAS (L, PA)

A second name used by a person. Sometimes called an "AKA" ("also known as").

ALIBI (L)

Evidence intending to show that the defendant was in a different place at the time the offense was committed.

ALIENATION (L)

The voluntary and absolute transfer of title and possession of real property from one person to another.

ALLEGATION (L)

A statement of fact made in a legal proceeding, which the person stating it intends to prove. An assertion, as compared with proof.

ALLELE (Cr's)

Any of several alternative forms of a gene located at the same point on a particular pair of chromosomes. For example, the genes determining the blood types A and B are alleles.

ALLOCATION OF RESPONSIBILITIES (PA)

Responsibility for work performance allocated to elements of the department on some logical basis. There are three primary bases for determining appropriate allocations of responsibilities:
1. Function or purpose
2. Process or method
3. Clientele

ALLOY (Cr's)

Metals mixed by fusing.

ALPHA RAY (Cr's)

A type of radiation emitted by a radioactive element. The

radiation is composed of helium atoms minus their orbiting electrons.

ALVEOLUS   (Cr's)

A small sac in the lungs through whose walls air and other vapors are exchanged between the breath and the blood.

AMBULANCE CHASER   (L)

An attorney who solicits law practice, especially personal injury claims. An agent for such an attorney.

AMEND   (L)

To alter, to improve upon.

AMICUS CURIAE   (L)

Literally, "friend of the court." A participant in a court case who argues legal points relevant to the case, on the basis that the decision will affect the interest which the group represents.

AMENORRHEA   (Cr's)

Absence of menstruation.

AMNESTY   (L)

A general pardon offered to groups of individuals.

AMORPHOUS SOLID   (Cr's)

A solid in which the constituent atoms or molecules are arranged in random or disordered positions. There is no regular order in amorphous solids.

ANALGESIC   (Cr's)

A drug or substance that lessens or eliminates pain.

ANAMNESTIC   (Cr's)

Pertaining to past history of disease.

ANARCHY   (L)

Absence of government; general disorder in society.

ANASTOMOSIS   (Cr's)

A communication between two vessels.

ANEURYSM   (Cr's)

Saccular dilatetion of a blood vessel or part of the heart.

ANGINA PECTORIS   (Cr's)

Spasmodic chest pain, often associated with a sensation of impending death, usually due to inadequate oxygen supply of the heart muscle.

ANGIOGRAPHY   (Cr's)

Study of the vessels, chiefly the visualization of blood vessels by X rays.

ANGIOMA   (Cr's)

A tumor composed of blood or lymph vessels.

ANNUL   (L)

To make void, to invalidate or cancel.

ANOMIE   (Cr'y)

The situation in which the values and frame of reference of the individual do not fit the culture or society in which he lives; thus he is unable to adjust to the expectations of his society. The result is crime and delinquency.

ANOXIA   (Cr's)
Oxygen deficiency.

ANTERIOR   (Cr's)
Situated toward the front.

ANTECEDENT   (L)
Priorto, preceding.

ANTHROPOMETRY   (Cr's)
A system of identification of individuals by measurements of parts of the body, developed by Alphonse Bertillon.

ANTIBODY   (Cr's)
A protein that destroys or inactivates a specific antigen. Anti--bodies are found in blood serum.

ANTICOAGULANT   (Cr's)
A substance that prevents coagulation or clotting of the blood.

ANTIGEN   (Cr's)
A substance, usually a protein, that stimulates the body to pro--duce antibodies against it.

ANTISERUM   (Cr's)
Blood serum in which there are specific antibodies.

ANTIMONY   (Cr's)
A metallic used to alloy lead in bullets for hardening the pro--jectile.

ANTISOCIAL BEHAVIOR   (Cr'y)
1. Behavior believed by the members of a group to be against the interests of their group. The behavior reflexts a rejection of social norms and values accepted and considered important by group members.
2. Behavior that is disruptive or potentially disruptive to the smooth functioning or survival of a group, regardless of whether or not group members recognize that the group's welfare is threatened. I this sense antisocial behavior is determined by outside observers and may include behavior not disapproved by group members.

ANVIL   (Cr's)
A small piece of metal, arrowhead in shape which is placed in--side the primer cup and forms the point of resistance as the firingpin strikes the primer, thereby creating friction which dis--charges the priming composition.

APOPLEXY   (Cr's)
Stroke.

APPARENT DANGER   (L)
As used with reference to the doctrine of self--defense in

homicide, means such overt actual demonstration, by conduct and acts, of a design to take life or do some great personal injury injury, as would make the killing apparently necessary to self-- preservation.

APPEAL (L)

A petition to a higher court to modify the judgement of a lower court.

APPEAL BOND (L)

Security in a given amount to be posted by an appellant as a requirement for perfecting an appeal.

APPEARANCE (L)

The initial court response by a defendant in a lawsuit. May be in person or by attorney.

APPELLANT (L)

He who initiates an appeal from one court to a higher court.

APPELLATE COURT (L)

A judicial tribunal which reviews cases originally tried and de-- cided by inferior tribunals. The appellate court acts without a jury and is primarily interested in correcting errors in proce-- dure or in the interpretation of law by the lower courts.

APPELLATE JURISDICTION (L)

The authority of a court to review the decisions of other courts and uphold, reverse, modify, or return them to a lower court for retrial.

APPELLEE (L)

The party in a lawsuit against whom an appeal has been taken.

APPREHEND (L, PA)

To seize a person; to arrest.

APPREHENSION (L, PA)

The seizure, taking, or arrest of a person on a criminal charge.

APPREHENSION OF OFFENDERS (PA)

The major police activity which views quick apprehension as the means to discourage the would--be offender. The certainty of arrest and prosecution has a deterrent quality which is in-- tended to make crime seem less worthwhile. Additionally, apprehension enables society to punish offenders, lessens the prospect of repetition by causing suspects to be incarcerated, and provides an opportunity for rehabilitation of those con-- victed.

APPROVER (L)

An accomplice in crime, who, while confessing himself guilty, accuses others of the same offense, and who give such testi-- mony.

AQUEDUCT (Cr's)

Narrow canal which connects the third and fourth ventricle of the brain.

ARACHNOID (Cr's)

Soft, spider web–like membrane covering the brain.

ARBITRARY PUNISHMENT (L)

Punishment left to the discretion of a judge and not defined by statute.

ARBITRATOR (L)

An impartial person chosen by the parties to solve a dispute between them.

ARCHES, FINGERPRINTS (Cr's)

Patterns, in which the ridges go from one side to another, never turning back to make a loop. As a rule, there are no deltas.

AREA (PA)

A section or territorial division of a large city, each comprised of designated districts. In some departments, area commanders are appointed to exercise close command and supervision of district commanders. In other departments this echelon of command is eliminated by having areas supervised and con–trolled by deputies of the patrol–division chief, operating directly under his control and out of his office.

ARGUMENT (L)

A statement to a court, judge, or jury, of counsel's reasons why the client should prevail in a lawsuit.

ARGUMENTATIVE (L)

Suggesting conclusions to be drawn from the facts.

ARMS (Cr's, L)

Weapons. Anything used to inflict injury on the person of another.

ARRAIGN (L)

To bring a prisoner to court for the purpose of having him answer the charge against him. The initial court appearance of a person who is charged with a crime.

ARRAY (L)

The persons summoned to court for jury duty.

ARREST (L, PA)

The apprehension or detention of a person in order that he may be held to answer an alleged crime before a magistrate.

ARREST OF JUDGEMENT (L)

The refusal of a court to give judgement, regardless of the ver-- dict. Used when it appears that the plaintiff is not entitled to the verdict.

ARSON (L)

The malicious burning of another's house.

See also: Burning

ARTERY (Cr's)

A blood vessel that carries blood away from the heart.

ARTERITIS (Cr's)

Inflammation of an artery.

ARTICULO MORTIS (L)

At the time of death.

ASHURST–SUMNERS ACT OF 1935 (Cor, L)

A federal law which prohibited companies from accepting prison–made goods for transportation into any other state in violation of the laws of that state and required use of the "prison--made" label for any such goods involved in interstate commerce. The effect of this law was to exclude almost all prison–made products from interstate commerce.

ASPERMIA (Cr's)

The absence of sperm; sterility in males.

ASPHYXIA (Cr's)

Asphyxia or suffocation is suspension of breathing due to a deficiency of oxygen in the red blood cells. Among the forms which asphyxia may take are drowning, hanging, strangulation, choking, and smothering.

ASPORTATION (L)

Carrying away or removing property in the commission of a theft.

ASSASSINATION (Cr'y)

The murder of a high public official.

ASSAULT (L)

A threatening gesture, with or without threatening words. An attempted battery.

ASSENT (L)

Approval of something done. Expressly declared or implied.

ASSIMILATIVE CRIMES STATUTE (L)

A law of Congress which provides that, in the absence of an appropriate federal penal law, an offense committed on a fed--eral reservation shall be punishable under laws of the State in which the reservation is located.

ASSIZE OF CLARENDON

Also called Constitutions of Clarendon. A meeting summoned by Henry II in 1166 A.D. to formalize court procedures.

ASSOCIATE (L)

An attorney who is practicing law with another attorney or a law firm.

ASSOCIATIVE EVIDENCE (L)

The type of evidence which links the suspect to the crime scene or offense. For example, safe lining found in a suspect's shoe may associate the owner with the scene of a safe burglary where an identical type of lining was found on the floor.

ASSURED CLEAR DISTANCE AHEAD (L)

A legal requirement providing that no person shall drive a motor vehicle upon public roads at a rate of speed greater than will permit him to bring it to a stop within the assured clear distance ahead.

ASYSTOLE   (Cr's)

Inability of heart to contract.

AT LARGE   (L)

Free, out of prison, not in custody.

ATAXIA   (Cr's)

Inability to perform coordinated voluntary movements as occurs in some nervous disorders.

ATHEROMA   (Cr's)

Fatty degeneration of the inner layer of an artery.

ATOM   (Cr's)

The smallest unit of an element, not divisible by ordinary chemical means. Atoms are made up of electrons, protons, and neutrons plus other sub–atomic particles.

ATOMIC MASS NUMBER   (Cr's)

The sum of the number of protons and neutrons in the nucleus of an atom.

ATOMIC NUMBER   (Cr's)

The number of protons in the nucleus of the atom. Each ele--ment has its own unique atomic number.

ATTAINDER, BILL OF   (L)

A legislative act, directed against a certain person, pronouncing him guilty without trial.

ATTEMPT   (L)

An effort to commit a crime amounting to more than mere preparation or planning for it, which, if not prevented, would have resulted in the completion of the act attempted.

ATTORNEY   (L)

An attorney at law. A person authorized by another to act in his place.

ATTORNEY AT LAW   (L)

A person licensed to practice the profession of law.

ATTORNEY GENERAL   (L)

The chief legal officer of the United States or of a state. A federal or state cabinet official.

AUBURN SYSTEM   (Cor)

A correctional system established in 1815 at the Auburn, New York prison. This system imposed silence, individual confine--ment at night, congregate work during the day, harsh discipline and strong security measures. It was adopted by most Ameri--can states because it was more economical and administratively feasible than the Pennsylvania System.

See also: Pennsylvania System.

AUTHORITIVE INSPECTION (PA)

Inspection conducted by those in direct control of the persons and things being inspected, to see that tasks are satisfactorily performed.

AUTO ACCESSORY THIEF (Cr'y)

Persons who steal cars for the purpose of removing and selling the accessories or parts, such as tires, wheels, or radios. The term "car clouting" is used in many areas to describe this par-- ticular form of larceny.

AUTO LOADING (Cr's)

An automatic loading gun which fires, extracts, ejects, and re- loads once with each action of the firing mechanism. After each shot, pressure on the trigger must be released and reapplied before succeeding shot will fire.

AUTOLYSIS (Cr's)

Disintegration of tissue.

AUTOMATIC (Cr's)

Applied to small arms utilizing forces of gas pressure or recoil so after the first shot is fired, the fired case is ejected and the next round is loaded, fired and ejected. This cycle is repeated continuously until ammunition is exhausted or the pressure on the trigger is released.

AUTO THEFT (L)

A form of grand larceny, defined as an attempted or unlawful stealing and/or driving away of a motor vehicle.

AUTOPSY (Cr's)

Examination of a dead person to determine, among other things, the cause of death.

AUTREFOIS ACQUIT (L)

A plea in a criminal case, arguing that the defendant has already been acquitted on the same charge.

AUTREFOIS CONVICT (L)

A plea in a criminal case arguing that the defendant has already been convicted on the same charge.

AUXILIARY SERVICES (PA)

All services which assist the line officer in the performance of his duty. They include records, identification, communica-- tions, detention, property and evidence, and crime laboratory.

BACKING A WARRANT (L)

Endorsing a warrant issue by a court in another county, authorizing service in the county where sent.

BAD CHECK PASSER (PA, Cr'y)

One who passes worthless checks with the intent or tending to defraud others.

BADGER (L)

To continuously harass someone, including victims, witnesses and others.

BAIL (L)

A device to free a defendant while insuring appearance at trial by requiring the deposit of cash bond, or other security.

BAILABLE OFFENSE (L)

A crime for which a defendant is entitled to be set free if bail is set. Generally, all except capital offenses.

BAILEE (L)

One to whom personal property is entrusted for a distinct pur—pose.

BAILIFF (L)

An office assigned to court duty for the purpose of peace keeping, prisoner custody, and whatever the judge may require.

BAILOR, OR BAILER (L)

One entrusting property to another for a specific purpose.

BALLISTICS (Cr's)

The science of the flight of projectiles.

BAN (L)

A public notice, summons or edict, whereby something is com—manded or prohibited.

BANC (L)

A bench. The sitting together of all judges of a court to hear a case. Also, en banc.

BANCUS SUPERIOR (L)

The Upper Bench, or Superior Court.

BAR (L)

The embodiment of the legal profession.

BAR ASSOCIATION (L)

A professional organization composed of licensed attorneys.

BARGAIN (L)

A mutual voluntary agreement between two parties for the exchange or purchase of some specified goods. It also implies negotiation over the terms of an agreement.

BARIUM (Cr's)

Metallic element with the chemical symbol of Ba, atomic number of 56 and atomic weight of 137.34 found in the primer compound; one of the elements detected by the neutron ativation analysis (NAA).

BARREL TIME   (Cr's)

Time measured from the fall of the hammer to the passage of the projectile from the muzzle of the gun.

BARRISTER   (L)

An advocate.

BASE   (Cr's)

A compound capable of accepting a hydrogen ion (H+).

BASTARD   (L)

One born out of wedlock. An illegitimate child. In some states defined by law.

BASTARDIZE   (L)

A legal declaration of bastardy.

BATTERY   (L)

An unlawful touching, striking, beating, or wounding of another's person or clothes without consent of the latter.

BATTERY CUP   (Cr's)

A small cup containing the primer.

BAWD   (L)

One keeping a house of prostitution, or bawdy house, and pro- viding prostitution services.

BEARING SURFACE   (Cr's)

Part of the bullet that comes in contact with the lands and grooves as it moves through the barrel; that portion of the bullet that mirrors the engraving of the rifling in the barrel.

BEAT   (PA)

An area assigned for patrol either by foot or otherwise.

BECCARIA, CESARE BONESANA, MARQUIS DE   (Cr'y)

Criminologist, 1738--1794, founder of the classical school of criminology. He argued that the existing crimino-legal system was arbitrary and allowed abusive practices. Beccaria held that punishment should only be applied in proportion to the serious- ness of the crime. Punishment is legitimate only when it is used by the state to defend the total sovereignty against the acts of any individual. Ultimately, punishment must be based upon law, which in turn is enacted by the legislature who represents the broader society. The type and degree of punishment should vary in proportion to the individual's threat to society. The goal of punishment is the deterrence of potential offenders and to prevent further harm by current offenders. To accomplish these ends, punishment must be prompt, inevitable, and equal. Finally, the death penalty is not a part of the original social contract and usurps the individual's right to life.

BECKE LINE

A bright halo that is observed near the border of a particle immersed in a liquid of a different refractive index.

BEHAVIOR MODIFICATION (Cor)

An approach based on the assumption that criminal behavior is learned and can be altered; desirable behavioral change can occur within the institution.

BELIEF (L)

A conviction based on evidence; a fact exists, an act was done, a statement is true.

BENCH (L)

A tribunal of justice. Judges as a group, distinguished from the bar.

BENCH WARRANT (L)

A judicial order issued for the arrest of an individual.

BENEFIT OF COUNSEL (L)

More than mere appointment of counsel to represent accused; such counsel to be given reasonable time for preparation to represent accused at trial.

BEQUEATH (L)

A gift of personal property or a gift of personally by means of a will.

BERTILLON SYSTEM (Cr's)

A system for the identification of persons by bodily measure--ments and photographs used in France and other countries; superceded by fingerprint identification.

BEST EVIDENCE (L)

Primary original evidence; the highest evidence to which the nature of the case is susceptible.

BESTIALITY (L)

Carnal intercourse between humans and animals.

See also: Buggery.

BET (L)

An agreement between two or more persons that some valuable thing shall become the property of one or some of them, on the future happening of a present uncertain event.

BETA RAY (Cr's)

A type of radiation emitted by a radioactive element. The radia--tion consists of electrons.

BEYOND A REASONABLE DOUBT (L)

In evidence means entirely satisfied to a moral certainty; clear, precise, and indubitable.

Guilt must be established "beyond a reasonable doubt"; facts proven must, by probative force, establish guilt.

BIFURCATION (L)

Division into two branches. Dividing a criminal trial into hear-ings on guilt and penalty issues.

BIGAMY (L)

Having two husbands or two wives concurrently.

BILL OF EXCEPTIONS (L)

A written statement of objections to decisions of the trial court upon questions of law arising during the progress of the trial so as to put the decision objected to on record for the information of the court having cognizance.

BILL OF PRIVILEGE (L)

Formerly the form of proceeding against an attorney of the court not liable to arrest.

BILL OF REVIEW (L)

A claim filed in court to have a decree of the court reviewed, modified, or reversed.

BILL OF RIGHTS (L)

The first ten amendments to the United States Constitution. (2) A statement of personal rights and privileges in the state constitutions of many of the United States. Derived from the Magna Charta.

BILL TO PERPETUATE TESTIMONY (L)

A petition filed to preserve testimony with reference to some matter not in litigation, but may come to be at a later time.

BILL TO TAKE TESTIMONY "DE BENE ESSE" (L)

A petition to record testimony material to a case pending when there is cause to believe the testimony may otherwise be lost before trial.

BILLA CASSETUR (L)

The bill may be quashed.

BIND (L)

To hold by legal obligation; e.g., to bind over a party accused of a crime to appear before a grand jury or court.

BIOGENIC THEORIES (Cr'y)

Theories of crime causation regarding man as a biological being; criminals look different from noncriminals, criminals have a different genetic or chromosomal make–up than noncriminals.

BIREFRINGENCE (Cr's)

A difference in the two indices of refraction exhibited by some crystalline materials.

BIRTH (L)

The act of entering life with an independent circulation.

BLACKMAIL (L)

An act wherein money is obtained by threats of consequences other than force.

See also: Extortion.

BLACK POWDER (Cr's)

A mixture of saltpeter (potassium nitrate), charcoal (carbon), and sulphur in the approximate proportions of 75:15:10.

BLACKSTONE, WILLIAM (Cr'y)

A criminologist who recodified English criminal law, defined specific crimes, and formulated punishments resulting from different offenses.

BLOOD FEUD (L)

Avenging the slaughter of kin on the person who slaughtered him or his belongings.

BLOW JOBS (Cr's, PA)

The criminal use of explosives to open safes. Safe cracking.

BOGUS (L)

Spurious, pretended or deceptive.

BOLT (Cr's)

Specifically of bolt action firearms, it is a cylindrical or oblong block of steel so designed that it may be pushed forward and locked to seal the breech for firing, then pulled back to permit ejection of the fired case and loading of another shell.

BOLT ACTION

A firearm in action in which breech closure is achieved by longitudinal of breech bolt parallel to axis of the bore.

BONA FIDE (PA, L, Cr'y)

In good faith, honestly.

BONA GESTURE (Cor, L)

Good behavior.

BONA GRATIA (L)

Voluntarily.

BONA WAVIATA (L)

Goods thrown away by a thief in his flight, for fear of being apprehended.

BOND (L)

A written obligation. In court, promised by parties, usually with surety, that the party will perform the orders of the court. Violation results in bond forfeiture and paid to the obligee of the bond.

BONDAGE (L)

A state of involuntary servitude.

BONDSMAN (L)

A surety; one who gives security for another.

BONO ET MALO (Cor, L)

A writ of jail delivery issued for every prisoner.

BOOKING (L, PA)

The administrative record of arrest.

BOOKMAKING (L)

The practice of receiving and recording bets.

BOOSTER BOX   (Cr'y)

A box designed to look like a wrapped package but with a hidden opening through which articles can be inserted.

BOOSTER CLOTHING   (Cr'y)

Garments designed to hold stolen merchandise.

BOOTLEG   (L)

To illegally manufacture, deal in or deliver a commodity, e.g., whiskey.

BORE   (Cr's)

The diameter of the gun barrel; the gage.

See also: Caliber, gage.

BORSTAL INSTITUTIONS   (Cr'y)

English minimum security schools for delinquent youths established in 1908.

BOUNTY   (L)

A premium paid by a government to encourage particular activities.

BRANDEIS BRIEF   (L)

A brief composed of economic or sociological facts rather than legal argument.

BRANDING   (L)

A method of marking animals for recognition. Formerly punishment by inflicting a mark on an offender with a hot iron.

BRAWLING   (L)

Quarreling or creating a disturbance.

BREACH   (L)

A breaking or violation.

BREECH BLOCK   (Cr's)

That part of the action which being locked into position sup-ports the cartridge in the chamber so that case may form an effective gas seal when firearm is discharged.

BREECH FACE   (Cr's)

The rear surface or face of the barrel.

BREACH OF PEACE   (L)

A violation of public order.

BREACH OF PRISON   (Cor, L)

Escape from lawful detention by a prisoner.

BREACH OF TRUST   (L)

The willful misappropriation by a trustee of a thing which has been lawfully delivered to him in confidence.

BREAKING   (L)

Parting or dividing by force.

BREECH   (Cr's)

The rear extremity of the rifle barrel.

BREVE   (L)

A writ.

BREVE DE RECTO (L)

Writ of right.

BREVE JUDICIALE NON CADIT PRO DEFECTU FORMAE (L)

"A judicial writ fails not through defect of form."

BREVE ORIGINALE (L)

An original writ.

BRIBERY (L)

Giving or receiving a gift to influence exercise of a judicial or public duty.

BRIDEWELL (Cor)

Also known as St. Brigit's Well, a sixteenth century workhouse used to hold minor offenders and beggars.

BRIEF (L)

A printed statement of a party's view of his case, submitted as an argument to the judge or judges of a court.

BROACH RIFLING (Cr's)

The method of forming the spiral grooves in the bore of a rifle barrel by cutting the metal with a multiple tooth called a broach.

BROCARDS (L)

Law maxims.

BROKER (L, Cr'y)

One who for commission or fee, brings parties together and assists in negotiating contracts between them.

BRONCHIECTASIS (Cr's)

Long–standing dilatation of the bronchi.

BRONCHOGENIC CARCINOMA (Cr's)

Cancer originating in a bronchus.

BRONCHUS (Cr's)

Main branch of the airway.

BROTHEL (L)

A house kept for purposes of prostitution.

BUCKET SHOP (L)

A gambling institution, ostensibly for stock brokerage, in which no purchases are made.

BUCK SHOT (Cr's)

Large lead balls for shotgun shells supplied in various sizes and load combinations intended for guard use, deer and other game animals. Pellets are cast or swaged and polished.

BUDGET REQUEST (PA)

The forms on which money requests are recorded may be pro–vided by the state but are usually prescribed by the city Finance Director, to correspond to the accounts and subaccounts main–tained in his office. Generally, he prepares blank forms on which city departments submit their budget requests. The form may have separate columns to show for each line item.

1. The appropriation for the current fiscal year.
2. The department request for the ensuing fiscal year.
3. The recommendation of the official, such as the City Manager, who presents the budget proposal to the City Council for action.
4. The appropriation finally authorized by the council.

For purposes of internal management, a department may find it desirable to prepare its own forms in greater detail.

BUGGERY   (L)

Pertains to anal intercourse.

See also: Bestiality, sodomy.

BULGING   (Cr's)

The swelling of a gun barrel.

BULLET   (Cr's)

Projectile of a rifle or pistol; one of the parts of the cartridge; term accurate only when referring to the projectile; composed of lead hardened by an alloy of tin and antimony. Sometimes semi jacketed or full jacketed with an outer layer of hard metal, usually a copper–zinc alloy; style variable e.g. boat–tail, flat nose, hollow point, round nose, spire point and wad center.

BULLET CORE   (Cr's)

Lead alloy pieces of prescribed shape and weight for assembly with jacket.

BULLET JACKET   (Cr's)

Covering over lead core. Usually gilding metal or steel. Nose is closed for metal case, open for expanding types with either lead exposed or protected or a separate tip inserted.

BURDEN OF PROOF   (L)

The duty of proving disputed facts of a case at trial.

BUREAU   (PA)

A department of government for the transaction of public business.

BURGLAR   (L)

One who commits burglary.

See also: Burglary.

BURGLARY   (L)

Breaking and entering into a dwelling with intent to commit a felony or theft.

BURN JOBS (safe cracking)   (Cr's)

Attempted opening of a safe by use of a cutting torch. Criminals must know the proper amount of air and acetylene to be applied to burn steel. Equipment includes oxygen and gas tanks, a burner, and an adequate footage of hose.

BURNING   (Cr's)
>Ignition of a combustible material with any appreciable burn–
ing. The ignition satisfies the requirement.

BUST   (PA)
>To arrest.

BUTT   (PA)
>The rear end of a rifle stock or spear. Also the mound of earth
used as a backing for a target.

BUTTON RIFLING   (Cr's)
>To form rifling in a barrel by displacing the metal with a hard
die drawn through the bore. The metal is not removed.

BY COLOR OF OFFICE   (L)
>Acts done of such a nature that the authority of office does
not validate their exercise.

CACHET, LETTRES DE (L)

Letters issued by French kings authorizing imprisonment or exile of a person.

CADAVER (Cr's)

A corpse; dead body.

CALENDAR (L)

A list of cases arranged for trial in court.

See also: Docket.

CALIBER (Cr's)

Diameter of bore measured in hundredths of an inch.

See also: Bore, Gage.

CAMOUFLAGE (PA)

Disguise.

CAMP (Cor)

Minimum security institution that operates around a work program.

CANNELURED BULLET (Cr's)

An elongated bullet with grooves around it for holding the lubricant or for crimping purposes.

CANONS OF ETHICS (L)

Various rules which governed the legal profession during the years 1908–1969. The legal profession is presently governed by the Code of Professional Responsibility which contains within it a sub--heading called canons.

CAPIAS (L)

A generic name for writs ordering the person to whom they are addressed to arrest a person therein named.

See also: Writ.

CAPIAS AD AUDIEN DUM JUDICIUM (L)

A writ issued in case the defendant be found guilty of a mis--demeanor, to bring him to the court to receive sentence.

CAPIAS AD RESPONDENDUM (L)

A writ issued for the arrest of a person against whom an indict--ment for misdemeanor was found. Formerly; issued against an absconding debtor, who was then made to give special bail.

CAPIAS PRO FINE (L)

A writ issued against a defendant who has failed to pay his fine.

CAPILLARY (Cr's)

Very find blood vessel; resembling a hair.

CAPITAL CRIME OR CAPITAL OFFENSE (L)

A crime punishable by death, e.g., first degree murder, armed robbery or high treason.

CAPITAL PUNISHMENT (L)

A penalty calling for loss of life.

CARBINE (PA, Cr's)

A rifle of short length and light weight.

CARBON MONOXIDE (Cr's)

An inodorous and very deadly gas formed by the oxidation of carbon at high temperatures or in a limited supply of oxygen. Carbon monoxide causes more deaths than all the other poisons combined.

CARDIAC (Cr's)

Relating to the heart.

CARNAL KNOWLEDGE (L)

See: Sexual intercourse.

CAROTID SINUS (Cr's)

Small organ located in the wall of carotid artery, the principal artery of the neck, serving as one of the mechanisms for adjust-- ing the blood pressure.

CARRY–AWAY JOBS (Safe cracking) (Cr's)

The safe is transported to a location where it can be opened at leisure. The thieves will use an ordinary vehicle. Occasionally, the suspension is modified to accept the extra weight to avoid an appearance of carrying a heavy load.

CASE (L)

A lawsuit or item of legal work. A case previously decided is a precedent case and a case on which a lawyer or judge is pre-- sently working is a problem case.

CASE LAW (L)

Judicial precedent generated by resolving unique legal disputes, as distinguished from statutes and constitutions.

CASE RESERVED (L)

A decision rendered as a matter of form so that the opinion of a higher court might be obtained.

CASE SYSTEM OR CASE METHOD (L)

The studying and teaching of law by the examination and dis-- cussion of the facts of precedent cases and the manner in which the courts resolved the disputes therein.

CATALYST

A substance that accelerates the rates of chemical reactions but is not itself permanently changed by the reaction.

CAUSA (L)

A cause; a reason; a writ of action pending.

CAUSA MORTIS (L)

By reason of, or in view of, death.

CAVEAT (L)

A formal notice given by a party interested to a Court of Judge against the performance of certain judicial acts.

CELLULITIS (Cr's)

Inflammation of subcutaneous connective tissue.

CELSIUS SCALE (Cr's)

The temperature scale using the melting point of ice as 0 and the boiling point of water as 100, with 100 equal divisions or degrees between.

CENTRAL POCKET OF LOOP (Fingerprints) (Cr's)

Looks like a simple loop; in the core, however, is at least one ridge which forms a convex curve toward the opening of the loop.

CEPI CORPUS (L)

"I have taken the body." Formerly a return upon an attachment or capias, when the person against whom the writ was issue was arrested.

CEREBELLAR TONSILS

Parts of the cerebellar cortex located adjacent to the margins of the foramen megnum.

CERTAINTY (L)

Clearness, confidence, definiteness.

CERTIFICATE (L)

A statement in writing, signed by a person having some official status, relative to a matter within his official knowledge or authority.

CERTIFIED COPY (L)

A paper verified to be a faithful replica of a document in the custody of the officer making the certification. It is signed by the officer and usually has an official seal affixed to it.

CERTIORARI (to be more fully informed) (L)

An original writ or action whereby a cause is removed from an inferior to a superior court for review. A dominant avenue to the United States Supreme Court.

CESSET EXECUTIO (L)

See: Stay of execution.

CESSET PROCESSUS (L)

See: Stay of proceedings.

CHAIN OF COMMAND (PA)

Levels of supervisory officials. The line of control divides at each level in the chain, since power is delegated to subordinates.

CHAIN OF EVIDENCE (Cr's, PA)

Assuring the admissability of physical evidence in court requires maintaining its integrity and relevance and accounting for its possession from crime scene to trial.

CHALLENGE (L)

An exception or objection. Challenges may be (a) for cause, which under law disqualifies the jury or juror from sitting; and (b) peremptory, those made without assigning any reason, and

which the court must allow. The number peremptory chal--
lenges allowed to each party is usually prescribed by statute.

CHAMBER (Cr's)

The end of a barrel receiving the shell or cartridge.

CHAMBERS (L)

Private office, adjoining a courtroom, in which a judge studies,
holds hearings and attends to other court business not requiring
a jury.

CHAMPION (L)

One who fights for another. (2) One who fights his own
battles.

CHANCE (L)

The happening of an event not ascertainable through foresight
or ingenuity; fortuity; risk.

CHANCE--MEDLEY (L)

A sudden affray, not intended. Sometimes applied to homicide
in self--defense.

CHANCE VERDICT (L)

A jury decision arrived at by casting lots or similar devices.

CHANGE OF VENUE (L)

Removal of a suit from one county or district to another for
trial; also applied to removal of a suit from one court to another
within the same jurisdiction.

CHARACTER EVIDENCE (L)

Testimony concerning the reputation of a person in his com--
munity, regarding reputation for truth and veracity.

CHARGE (L)

Instructions given by the court to a jury before it enters upon
its deliberations as to the principles of law which should guide
it in arriving at a decision. An accusation. A formal complaint,
information or indictment.

CHEAT (L)

Fraudulent, deceptive obtaining of the property of another.

CHECK OR CHEQUE (L)

An unconditional order to pay a sum to order or bearer, drawn
on a bank, payable on demand, and signed by the drawer.

CHEMICAL PROPERTY

Describes the behavior of a substance when it reacts or com--
bines with another substance.

CHIEF (L, PA)

Principal; one put over others; head of a department.

CHIEF ACCIDENT INVESTIGATOR (PA)

Investigator on the day shift who follows up on accident

investigations much as a detective continues preliminary in--
vestigations of crimes to ensure the adequacy of those investi--
gations by patrolmen and evidence technicians.

CHIEF CLERK   (PA)

The principal clerk who supervises the keeping of records and
other matters and implements orders from his superiors.

CHIEF JUSTICE   (L)

The presiding judge of a supreme court or court of appeals.

CHIEF JUSTICE OF THE UNITED STATES   (L)

The highest judicial officer of the United States; presides over
United States Supreme Court and Judicial Conference of the
United States; responsible for assigning judges from one
Federal court to another.

CHILD MOLESTER   (L, Cr'y)

One who injures or has questionable sexual dealings with a
child.

CHILLED SHOT   (Cr's)

Refers to hard shot; produced by mixing antimony with lead.

CHILLING EFFECTS   (L)

Self imposed limitations on the exercise of First Amendment
rights by citizens, who fearful of the possible application of
laws and sanctions, choose to circumscribe their legitimate
rights rather than risk prosecution.

CHOKE   (Cr's)

The decreasing diameter of a shotgun barrel toward the muzzle
to regulate the spread or pattern of shot.

CHOPPING JOBS (Safe cracking)   (Cr's)

The safe is turned upside down and the bottom or a wall is
chopped out. Regarded as the work of an amateur.

CHORIONIC VILLI   (Cr's)

Processes of the outer most envelope of the fertilized ovum
which attach the ovum to the wall of the uterus and provide
for metabolic interchange.

CHOROID PLEXUS   (Cr's)

Network of interlacing blood vessels protruding into the lateral
ventricles of the brain and concerned with the formation of
cerebrospinal fluid.

CHROMOSOME   (Cr's)

A rod like structure in the cell nucleus, along which the genes
are located.

CHRONIC POISONING   (Cr's)

Ingestion of small doses of poison over a long period of time,
resulting in gradual but progressive deterioration of body functions.

CIRCLE OF WILLIS   (Cr's)

Circle of arteries at the base of the brain.

CIRCUIT COURTS (L)
Courts with jurisdiction extending over several counties or districts.

CIRCUITS (L)
Judicial divisions of the United States or a state.

CIRCUMSTANTIAL EVIDENCE (L)
All evidence of an indirect nature. Existence of principal facts is inferred from surrounding circumstances.

CITATION (L)
Reference to a constitutional, statutory, precedential case or other persuasive material used in legal writing. (2) Summons to appear in court. (3) Compliment or award.

CITE (L)
To give or issue a citation.

CITIZEN (L)
One who has the freedom and privileges of a jurisdiction. (2) One who is a member of a body politic, owes allegiance to its government and may claim its protection.

CITY OR MUNICIPAL CORPORATION (L)
A public corporation established as a subdivision of a state for local governmental purposes, with various powers of government vested in its own officials.

CITY COURT (L)
Tries persons accused of violating municipal ordinances with jurisdiction over minor civil or criminal cases or both.

CIVILIAN (L)
A student, practitioner or professor of the civil law. (2) A person who is not in the military service.

CIVILIAN EMPLOYEES (L, PA)
Members who have not taken the oath of office and are not authorized to make arrest.

CIVIL LAW (L)
(1) Most often used to refer to property disputes between persons or groups. (2) Roman law, in contrast to English common law. (3) Early usage; secular law or the law of the state.

CIVIL LIBERTIES (L)
Rights recognized as properly belonging to all individuals subject to specified limits; e.g., the common good or the rights of others.

CIVIL RIGHTS (L)
Rights of citizens of the United States guaranteed by the Constitution of the United States, particularly Amendments I, XIII, XIV, and XV. (2). The rights of a citizen.

CIVIL SERVICE (L)

Government employees other than military, naval, legislative and judicial. Employees in the lower pay classification often have specific rights of tenure and promotion.

CLASS CHARACTERISTICS (Cr's)

Those unvariable characteristics of a particular make firearm or ammunition, e.g. number of grooves in rifling, direction of the twist of the rifling. Also applies to other evidence.

CLASSES OF POLICE ACTIVITIES (PA)

1. Patrol and observation
2. Supervision of public gatherings
3. Provision of miscellaneous field services
4. Response to calls
5. Investigation
6. Collection and preservation of evidence
7. Arrest of offenders
8. Preparation of reports
9. Presentation of court testimony

CLASSICAL CRIMINOLOGY (Cr'y)

Punishment must fit the crime; opposed to the death penalty, substituting imprisonment for it.

CLASSICAL SCHOOL OF CRIMINOLOGY (Cr'y)

Focused primarily on reform within criminal law, criminal procedures, and the general system of penalties; opposed arbi--trary and cruel punishment apparent in contemporary admini--stration of criminal justice; favored equality before the law, trial by jury, fixed penalties, and objective crime evaluation.

CLASSIFICATION (Cor)

Application of individual assignment of inmates to programs suited to their personal needs.

CLEAR AND CONVINCING PROOF (L)

Generally means proof beyond a reasonable, well--founded doubt.

CLEAR AND PRESENT DANGER (L)

Immediate serious violence is expected, advocated or past con--duct furnishes reason to believe such advocacy is contemplated.

CLEARLY PROVED (L)

See: Preponderance of evidence.

CLERICAL ERROR (L)

A mistake made in transcribing, or in the performance of other clerical operations.

CLERK (L)

An officer of a court who files pleadings, motions, orders and judgements, issues the process of the court and keeps records of legal proceedings.

CLEMENCY (L)

The power of pardon, commutation of sentence, reprieve, and amnesty.

CLIENT   (L)

One employing an attorney to appear for him in court, advise, assist, and defend him in any legal proceedings, and to represent him in legal business.

CLIP   (Cr's)

A metal case designed to hold a number of cartridges or shells to facilitate leading into repeating small arms.

CLOSE CUSTODY PRISONER   (Cor)

An inmate who must be locked up at night and must work in groups under close supervision within the prison proper.

CLUE   (PA, Cr's)

A thing or information which is apparently pertinent to the solution of case or crime.

COCHRAN–PATTERSON ACTS   (L)

Acts to forbid the transportation of any person in interstate or foreign commerce, kidnapped or otherwise unlawfully de-- tained, making such acts felonies.

COCK   (Cr's)

To set the action into position for firing, such as drawing back the hammer or firing pin against spring compression in prepara-- tion for firing.

CODE   (L)

A collection, compendium, or revision of laws. A complete system of positive law, scientifically arranged, and promul-- gated by legislative authority.

CODE OF PROFESSIONAL RESPONSIBILITY   (L)

The rules which govern the legal profession, consisting of nine canons, ethical considerations and disciplinary rules. Effective January 1, 1970.

COERCION   (L)

Constraint; compulsion; compelling one by physical force or treats to do an otherwise involuntary act.

COGITATIONIS PEONAM MENO PATITUR   (L)

No one suffers punishment for his thoughts.

COGNATI   (L)

Maternal relationship.

COGNIZANCE, OR CONUSANCE   (L)

Acknowledgement; recognition; jurisdiction; hearing a matter judicially. A judge is bound to take judicial cognizance of cer- tain matters without having them proved in evidence, e.g., the statutes of the state in which he holds court and the extent of his jurisdiction.

COGNOMEN   (L)

The surname or family name.

COHABIT (L)

To live together in the same house as man and wife.

COLLATION (L)

The comparison of a copy with its original to ascertain its validity.

COLLECTIVE BEHAVIOR (Cr'y)

Mobilization of a group for action.

COLLISION (L)

The striking together or against each other, of two or more objects.

COLLOQUIM (L)

(A talking together). A complaint or declaration for libel or slander that plaintiff was the one referred to thereby.

COLUMNY (L)

Slander, defamation.

COLLUSION (L)

A secret agreement between persons for some improper purpose.
See also: Combination.

COLORABLE (L)

That which is not what it purports or professes to be; deceptive.

COLOR OF RIGHT (L)

Semblance of right; apparent rightness.

COMBINATION (L)

A union of men for the purpose of violating the law.
See also: Collusion.

COMBINATION JOBS (Safe cracking) (Cr's)

Evidence that a safe has been opened by the combination, indicating that the safe was not locked properly, someone knew the combination or gained access to where the latter was kept.

COMBUSTION (Cr's)

Ballistics: The burning of powder in a barrel.

COMITY (L)

Voluntary acceptance of the decision of one court by another in similar circumstances without the requirement of legal pre--cedent.

COMITY OF NATIONS (L)

The obligation granted by courtesy to the laws of one nation within the territories of another, when they do not conflict with the laws of the latter.

COMMAND AUTHORITY (PA)

The chief of police will usually find his authority to impose disciplinary sanctions limited by city ordinance, Civil Service regulations, or policy of the municipal personnel office. He, as his command and supervisory officers, most always can reprimand a subordinate both orally and informally, or formally in writing. Invariably he has authority for summary suspensions under certain conditions, although these are usually "holding" actions designed to avoid further trouble during the time between a particular incident and formal, more deliberate action. Often, he may suspend an officer for a period of days or require extra service through withdrawing a number of an officer's leave days. The Chief often may delegate authority for disciplinary action of a lesser level of severity than he him--self may impose to subordinate officers.

COMMANDING OFFICER   (PA)

An officer in command of the department or any subdivision of it.

COMMENCE CRIMINAL PROSECUTION   (L)

Criminal prosecution may commence within statutory limitations when a complaint is filed in good faith and a warrant is issued.

COMMERCIAL SHOPLIFTER   (L)

One who steals merchandise and profits by its sale.

COMMINUTED FRACTURE

Fracture of bone into small fragments.

COMMISSION   (L)

Authorization to do an act. Evidence of appointment and authority to discharge duties of office. A body of persons appointed with necessary powers to do certain things. The act of perpetrating an offense. Compensation of a person employed to sell goods.

COMMISSIONER   (L)

A court officer authorized to perform certain judicial or administrative functions. A title given to heads of bureaus and officials charged with special duties.

COMMISSION FORM OF GOVERNMENT   (L)

Government by a body vested with the powers of municipal government.

COMMITMENT   (L)

The ordering of a person to a place of confinement.

COMMITTED IN PRESENCE OF OFFICER   (L)

A basis for arrest authorized by statute where circumstances are such as to present probable cause.

COMMITTEE   (L)

One or more members of a legislative body, corporate board of directors or association, appointed to consider and report upon certain matters or to carry out the resolutions of that body. A fiduciary appointed by a court to administer the assets of an incompetent person, analogous to a guardian (q.v.).

COMMON COUNTS (L)

Allegations to prevent variance of evidence.

COMMON INFORMER (L)

One who, without obligation, gives information leading to prosecution of offenders.

COMMON INTENT (L)

Natural definition of words.

COMMON KNOWLEDGE (L)

Knowledge of learning, history, experience, and facts of which every intelligent person is aware.

COMMON LAW (L)

That body of law originated, developed, formulated and ad-- ministered in England, and adopted by most of the states and peoples of Anglo--Saxon stock. Generally that part of law, juristic theory, and custom of any state or nation of general and universal application.

COMMON--LAW MARRIAGE (L)

Agreement by a man and woman to enter into marriage without ecclesiastical or civil ceremony, followed by assumption of marital duties and co--habitation.

COMMON NUISANCE (L)

See: Nuisance.

COMMON PLEAS (L)

Actions brought by man against man or by government when cause was of civil nature.

COMMUNICATIONS TASK (PA)

To receive and transmit information using devices of communi-- cation.

COMMUNITY BASED CORRECTIONS (Cor)

Correctional programs encompassing community--based facili-- ties and other community resources useful to correctional clients.

COMMUNITY CUSTODY PRISONER (Cor)

Daytime work release allowing inmate to leave institution and participate in community--based job.

COMMUNITY RELATIONS (PA)

The variety of ways to emphasize that the police are an impor-- tant part of the community they serve.

COMMUTATION (Cor, L)

Modification of a sentence to make the punishment less severe.

COMPETENCY (L)

The legal fitness or capacity of a witness to testify. The quality of evidence offered which makes it proper to be received.

See also: Credibility.

COMPETENT (L)

Legally qualified or capable.

COMPETENT COURT (L)

A court having lawful jurisdiction.

COMPETENT EVIDENCE (L)

The degree of legal qualification which the very nature of the thing to be proven requires.

COMPETENT WITNESS (L)

One who is legally qualified to testify.

COMPLAINANT (L)

One who makes a complaint; the plaintiff.

COMPLAINT (L)

The charge made before a proper officer than at offense has been committed by a person named or described. (2) Under modern rules of civil procedure, a pleading which must be filed to commence an action.

COMPLETED STAFF WORK (PA)

The study of a problem and the presentation of a solution, by a staff officer, in such form that all that remains to be done on the part of the head of the staff division, or the commander, is to indicate his approval or disapproval of the completed action.

COMPOUND (Cr's)

A pure substance composed of two or more elements.

COMPOUNDING A FELONY (L)

To enter into an agreement for a valuable consideration not to prosecute a felon.

COMPROMISE (L)

Settlement of an action or matters in dispute by agreement.

COMPULSION (L)

Force brought to bear to make a person do what he would otherwise not do.

COMPULSIVE DEVIANCE (L)

Deviance that the individual himself cannot control. The individual is compelled to continue or resume his deviant behavior despite the severe social penalties that result from it and despite his attempts to reform. Alcoholism and drug addiction are special forms of compulsive deviance.

COMPURGATOR (L)

One who, on oath, asserted another's innocence.

CONCEALED WEAPON (L)

A term for arms so placed that they cannot readily be seen under ordinary observation.

CONCEALMENT (L)

In contracts, the improper suppression of any fact or circumstance, by which one of the parties is induced to enter into the contract. The fraudulent hiding of one's property so that creditors may not levy on it to satisfy debts. Covering up or keeping secret the evidence of a crime.

CONCILIUM OR CONSILIUM (L)

Consultation; determination. Applied to the order setting a case down for argument on demurrer or in proceedings on a writ of error.

CONCLUDE (L)

To end; close up; determine.

CONCLUSION OF FACT (L)

An inference drawn from evidentiary facts.

CONCLUSION OF LAW (L)

A proposition arrived at by the application of artificial rules of law to facts pleaded.

CONCLUSIVE (L)

That which cannot be doubted.

CONCLUSIVE PRESUMPTION (L)

An inference which cannot be overcome by the introduction of evidence to the contrary.

CONCUBINE (L)

A woman who cohabits with a man as his wife without being married to him.

CONCURRENT JURISDICTION (L)

Authority shared by two or more legislative, judicial, or admin‐istrative officers or bodies to deal with the same subject matter.

CONCURRENT NEGLIGENCE (L)

Failure to exercise care by two or more persons, acting inde‐pendently, which failure combines to produce a single indivisi‐ble injury.

CONCURRENT WRIT (L)

A writ of summons of the same tenor as an original which re‐mains in force.

CONDEMNATION (L)

The taking of private property for a public or quasi‐public use, in return for fair compensation. A judgement or decree by which property seized for a violation of revenue or navigation laws is forfeited to the government. A judgement that a captured ship is a lawful prize.

CONDITIONAL RELEASE (Cor)

A type of release of prisoners without parole, but with certain conditions imposed.

CONDITIONS NECESSARY TO USE DEADLY FORCE (PA)

The arrest must be for a felony which normally causes or threatens death or serious bodily harm, or which involves the breaking and entering of a dwelling place.

The officer must reasonably believe that the arrest cannot otherwise be effected.

CONDONATION   (L)

A pardoning by a spouse of a conjugal offense by the marriage partner which prevents the offense from being made the subject of legal proceedings at any future time.

CONE   (Cr's)

The reduction of diameter in a barrel where the chamber joins the bore.

CONFEDERACY   (L)

A combination of two or more persons to damage or do injury to another or to commit some other unlawful act. A loose union of two or more states or nations.

CONFESSIO FACTA IN JUDICIO OMNI PROBATIONE MAJOR EST   (L)

A confession made in court is of greater effect than any proof.

CONFESSION   (L)

A direct acknowledgement of the truth of the guilty fact as charged.

CONFESSION AND AVOIDANCE   (L)

A plea admitting certain facts alleged by the opponent's preceding pleading, but avoiding their legal effect by alleging new matter.

CONFIDENCE GAMES   (L)

A form of fraud designed to separate a victim from his property or money through manipulation.

CONFIDENTIAL COMMUNICATIONS   (L)

Statements made by one person to another when there is a necessary relation of trust and confidence between them, which the person receiving them cannot be compelled to disclose.

CONFIDENTIAL INFORMANT   (L)

One who provides an investigator with confidential information concerning a past or projected crime.

CONFINEMENT   (L)

Confinement by either moral or physical restraint, threats of violence with a present force, or physical restraint of the person.

CONFISCATION   (L)

The appropriation of property taken from an enemy, or seized for a violation of law, to the use of the government.

CONFLICT   (Cr'y)

Occurs when two persons or groups maintain an animosity toward one another and where a rather hostile competition exists.

CONFLICTING EVIDENCE   (L)

Where there is a possibility that justification exists for drawing different conclusions from the same evidence.

CONFLICT OF INTEREST   (L)

A situation in which a government official (whether elected or appointed), by taking an action in his official capacity, would affect individuals or, more particularly, businesses with whom he has some connection in his capacity as a private citizen.

CONFLICT OF LAWS   (L)

Variance between laws of two states or countries relating to subject matter of suits brought in one of them, when parties to the suits, or some of them, or the subject matter, belong to the other.

CONFRONTATION   (L)

Bringing witnesses face to face with the accused; cross--exami--nation. The absolute right of cross--examination, i.e., con--frontation of witnesses, is basic to the American judicial system.

CONGENITAL   (Cr's)

Existing as such at birth.

CONGRESS, OR CONGRESS OF THE UNITED STATES   (L)

The name of the legislative body of the United States, com--posed of the Senate and House of Representatives.

CONJOINTS   (L)

Persons married to each other.

CONJURATION   (L)

A compact made by persons combining by oath to do public harm. The attempt to have conference with evil spirits.

CONNIVANCE   (L)

Guilty knowledge of, or assistance in, a crime. Consent, express or implied, by one spouse to the adultery of the other.

CONSANGUINEUS FRATER   (L)

A brother who has the same father.

CONSANGUINITY, OR KINDRED   (L)

Relationship of persons descended from some common ancestor.

CONSCIENCE   (L)

The moral sense of right and wrong inherent in every person by virtue of his existence as a social entity.

CONSENT   (L)

Voluntary accordance with, or concurrence in, what is done or proposed by another.

CONSENT AGREEMENT   (L)

The expressed or implied meeting of minds presupposing a mental capacity to act.

CONSENTIENTES ET AGENTES PARI POENA PLECTANTUR
     (L)

Those consenting and those perpetrating are liable to equal punishment.

CONSERVATORS OF THE PEACE (L)

Those appointed to preserve the public peace.

CONSOLIDATION (L)

The joining of several independent suits which involve common questions of law or fact, for the purpose of a joint hearing or trial. The fusing of many acts of a legislative body into one act.

CONSORTIUM (L)

Marital fellowship, company, companionship. The duties and obligations of marriage which the husband and wife take upon themselves toward each other.

CONSPICUOUS MASCULINITY (L)

An attempt to prove manhood by malicious and destructive acts.

CONSPIRACY (L)

An unlawful combination or agreement between two or more persons to carry into effect a purpose hurtful to some individual, or class or to the public at large.

CONSTABLES (L)

Persons appointed to keep the peace, serve writs, and levy executions.

CONSTABLEWICK (L)

The jurisdiction of a constable. Balewick.

CONSTAT (L)

It appears; a certificate of that which appears on the record.

CONSTITUENT (L)

A principal; one who appoints an agent or attorney. A voter or member of an electorate.

CONSTITUTION (L)

The fundamental and basic law of a state or nation which establishes the form and limitations of government and secures the rights of the citizens.

CONSTITUTIONAL (L)

In accordance with the constitution. Laws which contravene the constitution are null and void.

CONSTITUTIONALISM (L)

The doctrine that the power to govern should be limited by definite and enforceable principles of political organization and procedural regularity embodied in the fundamental law, or custom, so that basic constitutional rights of the individuals and groups will not be infringed.

CONSTITUTIONAL LAW (L)

Law derived from, related to, or interpretive of a constitution.

CONSTRUCTIO LEGIS NON FACIT INJURIAM   (L)

The construction of the law does, i.e., should be made to do, no injury.

CONSTRUCTION   (L)

The interpretation of a statute or written instrument.

CONSTRUCTIVE BREAKING   (L)

Burglarious entry by the use of collusion, trick, ruse, intimidation, or impersonation.

CONSUMMATION   (L)

The due completion of something.

CONTEMNER   (L)

Or Contemnor, one who has committed contempt of court.

CONTEMPORANEA EXPOSITIO EST OPTIMA ET FORTISSIMA IN LEGE   (L)

A contemporaneous interpretation is the best and most authoritative in the eye of the law.

CONTEMPT   (L)

A willful disregard or disobedience of public authority or an offense against the dignity and good order of the court. Similar authority is exercised by each house of the Congress of the United States, by state legislatures, and in some instances by administrative agencies. The contempt power is usually subject to judicial review.

See also: Contumacy.

CONTENTIOUS JURISDICTION   (L)

Authority to hear and determine matters between adversaries in an action or other judicial proceeding.

CONTEXT   (L)

The elements of a writing before and after a phrase or passage which may be looked at to explain its meaning.

CONTIGUOUS   (L)

(1) Actual contact or touching, as contiguous lands. (2) Close proximity.

CONTINGENCY   (L)

An unforeseeable but possible event; a fortuity.

CONTINUANCE   (L)

The adjournment of a cause from one day to another in the same or a subsequent term.

CONTINUOUS SPECTRUM   (Cr's)

A type of emission spectrum showing a continuous band of colors all blending into one another.

CONTRA   (L)

Latin, against; contrary to.

CONTRABAND   (L)

Goods exported or imported in violation of law. Goods

the possession of which constitutes a violation of law. (3) In international law, those goods which a neutral may not carry to a belligerent, e.g., munitions of war.

CONTRA BONOS MORES (L)

Against good morals.

CONTRACT SYSTEM (Cor)

A form of prisoner employment widely used from c. 1790 to c. 1865. Prisoners were let to private contractors under super--vision of prison personnel, while the contractor furnished the equipment and raw materials and supervised the work.

CONTRACULTURE (Cr'y)

A subculture that stands in opposition to important aspects of the dominant culture of the society.

CONTRA FORMAM STATUTI (L)

Contrary to the form of the statute.

CONTRA PACEM (L)

Against the peace.

CONTRA PROTERENTEM (L)

Against the one putting it forth.

CONTRIBUTORY NEGLIGENCE (L)

Failure of plaintiff to exercise care which contributes to his injury. In the majority of jurisdictions, contributory negligence will bar recovery by plaintiff.

CONTROL (PA)

Each delegation of authority should be accompanied by com--mensurate responsibility.

CONTROL CULTURE (Cr'y)

Those aspects of culture that make possible the orderly func--tioning of society by motivating and pressuring individuals to behave in accordance with social expectations.

CONTROLLING (PA)

Assurance of program development, support of policies, and conformance with procedures. Basically a supervisory matter but achieved through staff inspection processes.

CONTROL OF YOUTHFUL OFFENDERS (Cr'y)

To prevent development of delinquent tendencies in the young and aid in correction of such tendencies when they occur.

CONTUMACY (L)

A refusal to appear in court when legally summoned; disobedi--ence to the rules and orders of a court.

See also: Contempt.

CONVENTIONAL CRIMES (Cr'y)

Street crimes such as robbery, burglary, homicide, larceny, rape, and auto theft.

CONVERSION (L)

(1) The wrongful appropriation of the goods of another.
(2) Equitable conversion is the changing of the nature of pro–
perty, which may be (a) actual, e.g., by converting land into
money by selling it, or vice versa; or (b) constructive, where
such an operation is assumed to have, though it has not actually,
taken place, e.g., when an owner has agreed to sell land, and
dies before executing the conveyance, the executors are entitled
to the money, and not the heirs. Property constructively con–
verted assumes the same qualities as if the operation had been
actually carried out.

CONVEXITY OF BRAIN   (Cr's)
Curved exterior of the brain.

CONVICT   (L)
Proving and finding a person to be guilty of a felony or misde-
meanor. Persons found guilty of a felony or a misdemeanor.
Persons sentenced to death or imprisonment.

CONVICTION   (L)
The result of a criminal trial ending in a judgement of guilt.

CONVOLUTION   (Cr's)
Ridge on the surface of the brain.

COORDINATION OF EFFORT   (PA)
A commander's responsibility for coordination of personnel
within his span of control and with other element commanders
and supervisors.

COPY   (L)
A transcript of an original document.

CORAM   (L)
Before; in the presence of.

CORAM NOBIS   (L)
Before us; formerly a manner of appeal; applied to writs of
error.

CORAM NON JUDICE   (L)
Before one not the (proper) judge; a court which has no juris–
diction over the person, subject matter or process.

CORAM PARIBUS   (L)
Before his peers.

CORAM VOBIS   (L)
Before you; a writ of error directed to the court which tried
the cause; to correct an error in fact.

CORE   (Cr's)
The approximate center of the pattern area in a fingerprint.

CORESPONDENT, OR CO–RESPONDENT   (L)
A party accused of committing adultery with the accuser's
spouse. Often named as party to a divorce suit.

CORONER   (L)

An official possessing judicial and ministerial authority to hold inquests and act as the sheriff's substitute in the absence of the latter.

CORONER'S JURY   (L)

Citizens summoned for the purpose of holding an inquest.

CORPORAL PUNISHMENT   (L)

Physical punishment as distinguished from pecuniary punish- ment or a fine.

CORPUS   (L)

Body; the person; the whole; the element.

CORPUS COMITATUS   (L)

The whole county; power to deputize.

CORPUS DELICTI   (L)

The body of a crime. The material substance upon which a crime has been committed. The substantial fact that a crime has been committed.

CORPUS HUMANUM NON RECIPIT AESTIMATIONEM   (L)

A human body is not susceptible of appraisement.

CORRECTION   (Cor, L)

Punishment.

CORRECTIONAL ADMINISTRATION   (Cor)

Systematic organization and management of the basic necessi- ties and treatment programs of correctional institutions for presentation to correctional clients.

CORRECTIONAL CLIENT   (Cor)

A person in the correctional system subsequent to a finding of legal responsibility for damage to society.

CORRECTIONAL SYSTEM   (Cor)

The most isolated part of the criminal justice system; its insti-- tutions usually have thick walls and locked doors and are often located in rural areas. Its officials usually do not have everyday working relationships with officials from the system's other branches, and there is usually little supervision over their pro-- grams, isolated as they are from the public eye.

CORRECTIONS   (Cor)

One of society's attempts to rehabilitate and neutralize deviant behavior in adult criminals and juvenile delinquents.

CORROBORATIVE EVIDENCE   (L)

Additional testimony to reinforce a point previously the subject of proof.

CORROSION   (Cr's)

Deterioration by chemical action of the inside of a barrel; usually caused by products of combustion after firing.

CORRUPTION   (L)

Gross dishonesty or illegality; sometimes applied to influencing

a judge, juror or public officer to commit malfeasance or non--
feasance.

CORTEX (Cr's)

Outer layer of an organ.

COUNSEL (L)

One who gives legal advice; attorney–at–law. Collective noun;
all attorneys united in the management of a cause or advising
in a particular manner.

COUNSELING (Cor)

Use of interviews, psychological tests, guidance, and other
techniques to help solve personal problems and plan futures of
clients realistically.

COUNSELOR–AT–LAW (L)

An attorney-at-law.

COUNT (L)

Statement of a cause of action. A complaint has as many
counts as there are causes of action, or different statements of
the same cause of action. In criminal law, each part of an
indictment which charges a distinct offense.

COUNTER (L)

Contrary; opposed to.

COUNTER AFFIDAVIT (L)

A sworn statement in writing made in opposition to another
already made.

COUNTER BOND (L)

A bond (q.v.) given to indemnify a surety for signing one's
bond.

COUNTERCLAIM (L)

The defendant's claim against the plaintiff, which most courts
permit in response to the complaint.

COUNTERFEIT (L)

Fraudulent imitation made without lawful authority.

COUNTERMAND (L)

To revoke or recall.

COUNTERPART (L)

A corresponding part of duplicate. Where an instrument is exe–
cuted in several copies, one is the original and the others are
counterparts.

COUNTY (L)

Civil division of a state for judicial, administrative and political
purposes.

COUNTY COURT (L)

A tribunal with limited jurisdiction usually defined by various
state constitutions and statutes.

COURT (L)

An institution for the resolving of disputes. A place where justice is administered. The judge or judges when performing their official duties. Classifications; often consolidated:

a. Courts of record, producing a final record of proceedings

b. Courts not of record, wherein no final record is made

c. Courts of original jurisdiction, in which suits are initiated, and which have power to hear and determine causes in the first instance

d. Appellate courts, which take cognizance of causes removed from other courts

e. Courts of equity, which administer justice according to the principles of equity

f. Courts of law, which administer justice according to princi-- ples of common law

g. Civil courts, which give remedies for private wrongs

h. Criminal courts, in which public offenders are tried

i. Ecclesiastical courts, which formerly had jurisdiction over testamentary and matrimonial causes

j. Courts of admiralty, which have jurisdiction over maritime causes

k. Courts--martial, which have jurisdiction of offenses against the military or naval laws, committed by persons in that service.

COURT--BARON   (L)

An English court incident to every manor held any place within same, upon due notice.

COURT OF APPEALS   (L)

The highest courts of New York, Maryland, Virginia, and Kentucky. An intermediate appelate court in many states.

COURT OF COMMON PLEAS   (L)

A court of original and general jurisdiction.

COURT OF LAW   (L)

Any duly constituted tribunal administering the laws of the state or nation. A court of common law.

COURT OF STAR CHAMBER   (L)

An English court of ancient origin consisting of privy council-- lors, spiritual and temporal, two judges of common law, without a jury. Jurisdiction extended over riots, perjury, misbehavior of sheriffs, and other misdemeanors contrary to laws of the land; afterwards encompassing assertion of proclamations and orders of state, vindication of illegal commissions and grants of monopolies; holding for honorable that which it pleased, and for just that by which it profited, becoming both a court of civil rights and a court of revenue. Later abolished.

COURTS OF ASSIZE AND NISI PRIUS   (L)

English circuit courts composed of two or more judges of assize, sent twice a year to try matters of fact under dispute.

COVERTURE   (L)

Situation of a woman during marriage.

COVIN   (L)

Fraud, collusion.

CREDIBILITY   (L)

Veracity of a witness; the degree of credit assigned to testimony. For consideration by the jury.

See also: Competency.

CRIME   (L)

Commission or omission of any act, in violation of law, for which a penalty has been imposed as a sanction against such commission or omission.

CRIME CAUSATION, BIOLOGICAL DETERMINIST   (Cr'y)

Theory that the natural laws of heredity determine the eventual actions of the basic organism.

CRIME CAUSATION, CULTURAL DETERMINIST   (Cr'y)

Belief that man's behavior is merely a reflection of man's sociocultural world.

CRIME CAUSATION, DEMONOLOGICAL   (Cr'y)

Interpretation that assumes the presence of other wordly powers or spirits in the criminal event.

CRIME CAUSATION, INTELLECTUAL DETERMINIST   (Cr'y)

Assumption that crime has its origin in the general social system and the social contract.

CRIME CAUSATION, PHRENOLOGICAL EXPLANATION   (Cr'y)

Assumption that skull conformations reveal the person's facili‐ ties or propensities to behavior, tendencies being transmitted from parent to child.

CRIME CAUSATION, PSYCHOANALYTIC APPROACH   (Cr'y)

Theory that criminal behavior is a substitute response for re‐ pressed complexes produced by conflict in the unconscious mind creating feelings of guilt or anxiety, a desire to remove guilt feelings, and a wish to restore the proper balance of good against evil through punishment.

CRIME, COMMON LAW   (L)

Punishable by the force of common law, as distinguished statutory crime. Crime based upon formal "outlawing" of some act.

CRIME, CONTINUOUS   (L)

Consisting of a series of acts, which endure after the period of consummation, as the offense of carrying concealed weapons. Crimes "mala in se" are immoral or wrong in themselves, such as arson, rape or murder.

CRIME, FOLK   (Cr'y)

A legal violation quite common and not to be taken seriously, e.g., traffic law violations, white collar crime, chiseling, black market dealings, and other minor illegal actions. Folk criminals are quite numerous, unstigmatized, and differentially treated in the legal process.

CRIME INDEX   (Cr'y)

F.B.I. crime statistics (rate of crime for each 100,000 inhabi–tants) using seven crime classifications: murder, forcible rape, aggravated assault, burglary, larceny, and auto theft.

See also: Crime rates.

CRIME INVESTIGATION   (Cr's, PA)

The gathering of evidence, recovery of stolen property, and apprehension and prosecution of criminals.

CRIMEN   (L)

A crime.

CRIMEN FALSI   (L)

Forgery, perjury, counterfeiting, alteration of instruments, and other frauds.

CRIMEN LAESAE MAJESTATIS   (L)

Treason.

CRIMEN OMNIA EX SE NATA VITIAT   (L)

Crime vitiates all that springs from it.

CRIMEN REPETUNDARUM   (L)

Bribery.

CRIME, ORGANIZED   (Cr'y)

Crime committed by members of a formal organization devoted to activities in violation of law. Such criminal organizations have a rigid, formalized bureaucracy. These organizations often have influential arrangements with members of the local police and community leaders.

CRIME RATES   (Cr'y, PA)

The number of Index Crimes, either by individual classes or total per 100,000 population.

See also: Crime Index.

CRIMES MALA IN SE   (L)

Crimes "mala in se" are immoral or wrong in themselves, such as arson, rape or murder.

CRIMES MALA PROHIBITA   (L)

Crimes "mala prohibita" are prohibited by statute and consti-- tute crimes only because they are so prohibited.

CRIME, STATUTORY   (L)

Created by statute, as distinguished from the common law.

CRIME, WHITE COLLAR   (Cr'y)

Crime committed by a person of respectability and social status in the course of his occupation; e.g., embezzlement, fraud, graft, illegal combinations in restraint of trade, misrepresenta-- tion in advertising, infringement of patents, adulteration of food and drugs, fee--splitting by doctors, and bribery. Usually less severely punished than the more conventional crimes. There is less public resentment of white collar crime than of other types.

CRIMINAL   (L)

One who has committed a criminal offense, been adjudged guilty of crime or been legally convicted of said crime; an offense against the law, crime--related.

CRIMINAL ACT   (L)

A term equivalent to crime; sometimes used to soften the mean-- ing, or to imply a question of legal guilt. Intentional violation of a statute designed to protect human life is a criminal act.

CRIMINAL ACTION   (L)

The method by which a party charged with a public offense is accused and brought to trial and punishment. A criminal action is prosecuted by the state as a party, against a person charged with a public offense; at the instance of an individual, to prevent an apprehended crime against his person or property.

CRIMINAL CASE   (L)

An action instituted to punish an infraction of criminal law.

CRIMINAL CHARGE   (L)

An accusation of crime taking shape in a prosecution. Can be in the form of a written complaint, information or indictment.

CRIMINAL CONVERSATION, OR CRIM. CON.   (L)

Unlawful intercourse with a married person other than one's spouse, adultery.

CRIMINAL COURT   (L)

Where criminal cases are tried and determined; not for civil cases or persons charged with criminal offenses and being held for action by proper authority.

CRIMINAL GROSS NEGLIGENCE   (L)

Acts of commission or omission of a wanton or willful nature, showing reckless disregard of the rights of others, under cir-- cumstances reasonably calculated to produce injury the offender is charged with knowledge of the probably result of his acts.

CRIMINAL HOMICIDE   (L)

First-- and second--degree murder, nonnegligent (voluntary) and negligent (involuntary) manslaughter.

CRIMINAL INFORMATION   (L)

A proceeding brought by a public indictment or presentment to a grand jury.

CRIMINAL INTELLIGENCE (L)

Information or knowledge involving persons or organizations engaged or contemplating engagement in illegal activities.

CRIMINAL INTENT (L)

Malice evidenced by a criminal act.

CRIMINAL JURISDICTION (L)

The authority by which judicial officers take cognizance of and decide criminal cases.

CRIMINAL JUSTICE SYSTEM (Cr'y)

An operational apparatus designed to enforce standards of conduct in defense of individuals and the community.

CRIMINAL LAW (L)

Law enacted by recognized political authority that prohibits or requires specified behavior by all or by a designated category of persons in the society or community and provides specific punishment, administered by a constituted authority, for violators.

CRIMINAL, LEGALISTIC (Cr'y)

One who violates a law unintentionally through ignorance; e.g., a feeble--minded person; or because the law is so confusing that it is virtually impossible to obey. Persons accused of a crime to stop them from leading unpopular movements are sometimes also classified as legalistic criminals.

CRIMINAL LETTERS (L)

A form of criminal process similar to a civil summons.

CRIMINAL MOTIVE (L)

Mental self--inducement causing one to intend, and afterward commit, crime.

CRIMINAL PROCEDURE (L)

Formalized official activity that authenticates the fact of commission of a crime and authorizes punitive treatment of the offender.

CRIMINAL PROCEEDING (L)

Some step taken before a court against a person or persons charged with violation of criminal law.

CRIMINAL PROCESS (L)

That procedure instituted to (1) compel a person to answer for a crime or misdemeanor, (2) to aid in the detection or suppression of crime.

CRIMINAL, PROFESSIONAL (Cr'y, L)

A highly trained career criminal. Often involves a philosophy of crime and pride in one's work. Career in forgery, counterfeiting, and confidence games are particularly characteristic of professional criminals.

CRIMINAL PROSECUTION (L)

Court action instituted on behalf of the public, to secure conviction and punishment of one accused of crime.

CRIMINAL, PSYCHOPATHIC   (Cr'y, L)

One who commits a crime because he is psychologically unable
to control his behavior. Psychotics whose psychoses result in
illegal acts. They include kleptomaniacs, pyramaniacs, and
sexual psychopaths.

CRIMINAL SEXUAL PSYCHOPATHS   (Cr'y, L)

Those emotionally unstable persons who have a propensity
toward committing sex offenses.

CRIMINAL, SITUATIONAL   (Cr'y, L)

One who commits a crime due to overwhelming pressure
brought about by an unusual situation contrary to his normal
life pattern. Not likely to be a repeat offender.

CRIMINAL SYNDICALISM   (Cr'y)

The advocacy of unlawful methods for revolutionary purposes.
Statutes imposing severe penalties for such advocacy were
enacted in most states between 1917 and 1920.

CRIMINOLOGY   (Cr'y)

The study of criminal behavior, legal norms, and social atti--
tudes toward various types of crimes and criminals. Criminol--
ogy includes the sociology of law, the analysis of conflict
theories as theoretical explanations for the basic causes of crime
in society, the study of the social and psychological determi-
nants of crime, methods of apprehension and punishment, individual and social reform, and the prevention of crime.

CRIMPING   (Cr's)

A mechanical operation employed in loading metallic cartridges
consisting of slightly compressing the mouth or neck of a metal
case to hold its bullet securely in place. Applied also to shot
shells.

CRISIS   (Cr'y)

A serious interruption of the normal way of life of an individual
or group, resulting from the occurence of an unexpected situation for which the individual or group is not prepared, and
which raises problems for which customary reponses are not
adequate and requiring the development of new modes of
thought and action.

CROSS–EXAMINATION   (L)

The questioning of a witness by opposing counsel after direct
examination. The form of the questions is designed to elicit
evidence from a hostile witness.

CROTCH WORKER   (L)

A female commercial shoplifter who steals by placing merchandise under her dress, between her legs, and leaving the store.

CRUELTY (L)

Family law; act which imperil life, health, or physical comfort of a husband or wife. Cruelty to animals, i.e., abuse or mistreat-- ment, is an indictable offense by the laws of many states.

CRYSTALLINE SOLID (Cr's)

A sold in which the constituent atoms have a regular arrange- ment.

CUL DE SAC (L)

A dead end street, sometimes with a circular area at the end large enough for a vehicle to turn around in.

CULPA (L)

Fault; neglect.

CULPA LATO DOLO AEQUIPARATUR (L)

Gross negligence is held equivalent to intentional wrong.

CULPABLE NEGLIGENCE (L)

A degree of carelessness greater than simple negligence. A negligent act or omission accompanied by culpable disregard for the foreseeable consequences.

CULPAE POENA PAR ESTO (L)

Let the punishment be proportioned to the crime.

CUMULATIVE EVIDENCE (L)

Testimony offered to prove what has already been proven by other evidence.

CUMULATIVE POISONING (Cr's)

Slow additions of poison followed by a sudden increase in intensity of its action.

CUMULATIVE SENTENCE OR CONSECUTIVE SENTENCE (L)

Additional judgement to take effect after expiration of an original judgement.

CURATIVE ACT (L)

A law passed intended to correct irregularities in a law pre-- viously passed.

CURIA (L)

The court.

CURIA ADVISARE VULT (L)

The court wishes to consider the matter; an entry reserving judgement until some subsequent day.

CURTILAGE (L)

Real property joining a dwelling house.

CUSTODIA LEGIS, OR IN CUSTODIA LEGIS (L)

In the custody of the law.

CUSTODIAL ZONING (Cor)

Time and space differentiations between groups of inmates in the yard and physical plant.

CUSTODY (L)

The care and keeping of anything; also, the detainer of a man's
person by virtue of lawful process or authority; actual imprisonment. Detention; charge; control; possession. Also, the
mere power, legal or physical, of imprisoning or of taking
manual possession.

CUSTOM   (Cr'y, L)
A compulsory practice of the people which has acquired the
force of law.

CUSTOMARY LAW   (Cr'y, L)
Law derived from long--established usages and customs; dis--
tinguished from written law.

CUTANEOUS   (Cr's)
Pertaining to the skin.

CYANOSIS   (Cr's)
A bluish discoloration of the skin and tissues due to lack of
adequate oxygenation of the blood.

DACTYLOSCOPY (Cr's)

The study of fingerprints and their use as a means of identification.

DAMAGE (L)

Injury to person, property, or reputation, caused by a wrongful act or negligence, or by accident.

DANGEROUS INSTRUMENTALITY (L)

Devices designed to do harm but excluding devices dangerous only by negligence.

DATE (L)

The designation of the time of execution of an instrument.

DAY IN COURT (L)

The right of a person to make complaint or present defense in court and be heard.

DEADLY FORCE (L, PA)

Employment of instrumentation designed to produce death or from which it can be reasonably expected that such will be the result.

DEATH (L)

(1) Cessation of all vital signs, by clinical determination of a physician. (2) Irreversible coma, requiring: a) no receptivity or responsiveness to externally applied stimula and inner need; b) no movement, breathing, or reflexes; and c) a flat electro-encphalograph reading; all tests to be repeated at least 24 hours later with no change.

DEATH BY ACCIDENTAL MEANS (L)

The termination of life by an unexpected, chance event.

DEBET QUIS JURI SUBJACERE UBI DELINQUIT (L)

Everyone ought to be subject to the law of the place where he offends.

DEBT (L)

Something owed, an obligation.

DECEDENT (L)

A deceased person.

DECEIT (L)

Facts withheld, misrepresented or falsely intimated to be true. (2) Formerly; common law action to recover damages for loss caused by misrepresentation or fraud.

DECIPI QUAM FALLERE EST TUTIUS (L)

It is safer to be deceived than to deceive.

DECISION (L)

Determination or judgement of the court, as opposed to reason-ing employed in its opinion.

DECLARANT (L)

One who makes a declaration.

DECLARATION (L)

A public declaration. The written statement by a plaintiff of cause for action. A statement made by a party to a transaction or event, frequently admissible in evidence.

DECLARATORY JUDGMENT (L)

A binding judicial declaration of the existing rights of parties under statute, contract, will, or other document.

DECOY (PA, Cr'y)

One whose role is to lure a person into a situation where he may be the victim of a crime.

DECREE (L)

The judicial decision of a litigated cause by a court of equity.

DEDIMUS POTESTATEM (L)

We have given the power. Formerly a writ or commision empowering the persons to whom it is directed to do a certain act.

DEFACTO (L)

In fact, actually.

DEFAMATION (L)

The uttering of spoken or written words tending to injure the reputation of another for which action for damages may be brought.

DEFAULT (L)

Fail to appear in court at an appointed or certain time, failure to discharge a duty.

DEFECT (L)

A lack of perfection or completeness; an imperfection, flaw or failing. To change one's loyalty or to desert.

DEFECTUS SANTUINIS (L)

Latin, failure of issue, i.e., lack of children.

DEFENDANT (L)

The party against whom an action is brought, warrant issued or indictment found.

DEFENSE (L)

Forcible resistance of an attempt to injure or commit a felony. (2) Any fact or argument of law which exonerates a person from criminal prosecution or the claims asserted against him in a civil lawsuit. (3) The conduct of a trial on behalf of a defendant.

DEFENSE COUNSEL (L)

Counsel for the defendant.

DEFRAUD (L)

Acts, omissions or concealments involving a breach of duty, trust or confidence, injurious to another, or by which undue and unconscionable advantage is taken of another. (2) To cheat, trick or dupe.

DE HOMINE REPLEGIANDE (L)

Formerly a writ to take a man out of prison or out of the cus-- tody of a private person.

DE JURE (L)

By right; lawful.

DE JURE JUDICES, DE FACTO JURATORES, RESPONDENT (L)

The judges answer concerning the law, the jury concerning the facts.

DELEGATE (L)

One authorized to act for another. One elected to repre- sent others in deliberative assembly, such as a political conven- tion.

DELEGATION (L)

A body of representatives of a particular nation, state, district, or county in a legislative or other assembly, or at the court of a foreign power.

DELEGATION OF AUTHORITY (RULE) (PA)

One is only held responsible for the accomplishment of orders when the authority necessary for their accomplishment has previously been delegated to him.

DELETION (L)

Erasure, obliteration or removal.

DELIBERATELY (L)

Intentionally.

DELINQUENCY (Cr'y)

Any violation of the law by an adult or child; usually refers to juvenile delinquency.

DELINQUENCY, JUVENILE (Cr'y)

Violation of a law or city ordinance by an individual below the legal adult age of the community; essentially a legal concept. Much juvenile delinquent behavior, when performed by an adult, is considered criminal behavior. The legal age dividing juvenile delinquency from adult crime varies from state to state. Punishment is influenced by attitudes of the local community and degree of tolerance.

See also: Delinquent child.

DELINQUENT CHILD (L, Cr'y)

A person younger than a specified age, who has violated any law or is incorrigible.

See also: Delinquency, juvenile.

DELINQUENT OFFENSES (Cr'y, L)

More extensive than adult crimes; covering behavior often

permitted adults.

DELINQUENT SUBCULTURE   (Cr'y)

A behavior form which children learn as they become members of groups in which delinquent conduct is already established and operative.

DELIVERY   (L)

(1) The actual, or constructive act of transferring possession. (2) Transfer of a deed from grantor to grantee, or one acting in his behalf, which is absolute, immediately; or conditional, when the deed is handed by the grantor to a third person, to be by him handed to the grantee when certain specified conditions shall be performed. (3) With respect to instruments, documents of title, chattel paper or securities, voluntary transfer of possession.

DELTA   (Cr's)

A triangular--shaped detail found in all fingerprints, but not in arches. Formed by bifurcation of a ridge or through wide separation of two ridges which have, up to the point of the delta, run side by side.

DE LUNATICO INQUIRENDO   (L)

Formerly a writ for ascertaining whether a party charged is a lunatic or not.

DE MANUCAPTIARE   (L)

Formerly a writ commanding the sheriff to take sureties for a prisoner's appearance and to set him free.

DEMENTIA   (Cr'y)

Mental deterioration.

DE MINIMUS NON CURAT LEX   (L)

The law does not concern itself with trivial matters.

DEMOCRACY   (Cr'y, PA)

Among the values which democracy has been thought to embody are the importance of individual man, the peaceful voluntary adjustment of disputes, the insuring of peaceful change in a changing society, the orderly succession of rulers, a minimum use of coercion, recognition of diversity and pluralism, and the attainment of justice.

DEMUR   (L)

To stay, or abide. To object formally to a pleading.

DEMURRER   (L)

A formal response to a pleading, admitting the truth of the allegations, for the purposes of argument, but asserting that no cause of action, or defense, is stated by the allegations of the pleading. It imports that the party demurring will not proceed until the court decides whether he is bound to do so. Demurrers are either general, where no particular cause is assigned and insufficiency is stated in general terms, or special, where particular defects are pointed out. Demurrers may be to the whole or any part of a pleading. Under modern rules of civil procedure, the demurrer has been replaced by a motion to dismiss for failure to state a claim.

DENIZEN   (L)

An alien with some privileges of a citizen. An inhabitant or resident.

DE NOVO   (L)

Anew; afresh. A trial do novo is a trial which is held for a second time, as if there had been no former decision.

DENSITY   (Cr's)

A physical property of matter that is equivalent to the mass per unit volume of a substance.

DE ODIO ET A TIA   (L)

Formerly a writ commanding the sheriff to inquire whether a person charged with murder was committed upon just cause of suspicion, or merely on account of someone's hatred and ill will.

DEPARTMENT   (PA)

An administrative subdivision of a nation or government.

DEPARTMENT RULES   (PA)

Rules established to control the conduct of members of the force; may be embodied into the duty manual or published as a separate volume.

DEPOSE   (L)

To give testimony under oath. To oust from public office.

DEPOSITION   (L)

Testimony reduced to writing under oath or affirmation, before a public officer, in answer to questions submitted by the party desiring the deposition and the opposite party.

DEPRESSANT   (Cr's)

A substance used to depress the functions of the central nervous system. Depressants calm irritability and anxiety, and may induce sleep.

DEPTH OF FOCUS   (Cr's)

The thickness of a specimen entirely in focus under a microscope.

DEPUTY   (L, PA)

One who acts in place of another in the administration of a public office. Usually has power to do any act which the principal might do, and, acts in his name.

DERANGEMENT   (Cr'y)

Insanity.

DERELICT   (L)

Abandoned, deserted.

DERIVATIVE PENALIZATIONS (Cr'y)

Unintended negative results from infliction of an intended sanction.

DERMAL NITRATE TEST (Cr's)

(Paraffin gauntlet test.) A procedure designed to determine whether a suspect has recently discharged a firearm.

DESERTION (L)

Intentional abandonment of an obligation. Often defined by statute or court decision.

DETECTIVE (PA)

A plainclothes officer engaged in investigating civil and criminal matters.

DETENTION HOME (Cr's)

Juvenile hall. A secure but nonjail-like short term facility, separate from any jail and from any public building other than a juvenile court.

DETERRENCE THEORY (Cr'y)

The theory that the main purpose of punishment is to prevent crime; the knowledge that severe punishment will follow com-- mission of a crime is the most effective way to discourage po-- tential criminals from committing crimes, and the experience of severe punishment is the most effective way of discouraging criminals from committing additional crimes.

DETONATING CORD (Cr's)

A cord like explosive containing a core of high explosive material, usually PETN. Also called Primacord.

DEVIANT BEHAVIOR (Cr'y)

Behavior different from the majority of a society.

DE VENTRE INSPICIENDO (L)

Formerly a writ to inspect the body, when a woman claimed to be pregnant.

DIASTOLE (Cr's)

Period of heartbeat during which the heart chambers are dilated and fill with blood, to be emptied during systole.

DICTUM OR OBITER DICTUM (L)

A statement by a judge concerning a point of law which is not necessary for the decision of the case in which it is stated. Usually, dictum is not as persuasive as is its opposite, i.e., holding (q.v.).

DIES (L)

A day.

DIES A QUO (L)

The day from which.

DIES GRATIAE (L)

Days of grace.

DIFFERENTIAL ASSOCIATION   (Cr'y)
>   Edwin H. Sutherland's argument that crime is learned in a systematic manner as persons associate within deviant groups.

DIFFERENTIAL OPPORTUNITIES   (Cr'y)
>   The differential potential for fullfilling cultural goals through institutionalized procedures.

DIGEST   (L)
>   A methodically arranged and indexed compilation of abstracts of decisions, intended to aid an attorney in finding precedent cases which are relevant to his problem cases.

DILAUDID (DIHYDROMORPHINONE HYDROCHLORIDE)   (Cr's)
>   Closely allied to morphine in chemical nature and physiological effects. Effective in doses considerably smaller than morphine. Withdrawal symptoms qualitatively identical to abstinence from morphine.

DILIGENCE   (L)
>   Care or persistence.

DIMINUTION   (L)
>   Decrease or reduction.

DIPLOIC VEINS   (Cr's)
>   Veins passing in the spongeous bone between the internal and external layers of the skull.

DIPLOMATIC IMMUNITY   (L)
>   Immunity of all accredited foreign diplomatic officials, subor-- dinates and servants, from arrest.

DIRECT ATTACK   (L)
>   An application or motion to amend, vacate or appeal a judge-- ment.

DIRECT CONTEMPT   (L)
>   Words spoken or acts done in the presence of a judge, while court is in session, tending to embarrass or prevent justice.

DIRECTED VERDICT   (L)
>   Determination by a jury, at the direction of the court, where there has been a failure or overwhelming weight of evidence, or where the law, as applied, favors one of the parties.

DIRECT EVIDENCE   (L)
>   That means of proof tending to show existence of a fact in question, without intervention of proof of any other fact; distinguished from circumstantial evidence, often called "in-- direct."

DIRECT EXAMINATION   (L)
>   Initial questioning of a witness by the party calling him.

DIRECTING   (PA)
>   An independent process at a point of action facilitating

movement toward goals at every level of a police agency not restricted to supervisory, command, or administrative person-- nel.

DIRECTION LINE   (Cr's)

Direction in which the subject is moving.

DISAGREEMENT   (L)

A dispute, difference or variance.

DISBAR   (L)

To cancel the privilege to practice law, as a result of miscon-- duct.

DISCHARGE   (Cor)

A court order (1) freeing a person held to answer a criminal charge. (2) Relief of a jury from further consideration of a case.

DISCIPLINE   (PA)

A function of command exercised to develop acceptance of direction and control; a positive form of training and an impor-- tant tool for elimination of weakness and development of self-- control.

DISCONTINUANCE   (L)

The failure to proceed in, or the voluntary dismissal of, a case.

DISCOVERY   (L)

A method by which opposing parties to a lawsuit may obtain full, factual information concerning the entire area of contro-- versy to disclose the genuine points of factual dispute and facil-- itate adequate preparation for trial.

DISCREDIT   (L)

To cast doubt on the veracity of testimony by attacking the witness's reliability as an accurate source of information.

DISCRETION   (L)

Use of private and independent judgement; authority of a trial court not controlled by inflexible rules, but exercised as the trial judge believes best under the circumstances, subject to re-- view. Ability to distinguish between good and evil.

DISCRIMINATION   Cr'y)

Differential treatment owing to membership in a particular social group.

DISMISS   (L)

To send a defendant or action out of court; final, i.e., after a full hearing on the merits, or without prejudice, i.e. when plaintiff is at liberty to bring another action for the same cause.

See also: Dismissal.

DISMISSAL (L)

An order or judgement finally disposing of an action.

See also: Dismiss.

DISORDER (PA, L)

Disturbance of the peace.

DISPATCHER (PA)

Aids the commanding officers of all divisions in communicating their orders to officers in the field.

DISPENSATION (L)

Legal exemption; permission to act in an otherwise legally for-- bidden manner.

DISPERSION (Cr's)

The separation of light into its component wavelengths.

DISSECTING ANEURYSM (Cr's)

Hemorrhage which breaks into the wall of a blood vessel and proceeds between its layers.

DISSENTING OPINION (L)

A judicial opinion in disagreement with the majority of a court tribunal by one or more members. Such opinions may be a foreshadowing of changes of rules of law.

DISTRICT (L)

A geographical subdivision of a political entity for administra-- tive, political or judicial purposes.

DISTRICT (PATROL) (PA)

A geographical subdivision of the city for patrol purposes usually with its own station and commanded by a captain charged with the basic responsibility for administering, direct-- ing, and controlling the patrol force in that district. However, where the size of platoons justifies assignment of captains as watch commanders districts should be commanded by persons having the exempt title of district commander.

DISTRICT ATTORNEY (L)

An officer appointed for each judicial district of the United States, whose duty it is to prosecute, in such district, all persons charged with violating the laws of the United States, and to represent the United States in all civil actions pending in such district to which the United States is a party.

DISTRICT COURTS (L)

Trial courts established in United States judicial districts. Some states constitute a single district but larger states are divided into two or more. State courts established for hear- ing and deciding causes within their jurisdiction. In some, jurisdiction is chiefly appellate, in others it is original.

DIVERSITY (L)

A plea by a prisoner, alleging mistaken identity.

DIVISION (PA)

A primary subdivision of a bureau or office of the chief having a department—wide function for general police service of specialized activity. In departments without district stations, each division is usually commanded by a captain; in depart-- ments having district stations a division is usually commanded by a chief, a director, or a supervising captain.

DIVISION OF OPINION   (L)

A disagreemnt between the judges constituting a court prevent-- ing a judgement from being rendered in a matter before them.

DIVISIONS OF FUNCTIONS   (PA)

Line departments perform much of the day--to--day personnel management practices as a function of supervision and com-- mand.

DIVORCE   (L)

Judicial severance of the tie of matrimony. It may be an abso-- lute divorce of nullity of marriage, which is complete; or a legal separation which does not entitle the parties to marry again.

DOCK   (L)

In some courts; the prisoner's bench.

DOCKET   (L)

An agenda for court proceedings, an abstract or brief entry in a court of record, or a book of brief entries of acts done in court.
See also: Calendar.

DOCTRINE   (L)

A principle of law, often developed through court decisions; a precept or rule.

DOCUMENT   (L)

A deed, agreement, letter, receipt or other instrument in writing used to prove a fact. Civil law; evidence delivered in due form of whatever nature.

DOE, JOHN   (L)

One of the forms used to designate a party to a civil suit or criminal prosecution, whose name is not known.

DOLI CAPAX   (L)

Capable of distinguishing between right and wrong.

DOLI INCAPAX   (L)

Incapable of distinguishing between right and wrong.

DOLOSUS VERSATUR IN GENERALIBUS   (L)

He who wishes to deceive deals in generalities.

DOLUS   (L)

An act which deceives another to his harm, or violates a confidence. Used generally in the sense of willful deceit, fraud, i.e., Dolus malus.

DOMESTIC   (L)

Relating to the home, household or one's state or nation.

DOMICILE   (L)

One's place of legal and/or permanent residence.

DONOR (L)

One who makes a gift or confers power of appointment.

DORMANT (L)

Sleeping; silent; not acting.

DORMANT CLAIM (L)

A claim abeyance; not in force.

DOUBLE ACTION (Cr's)

Cocking and firing of firearm with one continuous pull of finger.

DOUBLE JEOPARDY (L)

Common--law and constitutional prohibition against second prosecution after a first trial for the same offense.

DOUBT, REASONABLE (L)

That state which, after comparison and consideration of all evidence, leaves the minds of jurors in such condition that they cannot feel an abiding conviction to a moral certainty of the truth of the charge; such doubt as would cause a reasonable and prudent man to pause and hesitate to act upon the truth of the matter charged.

DRIVER INDEX (PA)

An index containing the names of persons involved in automobile accidents or arrested or served with citations, notices of violation, or written warnings.

DROIT (L)

Law; a right.

DROP (Cr's)

As applied to a gunstock, it means downward bend.

DROP SHOT (Cr's)

Soft shot.

DRUG ADDICTION (L)

The condition of one who habitually or compulsively uses narcotics to such extent as to negate all self--control.

DRUNKENNESS (L)

The condition of one whose mind is affected by ingestion of alcoholic beverages; intoxication; inebriation.

DUCES TECUM (L)

A type of subpoena requiring presentation of documents.

DUE PROCESS OF LAW (L)

Compliance with the fundamental rules for fair and orderly legal proceedings. Legal proceedings which observe rules designed for the protection and enforcement of individual rights and liberties.

DUODENUM (Cr's)

The left part of the small intestine.

DUPLICATE (L)

One of two alike documents; an executed copy.

DUPLICITY   (L)

Deception or double-dealing. Formerly the union of more than one cause of action or defense in a single pleading.

DURA MATER   (Cr's)

Hard, outermost of three membranes covering the brain.

DURESS   (L)

Unlawful constraint execised upon one forced to do some act that otherwise would not have been done. It may be either "duress of imprisonment," where the person is deprived of liberty to force compliance, or by violence or actual injury, or duress per minas, consisting in threats of imprisonment or great physical injury or death. Duress may also include the same injuries, threats, or restraint exercised upon the man's wife, child, or parent.

DUTY   (L)

Obligation; correlative to a right. That which a person is obliged to do or refrain from doing. A responsibility which arises from the unique relationship between particular parties. What one should do, based on the probability of foreseeability of injury to a party. A tax.

DUTY MANUAL   (PA)

Describes procedures and defines the duties of officers assigned to specified post or positions. Duty manuals and changes in them should be made effective by general order; the changes should be incorporated into the first revision of the duty manual.

DWELLING   (L)

Any building or habitation or part thereof in which a person is then "temporarily or permanently residing;" includes a room or an apartment in a hotel which the guest and his family are entitled to occupy exclusively. Limited to that part of the building or other habitation actually used for residential pur–poses.

See also: Dwelling House.

DWELLING HOUSE   (L)

A building used as a residence.

See also: Dwelling.

DYER ACT   (L)

A federal prohibition making illegal the transportation of stolen motor vehicles in interstate or foreign commerce.

DYING DECLARATION   (L)

Hearsay evidence admissible in some courts under certain cir--cumstances, of a statement made by a person aware of his immi--nent death.

DYSPNEA   (Cr's)

Shortness of breath, labored respiration.

EADEM EST RATIO, EADEM EST LEX (L)

The same reason, the same law.

EARNINGS (L)

Compensation; the exact meaning depending upon the context in which it is used.

EARWITNESS (L)

One attesting to something that he has heard himself.

EASEMENT (L)

A right of one owner of land to make lawful and beneficial use of the land of another, created by an express or implied agree--ment.

EAT INDE SINE DIE (L)

Words sometimes used on the acquittal of a defendant, that he may go thence without a day, i.e., be (finally) dis--missed.

EAVESDROPPING (PA, Cry)

Clandestine hearing of a conversation that was not intended for the hearer; wiretapping.

ECTOPIC (Cr'y)

Out of the normal position.

EDEMA (Cr's)

Swelling due to accumulation of fluid in tissue.

EFFECTUS SEQUITUR CAUSAM (L)

The effect follows the cause.

EI INCUMBIT PROBATIO, QUI DICIT, NON QUI NEGAT (L)

The proof lies upon him who affirms, not upon him who denies.

EJECTMENT (L)

Dispossession, expulsion.

EJECTOR (Cr's)

That part of the mechanism of a firearm which throws the expended casing from the arm.

EJUS EST NON NOLLE QUI POTEST VELLE (L)

He may consent tacitly who may consent expressly.

ELECTION (L)

The making of a choice or selection, e.g., the choice of a public official.

ELECTOR (L)

One with the right to vote.

ELECTROCUTE (Cr'y)

To kill by electricity.

ELECTRON ORBITALS (Cr'y)

The pathway of electrons as they move around the nuclei of atoms. Each orbital is associated with a particular electronic energy level.

ELECTROPHORESIS (Cr's)

A technique for the separation of molecules through their migration on a support medium while under the influence of an electrical potential.

ELEMENT (Cr'y)

A collection of atoms all having the same atomic number. An element cannot be broken down into simpler substances by chemical means.

ELISORS (L)

Those persons appointed to perform the duties of the sheriff and coroner when the latter have been challenged for interest or partiality.

ELOIGN (L)

To remove; to take to a distance.

ELONGATA (L)

A return sometimes made by a sheriff in replevin, meaning that the personal property sought is not to be found, or has been removed to a place unknown to him.

ELONGATED BULLET (Cr's)

Longer than wide; it is evolved from the round bullet.

ELONGATUS (L)

Sometimes a sheriff's return to a writ, meaning that the man is out of the sheriff's jurisdiction.

EMBEZZLEMENT (L)

The appropriation to one's own use, that person being an agent or employee, of money or property received by him for and on behalf of his employer. It differs from larceny, in that em-- bezzled property is not at the time in the actual or legal posses-- sion of the owner.

EMBOLISM (Cr's)

Sudden obstruction of a blood vessel by an embolus.

EMBOLUS (Cr's)

An abnormal particle (such as an air bubble or fat particle) cir-- culating in the blood.

EMBRACERY (L)

Attempt to corrupt a jury. The person making the attempt is called an embraceor.

EMINENT DOMAIN (L)

The right of a government to take private property for public use, in return for fair compensation.

EMISSION SPECTRUM (Cr's)

Light emitted from a source and separated into its component colors or frequencies.

EMOTIONAL CATHARSIS (Cor)

Generally speaking, the caseworker allows the client to talk about his ambitions, demands, hopes, and fears and generally get things off his chest.

EMPIRICAL   (L)

Based upon facts gathered from observation, experience or experiment.

EMPIRICAL RESEARCH   (L)

Investigation or inquiry which is based on empirical (q.v.) facts.

EMPLOY   (L)

The personal relationship in which one engages or uses another as an agent or substitute in transacting business, or the perfor-- mance of some service, including skilled or unskilled labor or professional services.

EMPLOYEE   (L)

One who does work for another.

EMPLOYER   (L)

One who hires another to do work for him.

EMPTIO   (L)

The act of buying.

EMPTOR   (L)

A purchaser.

EMPYEMA   (Cr's)

Presence of pus in a body cavity.

ENACT   (L)

To establish by law; to decree.

ENCEINTE   (L)

Pregnant; with child.

ENCEPHALOMYELITIS   (Cr's)

Inflammation involving the brain and the spinal cord.

ENCROACH   (L)

To intrude slowly or gradually upon the rights of property of another.

ENDOCARDITIS   (Cr's)

Inflammation of the inner lining of the heart.

ENDOCRINE   (Cr's)

A gland which secretes its product into the blood stream.

ENDOMETRIAL CAVITY   (Cr's)

Cavity of the uterus.

ENDOMETRIUM   (Cr's)

Inner lining of the uterus.

ENDOTHERMIC REACTION   (Cr's)

A chemical transformation in which heat energy is absorbed from the surroundings.

ENERGY   (Cr's)

In ballistics, the force or power of a charge.

ENFORCEMENT INDEX   (PA)

An arrest index; the ratio of traffic citations to injury accidents.

Useful in maintaining a suitable level of enforcement and en-
suring uniform application at locations and during the hours
when needed.

ENFORCEMENT TOLERANCE   (PA)

(1) That margin or degree of deviation needed to assure that a
violation has in fact occurred, allowing for reasonable human
and mechanical errors in measurement and judgement. (2) The
amount or degree of enforcement that may be maintained
indefinitely with public acquiescence.

ENGROSSED BILL   (L)

A legislative proposal in final form and ready for passage or
enactment into law.

ENJOIN   (L)

To require that something be or not be done, enforceable by fine
or imprisonment.

ENROLL   (L)

To record; to register; to enter into record any act, order or
judgement of a legal body.

ENTIRETY   (L)

The whole, as distinguished from moiety, i.e., the half or part.

ENTITLE   (L)

To give a right or title to.

ENTRAPMENT   (L)

The act of officers or agents of the government of inducing a
person to commit a crime not contemplated by him, for the
purpose of instituting criminal prosecution against him. The
mere act of furnishing the accused an opportunity, where
criminal intent was already present, is not entrapment.

ENTRY   (L)

"Entry" includes insertion of any part of the body into land
and buildings and may involve "the breaking or destruction of
any portion of the outer part of a building or enclosure used
for its protection or the change in location of any such part,
such as the moving or pushing aside of any object placed there
as a barrier." Insertion of a pole or hook may also constitute
entry.

ENVIRONMENT   (Cr'y)

Everything physical, social or cultural that stimulates and influences the behavior of the individual or group.

ENVIRONMENTAL MANIPULATION   (Cor)

Modification or removal of the client's problems from his
environment.

ENZYME   (Cr's)

A type of protein that acts as catalyst for certain specific reactions.

EPENDYMA   (Cr's)
   Lining membrane of the ventricles of the brain and the spinal
   canal.
EPENDYMITIS   (Cr's)
   Inflammation of the ependyma.
EPIDERMIS   (Cr's)
   Upper layer of the skin.
EPIDURAL   (Cr's)
   Situated over the dura.
EPIGLOTTIS   (Cr's)
   A thin plate of cartilege behind the tongue and in front of the
   glottis that covers the airway during swallowing.
EPINEPHRINE   (Cr's)
   Substance produced by the medullary portion of the adrenal
   gland. This hormone accelerates the heartbeat, causes vaso--
   constriction, increases blood pressure and the hearts output.
EQUALITY   (L)
   The condition extant when one has no unfair advantage over
   another. Uniformity or likeness.
EQUAL PROTECTION OF THE LAWS   (L)
   The equal protection of the laws of a state is extended to per--
   sons within its jurisdiction, within the meaning of the constitutional requirement, when its courts are open to them on the
   same conditions as to others, with like rules of evidence and
   modes of procedure, for the security of their persons and
   property, the prevention and redress of wrongs, and the en--
   forcement of contracts; when they are subjected to no restric--
   tions in the acquisition of property, the enjoyment of personal
   liberty and the pursuit of happiness, which do not generally
   affect others; when they are liable to no other or greater bur--
   dens and charges than such as are laid upon others; and when no
   different or greater punishment is enforced against them for a
   violation of the laws.
EQUITABLE   (L)
   Fair; reasonable; proper. Rights and duties historically enforced only in courts of equity. Preventive and remedial
   justice appropriate to the unique facts of a case, and rendered
   by a court, in contra--distinction to common law justice.
EQUITABLE ESTOPPEL   (L)
   A rule that if one person has induced another to take a certain
   course of action in reliance upon the representation or promises
   of the former, the former person will not be permitted to subse--
   quently deny the truth of the representation, or revoke such
   promises, upon which such action has been taken.
EQUITY   (L)

Fairness. A type of justice developed separately from common law, and tending to complement it. The current meaning is to classify disputes and remedies according to their historical relationship and development. A right or obligation attaching to property or a contract, with one person having better equity than another.

EQUITY OF A STATUTE   (L)

The spirit and intent of a statute, as opposed to the strict letter. Formerly, an English doctrine extending statutes to cases not within their express words, on grounds that such an extension would serve the purposes of the statute.

ERASURE, OR RASURE   (L)

Rubbing out or obliteration.

EROSION   (Cr's)

Wear to the inside of a barrel produced by flame and gases of powder ignited during firing.

ERRANT   (L)

Wandering, formerly descriptive of judges traveling a circuit.

ERRATIC   (Cr'y)

Irregular, unpredictable.

ERROR   (L)

A mistake in judgement. An incorrect ruling or instruction made by a judge in the trial of a case.

ERROR IN FACT   (L)

A voidable judgement rendered by reason of some fact unknown to the court and not apparent on the record.
     See also: Error in Law, Error of Law.

ERROR IN LAW   (L)

An error of the court in applying the law to the case on trial.
     See also: Error in Fact, Error of Law.

ERROR OF LAW   (L)

Erroneous conclusions of law drawn from facts, the existence of which the trier thereof was truly informed.
     See also: Error in Fact, Error in Law.

ERYTHROCYTE   (Cr's)

A red blood cell.

ESCAPE   (L)

The unlawful departure of a prisoner from custody; generally punishable as a misdemeanor, although the act of assisting another to escape is a felony.

ESOPHAGEAL VARICES   (Cr's)

Dilatation and tortuosity of the veins in the lower third of the esophagus (gullet), usually associated with cirrhosis of the liver.

ESOPHAGUS   (Cr's)

Gullet, muscular tube which conveys swallowed food from the

throat to the stomach.

ESPRIT DE CORPS   (PA)

Spirit of the body or the group, morale or loyalty.

ESTOPPEL   (L)

An admission or declaration, by which a person is prevented
from bringing evidence to prove the contrary, by matter of
record, which imports such absolute and incontrovertible verity
that no person against whom the record is produced is per--
mitted to deny it, by deed, because no person can dispute his
own solemn deed, which is, therefore, conclusive against him,
and those claiming under him, even as to facts recited in it, and
by matter in pais, e.g., a tenant cannot dispute his landlord's
title. This includes estoppel by misrepresentation or negligence.

ESTRAYS   (L)

Valuable animals found wandering at large, whose owner is un--
known.

ESTREAT   (L)

To enforce recognizance by sending an extract (estreat), or copy,
to the proper authority to be enforced.

ESTREPEMENT   (L)

Formerly a writ for the prevention of waste.

ETHMOIDAL PARANASAL SINUS   (Cr's)

Hollow space in the ethmoid bone of the skull.

EVICTION   (L)

The physical expulsion of someone from land by the assertion
of paramount title or through legal proceedings.

EVIDENCE   (L)

Proof, either written or unwritten, of allegations at issue be--
tween parties. It may be (a) direct, or indirect, which latter
includes circumstantial evidence (q.v.); (b) substantive, i.e.,
directed to proof of a distinct fact or corrobative, i.e., in sup--
port of previous evidence; (c) intrinsic, i.e., internal; or extrinsic,
i.e., not derived from anything to be found in the document
itself; (d) original or derivative, i.e., which passes through some
channel, e.g., parol, as opposed to original documents or evi--
dence.

EVIDENCE IN CHIEF   (L)

Primary proof relief upon to support a claim or defense.

EVIDENCE, LAW OF   (L)

Rules and principles regulating admissibility, relevancy, weight
and sufficiency of evidence in legal proceedings.

EXACTION   (L)

A reward or fee taken contrary to law, either by an officer or
by one pretending such status.

EXAMINATION   (L)

Preliminary judicial investigation of the grounds for an accusation against a person arrested for cime, by a magistrate, with a view to either discharging him or securing his commitment and appearance before the proper court for trial. Oral or written interrogatories of a witness on oath, by an attorney, court, or officer called an examiner or commissioner.

EXAMINED COPY   (L)

A copy of a record, public book or register, which has been compared with the original.

EXAMINER   (L)

An officer appointed by a court to take testimony under oath and reduce it to writing.

EXCESS   (L)

Something beyond what is right, proper or necessary.

EXCESSIVE BAIL   (L)

Bail in a sum more than reasonably sufficient to prevent evasion of law by flight or concealment; per se unreasonably great and clearly disproportionate to the offense involved, or shown to be so by the special circumstances of the particular case.

EXCLUSIONARY RULE   (L)

Legal prohibitions against the prosecution using evidence illegally obtained.

EXCULPATE   (L)

To exonerate, to clear of blame or guilt.

EX DELICTO   (L)

From the crime.

EXECUTE   (L)

(1) To accomplish, perform, complete. (2) To exercise authority. (3) To enforce. (4) To put to death as a matter of course.

EXECUTED   (L)

Done; completed; performed; vested.

EXECUTION OF A SENTENCE, SUSPENSION OF   (L)

The fixing of a sentence by a court and consequent holding in abeyance thereof during good behavior and of the offender.

EXEMPLIFICATION   (L)

An attested or certified transcript or copy of an official record, sometimes under the seal of a particular court of public office.

EXEMPTION   (L)

Immunity, or exception from operation of the law. Immunity from imposition of income tax, in an amount fixed by statute, allowed to a person for self and dependents.

EXERCISE OF JUDICIAL DISCRETION   (L)

The trial judge doing as he pleases, unguided by law.

EXHIBIT   (L)

A physical item of evidence. A document referred to in a pleading or affidavit, and therein identified by a letter or number.

EXHIBITIONISM (L, Cr'y)

Also known as indecent exposure, involving the public exposure of one's genitalia.

EXHUME (L)

To recover a dead body which has been properly buried.

EXITUS (Cr's)

Death.

EX MALEFICIO (L)

Out of misconduct.

EX MERO MOTU (L)

Of his own accord.

EX NECESSITATE LIGIS (L)

From the necessity of the law.

EX NECESSITATE REI (L)

From the necessity of the thing.

EX OFFICCIO (L)

By virtue of his office.

EXONERATION (L)

Acquittal; release; discharge; applied to criminal prosecutions, taxation and civil actions. Relieving an estate, or some part thereof, from liability or burden, by placing it on another estate or part, e.g., a testator is said to exonerate his personality from payment of his debts, if he charges them on another part of his estate, which is not primarily liable.

EXONERETUR (L)

An entry or notation of discharge of the bail, made on the bond when the condition is fulfilled.

EXOTHERMIC REACTION (Cr's)

A chemical transformation in which heat energy is liberated.

EX PARTE (L)

Of the one part; an action which is not an adverse proceeding against someone else.

EXPATRIATION (L)

The act, and right, of voluntarily forsaking one's own country and renouncing allegiance, with the intention of becoming a permanent resident and citizen of another country.

EXPERT (L)

One who has acquired by special study, practice and experience, peculiar skill and knowledge in relation to some particular sci-- ence, art or trade. A witness who, because of such special knowledge, is called to testify or give his opinion in cases de- pending on questions peculiar to such science, art, or trade.

See also: Expert Witness.

EXPERT EVIDENCE (L)

Authoritative testimony given in relation to some scientific, technical, or professional matter by experts.

EXPERT WITNESS (L)

One qualified to give expert opinion in relation to the signifi-cance of evidence before the court.

See also: Expert.

EXPLODE (Cr's)

To detonate, to set off explosives.

EXPLOSION (Cr's)

A chemical or mechanical action resulting in the rapid expan-sion of gases.

EX POST FACTO (L)

Made after the occurrence, e.g., legislation with retrospective application.

See also: Ex Post Facto Law.

EX POST FACTO LAW (L)

A law passed after the occurrence of a fact or commission of an act, which retrospectively changes the legal consequences or relations of that fact or deed.

See also: Ex Post Fac'to.

EXPRESS (L)

Something stated in direct words; not left to implication.

EXPRESS CONSENT (L)

Consent directly given, either viva voce or in writing; positive, direct, unequivocal consent, requiring no inference or implica-tion to supply its meaning.

EX PROPRIO MOTU (L)

Of his own motion.

EX PROPRIO VIGORE (L)

Of its own force.

EXPUNGE (L)

To physically destroy information in files, computers or other depositories.

EX REL OR EXRELATIONE (L)

On relation or information.

EXSANGUINATION (Cr's)

A drain of blood.

EXTENUATING CIRCUMSTANCES (L)

Such circumstances as render a delict or crime less aggravated, heinous, or reprehensible than it would otherwise be; a guilt palliative. May ordinarily be shown to reduce punishment.

EXTERMINATE (Cr'y)

To kill, to eradicate by killing.

EXTORTION (L)

The unlawful taking by color of office or of right, of anything of value which is not due. Often defined by statute.

See also: Blackmail.

EXTRACTOR (Cr's)

In ballistics, that mechanism which withdraws the casing from the chamber.

EXTRADEPARTMENTAL PLANS (PA)

Plans requiring action or assistance from persons or agencies outside the police department, or that relate to some form of community organization.

EXTRADITION (L)

The surrendering by one state to another of one accused or con--victed of an offense committed within the jurisdiction of the latter, upon demand of same.

EXTRADURAL (Cr's)

Situated over the dura.

EXTRAJUDICIAL (L)

That action done, given or effected outside the course of regular judicial proceedings; neither founded upon, nor unconnected with, the action of a court of law; as extrajudicial evidence, an extrajudicial oath. That which is done unnecessarily in the course of regular judicial proceedings. That which does not belong to the judge or his jurisdiction, notwithstanding which he takes cognizance of it.

EXTRANEOUS (L)

Not belonging to the matter in hand.

EXTRAORDINARY (L)

In excess of the usual or ordinary.

EXTRAORDINARY GRAND JURY (L)

Limited in scope of investigation by executive proclamation; must not be used as means of disclosing or intermeddling with extraneous matters.

EXTRAORDINARY REMEDY (L)

Forms of relief to which a court may resort to redress or pre--vent a wrong; relatively seldom used, because other measures will afford relief.

EXTRATERRITORIALITY (L)

The quality of some laws giving them operative force beyond the territory of the state or nation which enacted them, upon certain persons or rights.

EXTRAVASATION (Cr's)

Escape of blood from a vessel into the tissues, causing small hemorrhage.

EXTREME AND REPEATED CRUELTY (L)

Physical acts of violence producing bodily harm or suffering;

such acts as endanger life or limb, or raise a reasonable appre--
hension of great bodily harm, but not including bad temper,
petulance, rude language, want of civil attentions, or angry and
abusive words.

See also: Extreme Cruelty.

EXTREME CRUELTY (L)

A condition of extreme discomfort and wretchedness prevent--
ing spouse from discharging duties or seriously endangering
health; grave and serious misconduct which defeats the mar--
riage relation.

See also: Extreme and Repeated Cruelty.

EXTRINSIC (L)

External or from the outside.

EYEWITNESS (L)

One who gives evidence as to facts seen by himself.

FACE VALUE (L)

The apparent value of a statement, nominal value in case of bond.

FACIAS (L)

That you do, or cause.

FACSIMILE (L)

An exact copy.

FACT (L)

A thing done or existing; an actual occurrence in time or space or a mental or physical event. Not including the mere proba–bility thereof.

FAHRENHEIT SCALE (Cr's)

The temperature scale using the melting point of ice as 32 degrees and the boiling point of water as 212 degrees, with 180 equal divisions or degrees between.

FAILURE (L)

Want; neglect, nonsuccess.

FAILURE OF EVIDENCE (L)

Judically speaking, not only the utter absence of all evidence, but also a failure to offer proof, either positive or inferential, to establish one or more facts, the establishment of all of which is indispensable to the finding of the issues for the plaintiff.

FAILURE OF ISSUE (L)

Dying without children.

FAILURE OF JUSTICE (L)

Defeat of a particular right, or failure of reparation for a par–ticular wrong, from lack of inadequacy of a legal remedy for enforcement of one or redress of the other. Colloquially applied to a miscarriage of justice occurring as a result of a trial so pal––pably wrong as to shock the moral sense.

FAINT PLEADER (L)

A feigned action, or false plea.

FAIR AND IMPARTIAL TRIAL (L)

One where accused's legal rights are safeguarded and respected.

FAIR HEARING (L)

One in which authority is consistent with the fundamental principles of justice embraced by due process of law.

FAKE (L)

Frauduelnt, fictitious, forged.

FALSE (L)

Untrue or unjust.

FALSE ARREST, OR FALSE IMPRISONMENT (L)

Tortious restraint of one's liberty without proper authority.

FALSE PRETENSES (L)

Untrue utterances made for the purpose of obtaining something of value or to defraud.

FALSE RETURN (L)

Statements by a sheriff, constable or other court officer contrary to fact.

FALSIFY (L)

In taking accounts, to prove incorrect a debit or charge.
To make incorrect; to alter fraudulently.

FALSIFYING JUDGEMENTS (L)

Occasionally used to mean reversing judgements.

FALX (Cr's)

Fold of dura which separates the hemispheres of the brain.

FASTI DIES (L)

Those days upon which legal business might be transacted, i.e., lawful days.

FATAL (L, Cr's)

Deadly, resulting in death.

FATETUR FACINUS QUI JUDICIUM FUGIT (L)

He who flees judgement confesses his guilt.

FAVOR (L)

Bias; partiality; prejudice.

FEAR (Cr'y)

A strong, unpleasant emotion in response to painful, dangerous, or unexpected stimuli -- or anticipation of these. Motivates the individual to avoid or escape; social norms often require courageous behavior despite fear. Fear occurs as a reaction to social situations as well as physical threats. Usually experientially and culturally defined.

FEDERAL (L)

(1) Pertaining to the national government of the United States.
(2) An association of states or nations having various relationships with a unified or general government. Often, the states or nations will operate within specific spheres and the unified or general governemtn will concurrently operate within other spheres.

FEDERAL ACTS, OR FEDERAL LAWS (L)

Statutes enacted by Congress pertaining to matters within the legislative authority delegated by the Constitution, in conjunction with state laws as applicable.

FEDERAL QUESTION (L)

An issue within jurisdiction of Federal courts involving construction of the constitution, federal law, or a treaty.

FEDERAL RULES ACT (L)

The act giving the U.S. Supreme Court authority to devise and issue the Federal Rules of Civil Procedure.

FEIGNED ISSUE (L)

Formerly, a proceeding whereby an important point could, by consent of the parties, be determined by a jury, without bringing an action, or raising it in pleadings.

FELO DE SE   (L)

A felon with respect to himself. A person who commits suicide.

FELONIOUS HOMICIDE   (L)

Killing of another without legal justification or excuse.

FELONY   (L)

A grave crime of statutory or common law, punishable by death or imprisonment for more than a year. Formerly under common law, any violation punishable by forfeiture of land or goods in addition to the aforementioned sanctions.

FELONY–MURDER RULE   (L)

Any homicide adjunctive to a committed or attempted felony is first-degree murder. Legal malice is construed from commission of the felony.

FEME COVERT   (L)

A married woman.

FEME SOLE   (L)

An unmarried woman.

FERRI, ENRICO (1856–1929)   (Cr'y)

An early criminologist who theorized that crime resulted from interrelated anthropological or individual physical and social causes which lent themselves to intentional separation for examination.

FETISHISM   (Cr'y)

Abnormal sexual desire fixed upon a part of the body or object of apparel which, by manipulation or mere touching thereof, produces sexual gratification.

FETUS

An unborn child. Elapsed time after conception affects the definition.

FEUD   (Cr'y, L)

A permanent or long-lasting state of hostility, often involving periodic bloodshed, between social groups or sub-groups related by blood, geographical proximity, or traditional ties. Formerly (Great Britain), a land grant by a landholder to a servant or tenant for services rendered.

FIAT   (L)

A decree, order or warrant by constituted authority.

FIBRINOPURULENT   (Cr's)

Characterized by the presence of fibrin and pus.

FIDUCIARY   (L)

One authorized to act for another.

FIELD REPORTING   (PA)

A reporting system to show all work obtained as a result of

police action in a form appropriate for later use.

FILING (L)

The act of delivering a deed, mortgage, financing statement, pleading, motion, court order or other paper, to a duly authorized recipient.

FINDING (L)

The determination of a court or jury as to a question of fact at issue, as distinguished from a court's conclusions of law.

The discovery of property belonging to, and lost by, another.

See also: Finding of Fact.

FINDING OF FACT (L)

Determination of a fact by the court, averred by one party and denied by the other, and founded on evidence in case. A conclusion by way of reasonable inference from the evidence.

Also, the answer of the jury to a specific interrogatory propounded to them as to the existence of non--existence of a fact in issue.

See also: Finding.

FINE, CRIMINAL LAW (L)

A pecuniary punishment imposed by lawful tribunal upon a person convicted of a crime or misdemeanor. It may include a forfeiture of penalty recoverable in a civil action.

FINGERPRINTS (Cr's)

The prints or impressions produced by the friction ridges of the inner surface of the fintertips.

FIRING PIN (Cr's)

That part of a firing mechanism which strikes the primer to fire the cartridge.

FIRM (L)

Those persons collectively composing a partnership. The name or title under which a partnership transacts business.

FIRST IMPRESSION, CASE OF (L)

Controversy generating a new question of law.

FIRST INSTANCE, COURT OF (L)

The tribunal wherein action is first brought, as contrasted with an appellate court.

FIRST OFFENDER (Cor)

One who is prosecuted as a law violator the first time; one who violates the criminal law the first time.

FISSURE (Cr's)

Any cleft or groove, deep fold in the cortex of the brain which involves the entire thickness of the brain wall.

FIXTURE (L)

(1) In practice, especially between landlord and tenant, trade

84

and ornamental fixtures usually removeable by the tenant at the
end of his term, provided no material injury is done to the free--
hold. Written leases often make specific provisions concerning
the matter. (2) Formerly, personal chattel physically annexed
to a building or land, accessory to it and part and parcel of it.

FLASH POINT   (Cr's)
The minimum temperature at which a liquid fuel will produce
enough vapor to burn.

FLAT--POINT BULLET   (Cr's)
Bullet with a flat nose.

FLIGHT   (L)
Any leaving or self--concealment to avoid arrest or prosecution
after arrest.

FLUORESCE   (Cr's)
To emit visible light when exposed to light of a shorter wave
length i.e. ultraviolet light.

FLUOROSCOPE   (Cr's)
A small box with a viewing aperture for both eyes on one end
and calcium tungstate (or similar substance) screen on the other.
X--rays striking the screen fluoresce and present a shadow pic--
ture to the viewer.

FOCUS   (Cr's)
Localized area of disease.

FOETICIDE   (L)
Criminal abortion.

FOETUS   (L)
An unborn child. Elapsed time after conception affects the
definition.

FOLKWAYS AND CUSTOMS   (Cr'y)
Informal behavioral norms; habitual ways of doing things.
Tradition without moral significance enforced by informal
social control.

FOOT LINE   (Cr's)
The foot line shows the angle at which each foot is put down.
This is a straight line through the longitudinal axis of the foot--
print. The angle between the foot line and the direction line
is called the foot angle.

FOOT PATROL   (PA)
Patrol duties done by an officer on foot.

FORAMEN MAGNUM   (Cr's)
Large hold in the back of the base of the skull within which
the spinal cord connects with the medulla oblongate.

FORCE   (Cr'y, L)
An overt expression of power used to compel an individual or
group to follow a course or courses of action desired by another

individual or group. Force is often referred to as manifest power. It may take the form of physical manipulation (e.g., beating, imprisonment, death) or social pressure. Its legitimacy depends on whether or not in a specific instance its use is con--doned by the society or community as a whole.

FORCE AND ARMS, WITH   (L)

Words occasionally inserted in a declaration of trespass or indictment, though not absolutely necessary.

FORCIBLE ENTRY   (L)

The taking of possession of real property, by force, threat, or violence, by the actual owner or another.

FORCIBLE RAPE   (L)

Carnal knowledge forcibly and against one's will.

FOREIGN JUDGEMENT   (L)

A decision rendered by the court of a state or country, other than the one in which enforcement of the judgement is sought. Courts' records and judicial proceedings of state, properly authenticated, are entitled to the same faith and credit in the courts of any other state as in the courts from whence they came.

FOREIGN PLEA   (L)

A defense objection to the court's jurisdiction.

FORENSIC   (L)

Belonging to, or applied in, courts of justice.

FORENSIC MEDICINE   (L, Cr's)

The influence and application of medical science toward reso--lution of legal disputes.

FORFEITURE   (L)

A penalty for some illegal act imposing the loss of some right or property.

FORFEITURE OF A BOND   (L)

An order of court that a bond be paid in cash to the public trea--sury, because of the failure to perform the condition.

FORGE   (L)

To make a false instrument for the purpose of fraud and deceit.

FORGED BILL, CHECK, OR DRAFT   (L)

An instrument on which the signature are forged or otherwise falsely affixed.

FORGERY   (L)

The false making or alteration of an instrument purporting to be good and valid for the purposes for which it was created. The false or unauthorized execution of a document, with fraudulent intent.

FORNICATION   (L)

Extramarital intercourse between unmarried persons.

FORPRISE (L)

(1) An exception or reservation. (2) An exaction. (3) To swear to a falsehood. (4) To reject or renounce upon oath.

FORTHWITH (L)

Immediately; as soon as the nature of the case will permit.

FORUM (L)

A court of justice; the place where justice must be sought. Formerly, an open space in Roman cities, where the people assembled, markets were held, and the magistrates sat to transact their business.

FOSSA (Cr's)

Anterior, middle, posterior -- shallow depressions in the base of the skull which suit the contour of the brain.

FRATRICIDE (Cry, L)

The act of killing or murdering one's brother.

FRAUD (L)

Acts which have as their objective the gain of an advantage by deceitful or unfair means. They may be (a) actual, where there is deliberate misrepresentation or concealment; or (b) constructive, where the court implies, it, either from the nature of the contract or from the relation of the parties.

FRAUDULENT (L)

Descriptive of something which results in, or results from, a fraud (q.v.).

See also: Fraud.

FRAUS EST CELARE FRAUDEM (L)

It is fraud to conceal fraud.

FRAUS LATET IN GENERALIBUS (L)

Fraud lies hid in general expressions.

FREE (L)

Not bound; unrestricted; at liberty to act as one pleases.

FREQUENCY (Cr's)

The number of waves that pass a given point per second.

FREQUENTER (L)

One who visits often. Occasionally defined by statute.

FRESH PURSUIT (L)

To closely follow without unreasonable delay a fleeing suspect endeavoring to avoid immediate capture.

FRISK (L, PA)

A pat-down search, less than a full search of a suspect.

FROTTAGE (L)

Achievement of sexual excitement and satisfaction by rubbing against one of the opposite sex.

See also: Frotteurism.

FROTTEURISM (L)

The practice of rubbing one's genitals against another person, usually in a crowd, in order to achieve sexual stimulation.
See also: Frottage.

FRUIT OF THE POISONOUS TREE   (L)
The evidence which is the direct result or immediate product of illegal conduct on the part of an official is inadmissible in a criminal trial against the victim of the conduct under the due process clause of the fourteenth amendment.

FRUSTRA PROBATUR QUOD PROBATUM NON RELEVAT   (L)
It is useless to prove that which, when proved, is not relevant.

FRUSTRATION   (Cr'y)
The prevention or obstruction of an individual's attempts to satisfy his needs or desires. The term is also applied to the re--sulting emotional state, which is characterized chiefly by anger and anxiety.

FRUSTRATION--AGGRESSION HYPOTHESIS   (Cr'y)
The hypothesis that when a person is frustrated in the attain-ment of a desire he becomes aggressive, and if he cannot retali-ate against the source of his frustration (because he does not know the source, out of fear of the consequences, or the like), he will direct his aggression toward a less threatening substitute person or object.

FUGITIVE   (L)
(1) One who runs away. (2) One who, having committed a crime, flees from the jurisdiction within which it was com-mitted, to escape punishment.

FULL AUTOMATIC   (Cr's)
Firearms utilizing forces of the fired cartridges to extract, eject, load and fire the succeeding rounds continuously until process is interrupted by release of trigger or ammunition is exhausted.

FULL COCK   (Cr's)
Trigger mechanism engaging hammer or striker in position ready for firing.

FULMINATE   (Cr's)
One of the ingredients of the priming mixture.

FUNCTIONAL CONTROL AND SUPERVISION   (PA)
All elements of a police department have responsibility for the execution of certain functions. For example, a traffic unit may be responsible for follow--up investigations, the patrol force for effective patrol, the juvenile element for proper case refer-rals. Each one must also engage extensively in reporting and in some minimal record keeping, even where there is an effective central records system. All these, and other functions as well, should be carried out in accordance with departmental policies.

FUNDAMENTAL LAW   (L)

The Constitution. Also, organic statutes or laws intrinsically superior to ordinary law or regarded as being of superior obligation.

FUIOSI NULLA VOLUNTAS EST (L)

A madman has no free will, i.e., he is not criminally responsible.

FURTOM NON EST UBI INITIUM HABET DETENTIONIS PER DOMINUM REI (L)

There is no theft where the origin of the possession was with the consent of the owner, i.e., where the original possession is lawful, as in the case of a bailee.

GAG (Cr's)

Something placed over or in a person's mouth to prevent talking or making noise.

GAGE (Cr's)

(1) Diameter of the gun barrel; "12 Ga.," for instance, means
that 12 round lead balls of this diameter weigh one pound; lead
balls the size of a 10-gage gun weigh ten to the pound; of a 16-
gage gun, sixteen to the pound, etc. A pawn or
pledge.

GALLERY LOAD (Cr's)

A light or reduced charge in cartridges for use indoors.

GALLOWS (Cry)

A structure used for hanging criminals.

GAME OF CHANCE (L)

An event, project or contest determined entire, or in part, by
fortuitousness, and in which judgement, practice, skill or adroit-
ness have no office at all, or are thwarted.

GAME OF SKILL (Cr'y)

A project or contest determined entirely, or in part, by judgment,
practice, or skill.

GAMING, GAMBLING (L)

The wagering of something of value, on the outcome or occurrence of an event. In some cases, the outcome must result from
chance; in others, the event may be of any nature. Playing
at cards, dice, billiards, or other games, the winner taking the
money of the loser.

GANANCIAL PROPERTY (L)

Community property.

GANG (Cr'y)

A primary group that forms spontaneously, usually in urban
areas, for the purpose of friendship and common activities
often defined as being in conflict with the social order.

GANGRENE (Cr's)

Death of a part (usually a limb) due to loss of blood supply.

GAOL DELIVERY (L)

English. A commission for a judge to try prisoners and deliver
them out of jail.

GAS (Cr's)

A fluid which has no independent shape or volume and which
tends to expand indefinitiely.

GASTRIC (Cr's)

Pertaining to the stomach.

GASTROINTESTINAL (Cr's)

Pertaining to the stomach and the intestine.

GAUGE   (Cr's)
>Unit of measure for shotgun bore diameters, determined by the number of solid lead balls of the bore diameter obtainable from one pound of lead. Shells are head stamped to indicate the gauge of gun for which they are adapted.

GENDARME   (PA)
>A member of an armed police organization such as in France.

GENE   (Cr's)
>A unit of inheritance located on a chromosome.

GENERAL   (L)
>Common to many or all; extensive; not restricted; not special.

GENERAL ALPHABETICAL INDEX   (Cr's, PA)
>An index for the purpose of ascertaining the case number, the fingerprint classification, or previous record of any person having been the subject of police inquiry or action.

GENERAL APPEARANCE   (L)
>A submission of the defendant to the jurisdiction of the court for all purposes.

GENERAL ISSUE   (L)
>A response to a petition or a complaint without offering any special matter to evade it, e.g., the plea of not guilty.

GENERAL LAW   (L)
>A law that affects the community at large and does not omit any subject or place naturally belonging to such community.

GENERAL ORDER   (PA)
>Description of policy, program, or procedure, of broad applica-tion throughout the agency; a guiding document for a long period of time – binding until withdrawn or modified.

GENERAL OWNER   (L)
>One who has title to the property in question.

GENERAL VERDICT   (L)
>A jury decision; a finding for plaintiff or defendant, without specifying facts found from the evidence.

GENOCIDE   (L)
>Extermination of a particular human group.

GENOTYPE   (Cr's)
>The particular combination of genes present in the cells of an individual.

GESTATION   (L, Cr's)
>The period which elapses between conception and birth, usually about nine months of thirty days each, during which the fetal growth is carried within the womb. This period is added, where gestation exists, to that which is allowed by the rule against perpetuities.

GESTIO   (L)

Behavior or conduct.

GHETTO   (Cr'y)

In current usage, a segregated community, usually racially or culturally homogeneous, within a larger community. The iso-- lation of the community may either be enforced politically or economically or it may be voluntary.

GIFT   (L)

A voluntary transfer of real or personal property, without receiving valid consideration; a gratuitious transfer of owner- ship.

GIFT CAUSA MORTIS   (L)

A gift (q.v.), made by reason of, or in view of, death. Often revocable, if the donor (q.v.) does so during his lifetime.

GIFT INTER VIVOS   (L)

A gift (q.v.) which is irrevocable and made while the donor (q.v.) is alive.

GIST   (L)

The main point in question; the central issue.

GLIA   (Cr's)

The supporting tissue of the brain.

GLIOBLASTOMA MULTIFORME   (Cr's)

Type of glioma (brain tumor).

GLIOMA   (Cr's)

Brain tumor.

GLIOSIS   (Cr's)

Scarring in nerve tissue.

GLOTTIS   (Cr's)

The opening at the top of the windpipe located between the vocal cords.

GLYCOLYSIS   (Cr's)

The breakdown of sugars by the body.

GOOD BEHAVIOR   (L)

Orderly and lawful conduct; behavior such as is proper for a peaceable and law--abiding citizen. "Good behavior," as used in an order suspending sentence upon a defendant during good behavior, means merely conduct conformable to law, or to the particular law theretofore breached.

GOOD CONSIDERATION   (L)

As distinguished from valuable consideration; founded on mot motives of generosity, prudence and natural duty.

GOODS AND CHATTELS   (L)

Personal property, as distinguished from real property, e.g., merchandise for sale, household effects, office equipment and jewelry.

GOOD FAITH   (L)

A total absence of any intention to seek an unfair advantage or to defraud another party, an honest and sincere intention to fulfill one's obligations.

GRAND ASSIZE   (L)

Formerly, a peculiar kind of English trial by jury, giving the alternative of trial by battle.

GRAND JURY   (L)

A body of persons, not less than twelve, nor more than twenty-four, whose duty it is, on hearing evidence for the prosecution in each proposed bill of indictment, to decide whether sufficiency of a case is made on which to hold the accused for trial. It is convened by authority of a court and serves as an instrumentality of the court with authority to investigate and accuse but not to try cases. It was instituted under common law to protect the people from governmental oppression. In a few states, it has been partially abolished, but in others it exists by constitutional mandate. No person shall be held to answer for a capital or otherwise infamous federal crime, unless on a pre-sentment or indictment of a grand jury, except in casea arising in the land or naval forces, or in the militia, when in actual service in time of war or public danger; U.S. Constitution, Amendment V.

GRAND LARCENY   (L)

More serious that petit larceny; classified according to the value of the object. Usually defined by statute.

GRATIS   (L)

Free, without reward or consideration.

GRATUITOUS   (L)

Without legal consideration.

GREAT CARE   (L)

That amount taken by a prudent person with respect to his own property.

GREAT SEAL   (L)

An emblem of sovereignty, used to authenticate public documents. Each state of the United States and the national government use unique emblems for this purpose.

GRIEVANCE   (L)

One's allegation that something imposes an illegal obligation or burden or denies some equitable or legal right or causes injustice.

GROOVES   (Cr's)

The cavities inside a rifle barrel, usually resulting in an elongated spiral, by which a bullet, when expanded and forced forward, receives a spinning motion, making its flight accurate.

GROSS   (L)

Great, excessive, entire.

GROSS NEGLIGENCE   (L)

A high degree of negligence; such want of care as not even
inattentive and thoughtless men are guilty of with respect to
their own property.

GROUP THERAPY   (Cor)

A treatment process by which a psychiatrist or clinical psy--
chologist works with small groups, usually eight to twelve, for
purposes of therapy.

GUARDIAN   (L)

One appointed by a court and having control or management
over the person or property of another who is incapable of
acting on his behalf. Guardians ad litem are appointed by
the court to represent such persons, who are parties to a pend--
ing action.

GUILT   (L)

In criminal law, that quality which imparts criminality to a
motive or act, and renders the person amenable to punishment
by the law. Anxiety resulting from departure from norms
and values considered to have at least minimal validity.

GUILTY   (L)

Criminal, culpable. The status of one who has violated criminal
law of adjudged to have done so by due process of law.

GYRUS   (Cr's)

Convoluted ridge of the brain.

HABEAS CORPUS   (L)

Words used in various writs, commanding one who detains another to have, or bring, him before the court issuing the same and show cause for his detention.

HABEAS CORPUS ACT   (L)

The 1670 statute which established the right of habeas corpus writs in cases of illegal detention. The right existed previously, but its efficiency had been impaired. This act gave it renewed force.

See also: Habeas Corpus.

HABEAS CORPUS AD FACIENDUM ET RECIPIENDUM OR CUM CAUSA   (L)

A form of habeas corpus (q.v.), which issues when a person is sued in some inferior jurisdiction, and is desirous to remove the action into the superior court.

See also: Habeas corpus.

HABEAS CORPUS AD PROSEQUENDUM   (L)

A form of habeas corpus (q.v.), which is issued to remove a prisoner, in order that he might be tried in the proper jurisdic-- tion.

See also: Habeas corpus.

HABEAS CORPUS AD SATISFACIENDUM   (L)

A form of habeas corpus (q.v.), which is issued to remove a prisoner from one court to another, in order to charge him in execution upon a judgement of the last court.

See also: Habeas corpus.

HABEAS CORPUS AD SUBJICIENDUM   (L)

The celebrated prerogative writ of American and English law which is the usual remedy for a person deprived of his liberty. Its purpose is to test the legality of the restraints on a person's liberty, i.e., whether he is restrained of his liberty by due pro-- cess of law, not whether he is guilty or innocent. It is addressed to him who detains another in custody, and commands him to produce the body of the person in custody, with the day and cause of his caption and detention, and to do, submit to and receive whatever the court shall think fit. This writ is guaran- teed by U.S. Constitution Art. I, Sex. IX, and by the state con- stitutions.

See also: Habeas corpus.

HABEAS CORPUS AD TESTIFICANDUM   (L)

A form of habeas corpus (q.v.), which is issued to bring a witness into court, when he was in custody at the time of a trial.

See also: Habeas corpus.

HABEMUS OPTIMUM TESTEM, CONFIDENTEM REUM   (L)

We consider as the best witness a confessing defendant.

HABIT   (Cr'y)
> A learned pattern of response automatically repeated in appro--priate situations with a minimum of deliberate effort or reflec--tion.

HABITATIO   (L)
> The right of using a house as a dwelling.

HABITUAL CRIMINAL   (L)
> One who is convicted of a felony, has been previously con--victed of any crime (or twice so convicted), or (in New York) who is convicted of a misdemeanor and has previously been five times convicted of a misdemeanor. One subject to police surveillance and arrest on suspicion due to a previous criminal record and absence of honest employment.

HABITUAL CRIMINAL STATUTE, OR RECIDIVIST STATUTE (L)
> An act which imposes grater punishment for subsequent of--fenses than for the first.
>> See also: Habitual Criminal.

HABITUATION   (Cr's)
> A state of psychological dependence on a drug such as mari--huana or cocaine, or even tobacco.

HALFWAY HOUSE   (Cor)
> A pre--release guidance center where a small number of correc--tional clients live while they work in the community in a tran--sitional situation for a short time prior to release. An alter--native to institutionalization as opposed to probation.

HALLUCINATION   (L)
> Sensatory perception of an object which has no existence; a symptom of insanity.

HALLUCINOGEN   (Cr'y, Cr's)
> A substance that induces changes in mood, attitude, thought, or perception.

HAMMER   (Cr's)
> Pivoted member moving about axis which release gives impulse to firing pin.

HAMMURABI CODE   (Cr'y, L)
> The earliest written code relating to ancient penal practices; the Code of the Babylonian King Hammurabi, circa 2,000 B.C.

HAND   (Cr's)
> That part of a revolver which causes the cylinder to index about its axis.

HANDABEND   (L)
> A thief caught in the act, with the thing stolen in his hand.

HANDGUN   (Cr's)
> Short firearm intended to be aimed and fired from one hand.

Three types: automatic pistol, derringer and revolver.

HANDWRITING   (L)

Anything written manually by a person, e.g., with a pen or pencil.

HANES–COOPER ACT OF 1929   (L)

A federal law prohibiting prison made goods from inter--state commerce.

HANGFIRE   (Cr's)

Delayed or slow combustion.

HARRISON NARCOTIC ACT OF 1914   (L)

Federal law prohibiting importation, possession, unauthorized sale or purchase, and manufacture of heroin.

HAZARDOUS EMPLOYMENT OR HAZARDOUS OCCUPATION (L)

Work or service with incidental risks not present in other occu–pations.

HAZING   (L)

Harassment by abusive or ridiculous treatment.

HEAD SPACE   (Cr's)

The distance between the base of the cartridge and the face of the breech block.

HEAD STAMP   (Cr's)

Inscription, letters, gauge, brand, manufacturer, etc., stamped on metal head of shell.

HEARING   (L)

A court proceeding or the trial of a suit. Examination of witnesses incidental to the making of a judicial determination as to whether an accused person shall be held for trial.

HEARING EXAMINER   (L)

A public official authorized by law to set times for hearings, summon witnesses, administer oaths, hear testimony, receive evidence, and make findings of fact or conclusions of law, or both, for various governmental administrative agencies. Analogous to a Commissioner (q.v.) of a court.

HEARING IN CRIMINAL LAW   (L)

The examination of a prisoner charged with a crime or misde--meanor, and of the witnesses for the accused.

HEARING, PRELIMINARY   (L)

In criminal law; synonymous with "preliminary examination." The hearing given to a person accused of crime, by a magistrate or judge, exercising the functions of a committing magistrate, to ascertain whether there is evidence to warrant and require the commitment and holding to bail of the person accused.

HEARSAY EVIDENCE   (L)

Statements offered by a witness, based upon what someone

else has told him, and not upon personal knowledge or obser--
vation. Usually, inadmissible, but exceptions are made, e.g.,
in questions of pedigree, custom, reputation, dying declara--
tions, and statements made against the interest of the declarant.

HEAT OF COMBUSTION   (Cr's)
The heat evolved when a substance is burned in oxygen.

HEIR   (L)
A person who inherits or may by law inherit.

HELMINTHIC   (Cr's)
Pertaining to a wormlike parasite.

HEMATEMESIS   (Cr's)
Vomiting of blood.

HEMOGLOBIN   (Cr's)
A red blood cell protein responsible for transporting oxygen in
the blood stream and the red coloring of the blod.

HEMOLYTIC ANEMIA   (Cr's)
Anemia due to destruction of red blood corpuscules.

HEMOPERICARDIUM   (Cr's)
Blood in the heart sac.

HEMOPERITONEUM   (Cr's)
Blood in the abdominal cavity.

HEMOPTYSIS   (Cr's)
Spitting or coughing up blood.

HEPATIC CELLS   (Cr's)
Liver cells.

HEPATOMA   (Cr's)
Cancer of liver cells.

HERMAPHRODITE   (L)
A person who has the physical characteristics of both sexes.

HEROIN   (Cr's)
A synthetic drug made from morphine as a diacetyl derivative.
It is by far the most common drug occurring in cases of narcotic
addiction. In appearance it is usually a white, crystalline pow--
der; occasionally it is found in cubes or tablets.

HETEROZYGONS   (Cr's)
Having two different allelic genes on two corresponding posi--
tions of a pair of chromosomes.

HIGH CRIMES   (L)
Such immoral and unlawful acts as are nearly allied and equal
in guilt to felony, yet, owing to some technical circumstance,
do not fall within the definition of "felony."

HIGH ORDER EXPLOSIVE   (Cr's)
Explosive with a velocity of detonation greater than 1000
meters per second. For example, dynamite and RDX.

HIGHWAYS   (L)

Public ways, either on land or water, which every person has a
right to use, including alleys, county roads, city streets, state
and federal roads, and navigable rivers and streams.
HIJACK   (Cry)
To take by force goods, merchandise being transported.
HIRING   (L)
A bailment (q.v.) for compensation.
tion.
HIT AND RUN   (L, Cr'y)
Situation where a driver is involved in a traffic accident and
thereafter fails to comply with the laws regarding stopping,
giving aid or notifying police.
HOLDING   (L)
The principle which reasonably may be drawn from the decision
which a court or judge actually makes in a case. Resolution
of a unique dispute before a judge or court in a specific case.
Something which a person owns or possesses.
HOLD UP   (L, Cry)
Robbery involving the threat to use a weapon.
HOLLOW--POINT BULLET   (Cr's)
One wherein the leading portion has certain degree of con--
cavity for the purpose of increasing the mushrooming effect
upon impact.
HOLOGRAPH   (L)
A document or instrument, written entirely by the signer in
his own handwriting, which, on account of the difficulty with
which the forgery of such a document can be accomplished, is
in some jurisdictions, and for certain purposes, held as valid
without witnesses. The fact that it is entirely in the signer's
handwriting must be proven by witnesses, however.
HOLOGRAPHIC WILL   (L)
A will (q.v.) which is written entirely by the signer in his own
handwriting.
HOMICIDE   (L)
The killing of a human being. It may be (a) excusable, as when
committed by accident, and without any intent to injure; (b)
justifiable, if committed with full intent, but under such cir--
cumstances as to render it proper and necessary, as where the
proper officer executes a criminal in strict conformity with his
sentence or kills a man when forcibly resisting an arrest, or
where one kills another in defense of himself or his family, or
to prevent him from committing an atrocious crime attempted
with violence, such as rape or robbery; (c) felonious, when com--
mitted willfully and without sufficient justification. The latter
includes (1) suicide; (2) manslaughter, where one kills another

101

in a sudden quarrel, and without premeditation, or by accident while engaged in doing some lawful act not amounting to felony; (3) murder, i.e., wilful and premeditated killing with malice aforethought. This last offense is frequently divided by various state statutes into degrees, according to the atrocious-- ness of the motives with which, or the circumstances under which, the crime is committed.

HOMONYMOUS HEMIANOPSIA (Cr's)
Blindness which affects the nasal half of one eye and the temporal half of the other.

HOMOPHILY (Cr'y)
The tendency for friendships to form between persons with similar characteristics.

HOMOSEXUALITY (L)
Erotic love between two persons of the same sex.

HOMOZYGOUS (Cr's)
Having two identical allelic genes on two corresponding posi-- tions of a pair of chromosomes.

HORNBOOK (L)
A one--volume work containing the elementary principles of law, a handbook.

HOSTILE WITNESS (L)
One called to give evidence and who in unfriendly or inimical to the party whose attorney called him. Such a person is sub-- ject to cross--examination by the party calling him.

HOT PURSUIT (L, PA)
Law justifying pursuit and arrest of vessels and vehicles that have infringed the law, and the pursuit starts and continues.

HOUSE (L)
A dwelling, an institution, a family, a mercantile firm, or a col-- lection of persons.

HOUSE OF CORRECTION (Cor, L)
A place for the imprisonment of persons convicted of petty crime.

HOUSE OF ILL FAME (L)
A house resorted to for purposes of lewdness and prostitution.

HOUSEBREAKING (L)
The unlawful entering of a building of another with intent to commit a crime therein.

HUE AND CRY (L)
Formerly, the common law process of pursuing a person accused of felony, without a warrant and with horn and voice.

HUNG JURY (L)
A trial jury whose members are unable to agree upon a verdict.

HUSH MONEY (L)

A bribe to hinder information being given.

HYDROCARBON   (Cr's)

Any compound consisting only of carbon and hydrogen.

HYDROCEPHALUS   (Cr's)

Abnormal increase in the amount of cerebrospinal fluid in the brain, resulting in expansion of the brain ventricles.

HYPERGLYCIMIA   (Cr's)

High blood sugar.

HYPERINSULINISM   (Cr's)

High level of insulin in the blood.

HYPERPIGMENTATION   (Cr's)

Increase in amount of normal pigmentation.

HYPERPLASIA   (Cr's)

Increase in size of an organ due to increase in the number of cells.

HYPERSENSITIVITY ANGIITIS   (Cr's)

Allergic inflammation of blood or lymph tissues.

HYPERTENSION   (Cr's)

High blood pressure.

HYPERTROPHY   (Cr's)

Enlargement of an organ or part due to increase in size of cells.

HYPOGLYCEMIA   (Cr's)

Low blood sugar.

HYPOPIGMENTATION   (Cr's)

Decrease in amount of normal pigmentation.

HYPOTENSION   (Cr's)

Low blood pressure.

HYPOTHETICAL QUESTION   (L)

An interrogatory or inquiry propounded to an expert witness, containing a statement of facts assumed to have been proven, and requiring the witness to state his opinion concerning them.

HYPOVOLEMIC SHOCK   (Cr's)

Shock due to decreased blood volume.

HYPOXIA   (Cr's)

Low oxygen content.

HYSTERIA   (Cr'y)

A form of neurosis characterized by the experience of the symptoms of organic disease, such as paralysis, by an individual without evidence of physical disease or injury.

I.A.C.P. (PA)

International Association of Chiefs of Police.

IBID OR IBIDEM (L)

The same, e.g., the same volume, case or place.

ID CERTUM EST QUOD CERTUM REDDI POTEST (L)

That is certain which can be reduced to a certainty.

IDEM AGENS ET PATIENS ESSE NON POTEST (L)

It is impossible to simultaneously be the person acting and the person acted upon.

IDEM EST NIHIL DICERE ET INSUFFICIENTER DICERE (L)

It is the same thing to say nothing as it is not to say enough.

IDEM EST NON ESSE ET NON APPARERE (L)

Not to be and not to appear are the same, i.e., the court will not presume any alleged fact to exist, unless it has been shown by competent testimony.

IDEM SONANS (L)

Sounding the same; used of names misspelled which yet would not mislead, because the variance is trifling, or because they would be pronounced the same if spelled aright.

IDENTIFICATION (L)

The proof that a person or thing is that person or thing mentioned in the evidence.

IDENTIFICATION OF OFFENDERS (PA)

Since a criminal commonly flees the scene of his crime, a distinctive description should be obtained from the persons who are best able to recount his distinguishing characteristics, sex, age, build, weight, height, shape of nose, complexion, kind of lips, color of hair and eyes, shape of ears, nationality, occupation, degree of baldness, birth marks, skin blemishes, gait, speech, amputations, peculiar habits, clothing and jewelry worn, and direction and manner of escape are important. Unique or unusual characteristics have great value in identification. The above information should be broadcast over police radio without delay. A suspect's criminal record and fingerprint classification should be obtained, and his "mug" should be available.

IDEOLOGICAL MESSIANISM (Cr'y)

The belief that a given society's value system is so superior to any other that it should be imposed on other societies to the maximum extent possible by whatever means are required, including the use of force.

IDIOCY (L)

The condition of being of unsound mind from time of birth; congenital mental deficiency.

IDIOT (L)

One afflicted with idiocy (q.v.)

See also: Idiocy.

IGNITION TEMPERATURE (Cr's)

The minimum temperature at which a fuel will spontaneously ignite.

IGNORAMUS (L)

A word formerly written by a grand jury, on a proposed bill of indictment, when the grand jury refused to return an indictment. It means that a sufficient prima facie case was not made out. The endorsement now used is, "not a true bill," or "not found."

IGNORANTIA FACTI EXCUSAT: IGNORANTIA JURIS NON EXCUSAT (L)

Ignorance of the fact excuses; ignorance of the law excuses not.

ILLEGAL (L)

Contrary to the law, or forbidden by law. Occasionally, unlawful.

ILLEGAL CONDITIONS (L)

Provisions contrary to law, immoral, or repugnant to the matter of the transaction.

ILLEGITIMATE (L)

Not authorized by law; often applied to children born out of lawful wedlock.

ILLICIT (L)

Unlawful, or forbidden.

ILLUSORY (L)

Deceptive; having a false appearance.

IMBECILITY (L)

Unsoundness of mind characterized by deficiency of the higher intellectual and moral facilities.

IMMATERIAL (L)

Not material, essential, or necessary; not important or pertinent; not decisive; of no substantial consequence; without weight; of no significance.

IMMATERIAL AVERMENT, OR IMMATERIAL EVIDENCE (L)

A claim, or proof, without legal bearing on the point at issue.

IMMATERIAL ISSUE (L)

A question submitted for judicial resolution, which concerns a collateral matter, the decision of which will not settle the dispute between the parties.

IMMEMORIAL (L)

Beyond the memory of man.

IMMINENT DANGER (L)

In relation to homicide in self–defense; immediate danger, such as must be instantly met and cannot be guarded against by calling for the assistance of others or the protection of the law.

Such an appearance of threatened and impending injury as
would put a reasonable and prudent man to his instant defense.

IMMORAL CONTRACT   (L)

An agreement founded on an immoral consideration (contra
bonos mores), e,g., illicit cohabitation.

IMMUNITY   (L)

Exemption, as from serving in an office, or performing duties
which the law generally requires other citizens to perform.
The term aptly describes an exemption from taxation. A par--
ticular privilege.

IMPACT   (Cr's)

The force of a bullet striking an object.

IMPANEL, OR EMPANEL   (L)

To select a jury and record the names of its members.

IMPARL   (L)

To discuss a case with the opposite party, or his counsel, with a
view to an adjustment of differences and an amicable settle--
ment.

IMPARLANCE   (L)

Time which the court allows either party to answer the oppo--
nent's pleading.

IMPEACH   (L)

To charge a public official with crime or misdemeanor, or with
misconduct in office. To prove that a witness has a bad
reputation for truth and veracity, and is therefore unworthy of
belief.

IMPERATIVE   (L)

Obligatory.

IMPERFECT OBLIGATIONS   (L)

Moral duties not enforceable by law.

IMPERSONATE   (Cr'y, L)

To pretend to be someone else.

IMPERTINENCE   (L)

Allegations in a court pleading not responsive nor relevant to
the illues, and which could not properly be put in issue or
proven. Such matter may be ordered stricken from a pleading.

IMPLICATION   (L)

An inference of something not directly declared, but generated
by the things which are so declared.

IMPLIED AUTHORITY   (L)

Power or permission intentionally granted, but not expressly
declared.

IMPLIED CONSENT   (L)

A presumption that consent has been given manifested by sign,
action, fact or inaction or silence.

IMPLIED MALICE (L)

An inference or conclusion of hate or illwill from the facts and circumstances proved.

IMPLIED POWER (L)

Such power as may be reasonably necessary to make an express power effective.

IMPOSITION OF SENTENCE, SUSPENSION OF (Cor, L)

Withholding of a decision on length of prison term at time of conviction by the court. If it later becomes necessary to revoke the suspended sentence, the periof of imprisonment is fixed at that time.

IMPOTENCE, OR IMPOTENCY (L)

Physical inability of a man or woman to perform the act of sexual intercourse; often a ground for anullment of the marriage contract.

IMPOUND (L)

To place something in the custody of the law, until a question affecting it is decided.

IMPRISONMENT (L, Cor)

Confinement to prison; restraint of one's liberty for the purpose of detaining in custody one accused of crime or for punishing one convicted of crime.

IMPUTED NEGLIGENCE (L)

Negligence chargeable to a person by reason of relationship to the one actually negligent.

INADEQUATE (L)

Insufficient; not equal to full value.

INADMISSIBLE (L)

That which cannot be admitted or received, e.g., parol evidence is inadmissible to vary the terms of a written contract.

INALIENABLE (L)

Not transferable, not subject to being sold.

IN ARTICULO MOTIS (L)

At the point of death.

IN AUTRE DROIT (L)

In another's right.

IN CAMERA (L)

A case heard when the doors of the court are closed and only persons concerned in the case are admitted.

INCARCERATION (L, Cor, Cr'y)

Imprisonment; confinement in a jail or penitentiary.

INCENDIARY (L)

One who maliciously sets fire to a building.

INCEST (Cr'y, L)

Sexual relations between persons so closely related as to be prohibited by law. Heterosexual relationships, between those of a kin group, forbidden or disapproved of by cultural tradition.

INCIDENT (L)

Something dependent upon or pertinent to another more important thing, termed the principal An event or occurrence.

INCITE (L)

To encourage, stimulate or induce a person to commit a crime.

INCOGNITO (L)

In disguise.

INCOMMUNI (L)

In common.

INCOMPETENT (L)

Lack of ability, legal qualification, or fitness to discharge a required duty.

See also: Incompetent.

INCOMPETENT (L)

Disqualified, unable or unfit. A judge or juror is incompetent, when from interest in the subject matter he is an unfit person to decide a controversy. Testimony is incompetent when it is not such as by law ought to be admitted. A witness is incompetent, when by law he may not testify.

See also: Incompetency.

IN CRIMINALIBUS PROBATIONES DEBENT ESSE LUCE CLARIORES (L)

In criminal cases the proof ought to be clear as day.

INCRIMINATE (L)

To charge with crime; to expose to an accusation or charge of crime; to involve oneself or another in a criminal prosecution or the danger thereof; as, in the rule that a witness is not bound to give testimony which would tend to incriminate him.

INCRIMINATORY STATEMENT (L)

A statement which tends to establish guilt of the accused or from which, with other facts, his guilt may be infered, or which tends to disprove some defense.

INCULPATORY (L)

That which tends to incriminate or bring about a criminal conviction.

INCUMBENT (L)

One who occupies a public office.

INDECENCY (L)

Language or conduct offensive to modesty, by contemporary standards.

INDECENT EXPOSURE (L)

Exposure of the genitalia to one of the opposite sex under other than conventionally lawful circumstances.

IN DELICTO   (L)

In fault; guilty.

INDETERMINATE SENTENCE   (L, Cor)

A term of imprisonment leaving the exact period of punishment to be decided by executive authorities.

INDEX CRIMES   (PA, Cr'y)

Seven major offenses designated as "Part I" crimes used in the Uniform Crime Reports of the Federal Bureau of Investigation. Considered the most consistently reported to police, they are: murder, forcible rape, robbery, aggravated assault, burglary, larceny over $50, and auto theft.

INDICTMENT   (L)

An accusation in writing by a grand jury charging that a person therein named has done some act, or been guilty of some omission, which, by law, is a public offense, punishable on indictment.

INDIGENT   (L)

One who is needy and poor. One without sufficent property to furnish him a living or anyone able to support him to whom he is entitled to look for support.

INDIRECT EVIDENCE   (L)

Proof of collateral circumstances, from which a fact in contro--versy, not directly attested by witnesses or documents, may be inferred or presumed.

INDIVIDUAL CHARACTERISTICS   (Cr's)

Properties of evidence that can be attributed to a common source with an extremely high degree of certainty.

INDIVIDUAL DEVIATION   (Cr'y)

A product of psychic pressures.

INDORSEMENT   (L)

Something written on the back of an instrument in writing, and having relation to it. Especially, the writing put on the back of a bill, or promissory note, and signed, by which the party signing, called the indorser, transfers the property in the bill or note to another, called the indorsee. Indorsement may, how--ever, be in blake, i.e., not specifying the name of the indorsee, in which case it may be transferred from hand to hand without further indorsement, and is payable to bearer. Indorsement may also be made without recourse, and thereby, the indorser relieves himself from liability in case the bill or note is not paid.

INEQUITY   (L)

Unfairness, injustice.

INEVITABLE   (L)

That which cannot be foreseen or prevented, e.g., an accident (q.v.).

IN EXTREMIS   (L)

At the very end; at the last gasp.

IN FACTO   (L)

In fact.

INFAMY   (L)

The loss of character resulting from conviction of a major crime and which, under common law, renders the person in–competent as a witness or affects his credibility.

INFANT   (L)

One who is not of the age of majority (q.v.). Under common law, a person under twenty-one years of age, without regard to sex. The rights, privileges and disabilities of such persons are defined by various state statutes.

INFANTICIDE   (L)

A type of homicide (q.v.), consiting of the killing of a child after birth but prior to notification of live birth to authorities. After notification it becomes homicide as generally termed.

INFARCT   (Cr's)

Area of dead tissue caused by the interruption of the blood supply.

IN FAVOREM LIBERTATIS, OR INFAVOREM VITAE   (L)

In favor of liberty, or life.

INFERENCE   (L)

A truth or proposition drawn from another which is supposed or admitted to be true. A process of reasoning by which a fact or proposition sought to be established is deduced as a logical consequence from other facts, already proved or ad-- mitted.

INFERIOR COURT   (L)

Any court subordinate to the chief tribunal in the particular judicial system; but commonly a court of special limited, or statutory jurisdiction whose record must show the existence and ataching of jurisdiction in any given case, in order to give presumptive validity to its judgement.

IN FLAGRANTI DELICTO   (L)

In the commission of a crime.

INFORMAL   (L)

Deficient in legal form; lacking formality. An informality may, or may not, be of legal consequence. There is a tendency among courts to waive informality in some instances.

INFORMANT   (PA, Cr'y)

One who gives information to an investigator, regarding illicit activities of another.

INFORMATION (L)

A written accusation before a magistrate, made upon oath by a prosecuting officer, charging one or more persons with having committed a crime.

INFORMER (L, PA)

One who provides information concerning those who violate a law or penal statute, occasionally for the purpose of obtaining part, or the whole, of the penalty recoverable under the statute.

IN FORO CONSCIENTIAE (L)

At the tribunal of conscience; applied to moral obligations as distinct from legal.

IN FRAUDIM LEGIS (L)

In fraud of the law.

INFRA DIGNITATEM CURIAE (L)

Beneath the dignity of the court.

INFRINGEMENT (L)

Breach or violation of various intangible rights and privileges.

IN FUTURO (L)

In the future.

IN GENERE (L)

In kind; of the same kind.

INHABITED DWELLING (L)

A structure used exclusively or in part specifically for residential purposes.

INHERENT POWER (L)

Authority, right, ability, or faculty possessed without derivation from another.

INHERENT POWERS OF A COURT (L)

Those reasonably necessary for administration of justice.

INITIATIVE (L)

Laws adopted by popular vote, upon petition of a certain number of electors.

IN JUDICIO (L)

In a judicial proceeding.

INJUNCTION (L)

An order issued by a court of equity commanding a person to do, or to refrain from doing, an act which would injure another by violating his personal or property rights. It may be exercised pending outcome of a law suit or awarded as final determination of the suit.

IN JURE (L)

In law; by right.

INJUSTICE (L)

The withholding or denial of justice. In law, almost invariably applied to the act, fault, or omission of a court, ad distinguished from that of an individual.

IN LIEU OF   (L)

In place of.

IN LOCO PARENTIS   (L)

In the place of a parent; instead of a parent; charged, facitiously, with a parent's rights, duties, and responsibilities.

IN MALEFICIIS VOLUNTAS SPECTATUR NON EXITUS   (L)

In criminal acts the intention is to be regarded, not the result.

INMATE   (L, Cor)

One who dwells within another's house occupying separate rooms but with a common entrance and exit, or in a public in-stitution.

INMATE COUNCIL   (Cor)

Elected prison inmates who discuss policies and complaints with the prison administrator.

IN MISERICORDIA   (L)

At the mercy.

INNER CITY   (Cr'y)

The densely built up, highly urbanized section of a large city, including inner slums, rooming houses, "artistic–intellectual" settlements, and expensive apartment houses located near the center of the city.

INNOCENT   (L)

Free from guilt. A person not responsible for an event or occurrence. One without knowledge of a material fact.

INNUENDO   (L)

An indirect statement. The part of an indictment or pleading, in an action for libel, explaining the connection between the statement of alleged libel, and persons or things indirectly referred to in the statement, thereby showing the libelous nature of the latter.

IN ODIUM SPOLIATORIS OMNIA PRAESUMUNTUR   (L)

All things are presumed against one who destroys evidence.

INOPS CONSILII   (L)

Destitute of counsel.

INORGANIC COMPOUND   (Cr's)

A union of separate elements, ingredients, or parts, other than plant or animal.

IN PERSONAM   (L)

Against the person.

INQUEST   (L)

Judicial inquiry. Usually, an inquiry made by a coroner (q.v.) and jury concerning the cause of death of someone who has been killed, or has died suddenly, or under suspicious cir-cumstances, or in prison. Occasionally, an inquiry by a jury, concerning someone's mental condition. (4) A jury.

INQUISITION   (L)

An inquiry by a jury. The document which records the results of the inquiry.

IN RE   (L)

In the matter of, used in the name or style of court cases, other than actions between adverse parties.

INSANITY   (L)

A legal term for various forms of mental unsoundness, aberra-- tion or impairment. It implies disease or congenital defect of the brain, and embraces idiocy (q.v.), lunacy, and a great many other afflictions of the mind, e.g., mania (q.v.) in its various forms. Upon judgement of insaity the defendant cannot be held accountable for his behavior.

INSOLVENT   (L)

Bankrupt.

INSPECTION   (L)

A critical review or examination involving careful scrutiny and analysis ranging from simple observation to detailed inquiry or analysis of records and statistics. The right of a party to an action to examine objects of evidence relating to the pending action.

INSPECTION SERVICES   (PA)

Those services directed toward decreasing the potentiality of identifiable hazards.

INSTANTANEOUS CRIME   (L)

One fully consummated or completed in and by a single act such as arson or murder.

INSTIGATE   (Cr'y)

Stir up, cause to happen.

INSTRUCT   (L)

(1) To convey information. (2) The act of a trial judge in in-- forming the jury, concerning the law applicable to a case, which the jury is to decide. (3) To give orders or directions as a prin- cipal does to his agent.

INSTRUMENT   (L)

(1) A formal legal writing. (2) A negotiable instrument. (3) A negotiable instrument or a security (q.v.) or any other writing which evidences a right to the payment of money, and is not itself a security agreement or lease, and is of a type, which is in ordinary course of business, transferred by delivery with any necessary endorsement or assignment.

INSUFFICIENCY   (L)

The condition of an answer or affidavit not replying specifically or directly to the charge made or the question asked.

INSULATION THEORY (Cr'y)

A theory formulated by Walter Reckless and Simon Dinitz which suggests that, as persons undergo differential socialization experiences, they accept fundamental values and are increasingly insulated and reinforced in their practices.

INSULIN (Cr's)

Substance produced by the pancreas which regulates the blood sugar.

INTEGRATED BAR (L)

A mandatory association of lawyers licensed to practice in a particular jurisdiction.

INTEGRATION (L)

Unification or bringing together, especially; various racial groups.

INTENT, OR INTENTION (L)

Design; resolve; determination of the mind. To render an act criminal, a wrongful intent must exist, but the wrongful intent may be presumed, if the necessary or probable consequences of the act were wrongful or harmful, and the act was deliberately committed.

INTENTIO (L)

A count or charge.

INTERDICT (L)

An injunction.

INTERLOCUTORY (L)

Provisional, temporary.

INTERNAL AFFAIRS (PA)

A unit responsible for receiving and recording complaints against personnel, for initiating and completing the ensuing investigations, reporting the results to the Chief of Police, presenting cases to disciplinary boards, the personnel office, the Civil Service Commission, or the Prosecutor, and reporting on the disposition of cases to the complainant.

INTERNAL CAPSULE (Cr's)

Pathway of motor and sensory nerve fibres in the brain.

INTERPRETATION (L)

To construe, the assignment and declaration of the meaning of words or signs employed in a statute or instrument.

INTERROGATION (L, PA)

Questioning of one suspected of having committed an offense or who is reluctant to make full disclosure of information in his possession and pertinent to the investigation.

INTERROGATORIES (L)

Written question propounded on behalf of one party in an action to another party, or to someone not a party, before the trial thereof. The person interrogated must give his answers in writing, and upon oath. Verbal questions put to a witness before an examiner and answered on oath. Questions in writing, annexed to a commission to take the deposition of a witness, to be put to and answered by the witness under oath, whose answers are to be reduced to writing by the commis--sioner.

IN TERROREM (L)
For a threat, or by way of.

INTERSECTION (L)
The area embraced within the prolongation of the lateral boun--dary lines. of two or more highways, which join one another.

INTIMA (Cr's)
Innermost of three coats of a blood vessel.

INTIMIDATE (L)
To put one in fear, to frighten.

INTRACEREBRAL (Cr's)
Within the brain.

INTRA CRANIAL (Cr's)
Within the skull.

INTRAGALEAL (Cr's)
Within the soft tissues between the skull and the scalp.

INTRAMURAL (Cr'y)
Within the wall.

INTRINSIC (Cr's)
Situated within or belonging to the body.

INTRUSION (L)
A technical term for the entry of a stranger on land at the termination of a particular estate, and before the heir, or per--son entitled in reversion or remainder, can enter.

INVALID (L)
Not valid; of no binding force.

INVESTIGATOR (PA)
The key figure in a police examination into criminal matters.

INVOLUNTARY MANSLAUGHTER (L)
The unlawful and unintentional killing of another. The direct and proximate result of commission of an unlawful act.

IPSO FACTO (L)
By the fact itself; by the mere fact. By the mere fact of an act or a fact.

IRON GALLOTANNATE INK (Cr's)
Iron gallotannate or nutgall inks are true solutions and not merely suspensions of solid coloring matter in a liquid medium. Hence the ink is capable of penetration into the interstices of the fibers of the paper, thereby inscribing the writing in the

body of the paper and not on the surface alone, thus rendering its removal more difficult.

IRREGULAR   (L)

Done in the wrong manner, or without the proper formalities.

IRRELEVANCY   (L)

The absence of the quality of relevancy, as in evidence or pleadings. The quality or state of being inapplicable or imper-- tent to a fact or argument.

IRRELEVANT   (L)

Not pertinent; not tending to aid or support, e.g., evidence which does not tend to prove the fact at issue.

ISCHEMIA   (Cr's)

Local temporary deficiency of blood supply.

ISLAND (Fingerprints)   (Cr's)

One sweat pore with the surrounding part of the friction ridge is called an "island."

ISLET CELL ADENOMA   (Cr's)

Pancreatic tumor of islet cells which produce insulin.

ISO–ENZYMES   (Cr's)

Multiple molecular forms of an enzyme, each having the same or very similar enzyme activities.

ISONIPECAINE (Meperidine Hydrochloride)   (Cr's)

This drug is also known by the following trade names: Demeral, Dolantin, Dolantol, Endolat, and Pethidone. For relief of pain this drug lies somewhere between morphine and codeine in its effects.

ISOTOPE   (Cr's)

An action differing from another atom of the same element in th the number of neutrons it has in its nucleus.

ISSUE OF LAW   (L)

Can be decided only by a court of law.

ITINERANT   (L)

Traveling or wandering.

JACKET (Cr's)

A sheath, usually of metal, surrounding a bullet.

JAIL (L)

(Old English: gaol.) A legally designated county or city building regularly used for the confinement of persons held in lawful custody.

JAIL DUTIES (Cor)

To provide suitable custodial care of prisoners.

JAM (Cr's)

To become inoperative because of improper loading or ejection.

JEDBURGH JUSTICE, OR LYDFORD LAW (L)

Lynch law, punishment coming first and trial afterward.

JEOFAILE (L)

(Corrupted from j'ai faili, Fr., I have failed). Formerly an ex-pression used to avow an oversight in pleading or other law proceedings.

JEOPARDY (L)

Peril; danger; the condition of a prisoner being tried for an alleged crime.

JOHN DOE (L, Cr'y)

A fictitious name often used when the true name of a defendant is unknown.

JOYRIDER (Cr'y, L)

A youth who steals an auto for a joyride, abandoning it when the gas supply is exhausted.

JUDEX AEQUITATEM SEMPER SPECTARE DEBET (L)

A judge ought always to aim at equity.

JUDEX NON POTEST ESSE TESTIS IN PROPRIA CAUSA (L)

A judge cannot be a witness in his own cause.

JUDGE (L)

A public official with authority to determine a cause or ques--tion in a court of justice and to preside over the proceedings therein.

JUDGE ADVOCATE (L)

A military legal officer whose duties are analogous to those of a civilian judge or prosecutor, possibly with various other legal duties.

JUDGE--MADE LAW (L)

Common law as developed in form and content by judges or judicial decisions. Judicial decisions based on tortured constructions of the Constitution, or on the selection of unusual historical and legal precedents, or on unusual definitions of terms in "discovering" the law applying to a given case.

JUDGEMENT RECORD (L)

The pleadings and proceedings in a court up to and including the judgement, made and kept by the clerk, or a transcript thereof.

JUDGE PRO TEM (L)

One temporarily authorized to perform judicial duties.

JUDICANDUM EST LEGIBUS, NON EXEMPLIS (L)

We should judge by the laws, not precedents.

JUDICES NON TENENTUR EXPRIMERE CAUSAM SENTENTIAE SUAE (L)

Judges are not bound to explain the reason of their judgements.

JUDICIAL (L)

Relating to proceedings before a judge or in court.

JUDICIAL ADMISSION, CONFESSION (L)

A statement in due course of legal proceedings contrary to the interests of the person making it; can be used to decide the lawsuit against the person making it.

JUDICIAL DISCRETION (L)

When doubtful matters cannot be avoided by referring them to juries or to the political processes, judges shall decide them in accordance with the standards and values of the reasonable man.

JUDICIAL NOTICE (L)

The act by which a court, in conducting a trial, or framing its decision, will, of its own motion, and without the production of evidence, recognize the existence and truth of certain facts, having a bearing on the controversy at bar, which from their nature, are not properly the subject of testimony, or which are universally regarded as established by common notoriety, e.g., the laws of the state, historical events, and course of nature.

JUDICIAL POWER (L)

The power to hear and decide cases and controversies in accordance with the forms and procedures prescribed by the law of the land and to render judgement consistent with the substantive provisions of law, such judgement being definitive except for the legal right of parties to appeal to a higher judicial tribunal.

JUDICIAL PROCESS (L)

A set of interrelated procedures and roles for deciding disputes by an authoritative person or persons whose decisions are regularly obeyed.

JUDICIAL WRITS (L)

All writs or process, subsequent to the original writ issued out of chancery.

JUDICIA POSTERIORA SUNT IN LEGE FORTIORA (L)

The later decisions are the stronger in law.

JUDICIARY ACT (L)

The act of Congress of September 24, 1789, establishing federal courts.

JUDICIS EST JUDICARE SECUNDUM ALLEGATE ET PRO-BATA (L)

It is the duty of a judge to decide according to facts alleged and proved.

JUDICIS EST JUS DICERE NON DARE (L)

It is for a judge to declare, not to make law.

JUDICIUM A NON SUO JUDICE DATUM NULLIUS EST MOMENTI (L)

A judgement rendered by one not a proper judge is of no weight.

JURATION (L)

The act of swearing; the administration of an oath.

JURATORES SUNT JUDICES FACTI (L)

Jurors are the judges of fact.

JURIDICAL (L)

Relating to the administration of justice.

JURIDICAL DAYS (L)

Days on which courts are held and justice administered; court days.

JURIMETRICS (L)

The scientific investigation of legal problems.

JURIS (L)

L., of law; of right.

JURISDICTION (L)

The authority of a court to hear and decide an action or law-suit. The geographical court district. Limited power juris-diction, when the court has power to act only in certain specified cases; general, or residual, when it may act in all cases in which the parties are before it, except for those cases which pertain to another court; concurrent, when the same cause may be entertained by one court or another; original, when the court has power to try the case in the first instance; appelate, when the court hears cases only on appeal, certiorari, or writ of error from another court; exclusive, when no other court has power to hear and decide the same matter.

JURIS DOCTOR (L)

The first, or lowest, professional degree in legal education.

JURIS ET DE JURE (L)

Of law and from law.

JURISPRUDENCE (L)

Law. A body of law. Philosophy of law.

JURIST (L)

A judge. Formerly; one versed in Roman Law.

JURY (L)

A body of citizens, called jurors, sworn to deliver a true verdict upon evidence submitted to them in a judicial proceeding. Grand: summoned to consider whether the evidence, presented by the state against a person accused of crime, warrants his in-dictment. Petty or petit: the trial jury, either civil or criminal, usually twelve persons, but by various statutes a lesser number may constitute a jury in some courts. A special or struck jury is one selected especially for the trial of a given cause, usually by the assistance of the parties.

JURY BOX   (L)

A place in a courtroom where a jury sits, usually enclosed with a low rail.

JURY DIRECTIONS, OR JURY INSTRUCTIONS   (L)

A statement given by the judge, setting forth the law applicable to a particular lawsuit heard by a jury and about to be decided by it.

JURY PROCESS   (L)

The writ for the summoning of a jury.

JURY WHEEL   (L)

A revolving drum in which the names of persons subject to jury duty are placed, and from which the jury panels are drawn.

JUS DICERE, ET NON JUS DARE   (L)

To declare the law, not to make it.

JUS EX INJURIA NON ORITUR   (L)

A right cannot arise out of wrongdoing.

JUS IN PERSONNAM   (L)

A right against another person.

JUS LEGITIMUM   (L)

A legal right that may be inforced by due course of law.

JUS NATURAE   (L)

The law of nature.

JUSTA FORMAM STATUTI   (L)

According to the form of the statute.

JUSTICE   (L)

The goal of court decisions, which comes to light under compet-ing arguments. The constant and perpetual disposition to render every man his due; fairness; conformity to law; merited reward or punishment. A title sometimes given to judges, especially appellate judges.

JUSTICE OF THE PEACE   (L)

In some jurisdictions, a minor judicial officer with specifically enumerated powers, e.g., preventing breaches of the peace, and causing the arrest and commitment of persons violating the law. Under various state statutes, they may have limited jurisdiction to try certain cases.

JUSTICIABILITY   (L)

A court's ability to deal with a case in proper form for judicial decision or because courts can fashion a remedy if a right has been infringed upon.

JUSTIFIABLE   (L)

Lawful.

JUSTIFICATION   (L)

A reasonable explanation as to why the defendant did what he is charged with. In an action of libel, a defense showing the libel to be true; in an action of assault, showing the violence to have been necessary.

JUSTINIAN CODE   (L)

A code formulated by Emperor Justinian of the Byzantine Empire in 529–565 A.D. The standard of law throughout Europe during the Middle Ages. Common law as it is known today is basically derived from the Code of Justinian courts.

JUVENILE CORRECTIONAL SYSTEM   (Cor)

Juvenile institutions, usually training schools and having a high proportion of treatment personnel.

JUVENILE COURT   (Cr'y, L)

A court of law dealing only with illegal acts by children under the legal age of adulthood.

JUVENILE COURTS   (L)

Tribunals specially created by various state statutes to supervise dependent, neglected and delinquent children.

JUVENILE DELINQUENCY   (L, Cr'y)

Antisocial conduct and legally defined delinquency by youth under a defined age limit.

JUVENILE DELINQUENCY   (Cr'y)

Antisocial conduct and legally defined delinquency by youth under a defined age limit.

KANGAROO COURT   (Cor)

A mock court, e.g., composed of fellow prisoners in a jail.

KEYHOLE   (Cr's)

The shape of the hole caused by a bullet traveling off its long axis.

KICKBACK   (L)

The return of a part of one's compensation.

KIDNAPPING   (L)

The forcible abduction or carrying away of a person.

KLEPTOMANIA   (Cr'y)

An irresistible propensity to steal.

KNOWINGLY AND WILLFULLY   (L)

Conscious and intentional violation of a statute.

KYPHOSCOLIOSIS   (Cr's)

Abnormal curvature of the spine.

LAMINA (Cr's)

A thin, flat plate or layer.

LANDS (Cr's)

The raised spiral surfaces left by cutting grooves into the inner surface of a gun barrel to impart a spinning motion to the bullet.

LARCENY (L)

The unlawful taking and removing from the scene of personal property, without color of right or use of force, violence or fraudulent means and with intent to deprive the rightful owner thereof. Commonly classified as grand or petty, according to the value of the thing taken.

LARCENY BY TRICK (L)

Inducing another to part with possession of his personal prop--erty by trick or artifice.

LARYNX (Cr's)

The part of the airway containing the vocal cords.

LAST WILL OR LAST WILL AND TESTAMENT (L)

The will (q.v.) which a court accepts and records, i.e., probates.

LATENT (Cr's, L)

Hidden.

LATENT DEFECT (L)

A hidden defect not discoverable by observation.

LATENT FINGERPRINTS (Cr's)

Fingerprints not readily visible to the unaided eye but some--times seen aided by indirect light. On hard, smooth, nonabsor--bent surfaces they can be developed, that is, made visible, by various shades of fine–grain powders.

LATERAL (Cr's)

Pertaining to a side.

LATERAL POCKET LOOPS (Cr's)

Two loops opening at the same side.

LAW (L)

A system of standardized norms regulating human conduct, deliberately established for the purpose of social control. Laws are interpreted and enforced by formal public (political) authority, rather than by custom.

LAW, EX POST FACTO (L)

A retroactive law. Penalizing acts committed before the law was passed and not illegal at the time of occurrence.

LAWFUL (L)

That which is sanctioned or permitted by, or is compatible with law; legal.

LAW, REGULATORY (L)

Law not based on custom and tradition but enacted to meet new needs of a changing society. When there is rapid tech--

nological and social change, new conditions that require regula--
tion emerge for which there are no, inadequate, traditional
norms on which to base such regulations.

LAWSUIT   (L)

Any one of various proceedings in a court of law.

LEADERSHIP   (PA)

The ability to direct others to work together in the expeditious
realization of goals.

LEADING   (Cr's)

The presence of lead residue on the inner surface of a gun barrel.

LEADING CASE   (L)

A precedent so often followed as to be established as a principle
of law.

LEADING COUNSEL, OR LEAD COUNSEL, OR LEADER   (L)

The principal attorney having care of a case in which two or
more attorneys are employed.

LEADING QUESTION   (L)

An inquiry suggesting an answer. Used in cross--examination.

LEASE SYSTEM   (Cor)

A system of prisoner employment used throughout the South,
from the Civil War to 1936. Under this system, the prisoners
were leased to the highest bidder.

LEAVE OF ABSENCE   (PA)

An extended period during which an officer is excused from
active duty and during which time he receives no pay.

LEGAL   (L)

According, or relating, to law. Historically, distinguished from
EQUITABLE.

LEGAL FICTION   (L)

An assumption held to be true under the law even though in
fact it may be false; e.g., a law remains as it has always been
while in fact it has been modified considerably in its interpreta--
tion and application.

LEGALISTIC   (Cr'y)

The school of criminology which holds that a man is a criminal
by legal definition only; that is, the law is more important than
the act itself.

LEGALIZE   (L)

To make lawful   (q.v.)

LEGAL MALICE   (L)

Constructive malice, or malice in law.

LEGAL REALISM   (L)

A philosophy of law which critically analyzes judicial decision
making, to identify various psychological, sociological, eco--
nomic, political and other factors, which influence the resolution

of controversies; behavioral jurisprudence.

LEGAL TENDER (L)

Coins and paper money declared by statute to be good and sufficient for the payment of debts public and private.

LEGES POSTERIORES PRIORE CONTRARIAS ABROGANT (L)

Later laws abrogate prior contrary laws.

LEGITIMACY (L)

The condition of persons born of lawfully married parents. Lawfulness or legality.

LEGITIMATION (L)

Legal acknowledgement of children born out of wedlock.

LENGTH OF SERVICE (PA)

The period of elapsed time since the oath of office was last administered. Previous service may be added.

LE SALUT DU PEUPLE EST LA SUPREME LOI (L)

The safety of the people is the supreme law.

LESION (L)

A bodily injury. The degree of injury or duress sustained by a minor, or person of weak capacity, necessary to entitle him to avoid a deed.

LESSER INCLUDED OFFENSE (L)

A separate offense, all of the elements of which are alleged, among other elements, in an offense charged in an indictment.

LESS THAN DEADLY FORCE (L)

Less than deadly force; i.e., use of means not intended or likely to cause death.

LEX (L)

A law; the law; occasionally used as synonymous with jus, right.

LEX DILATIONES EXHORRET (L)

The law abhors delays.

LEX DOMICILII (L)

The law of the country where a person has his domicile (q.v.).

LEX EST DICTAMEN RATIONIS (L)

Law is the dictate of reason.

LEX EST NORMA RECTI (L)

Law is a rule of right.

LEX NON FAVET DELICATORUM VOTIS (L)

The law favors not the wishes of the dainty. In deciding whether an alleged nuisance should be restrained by injunction, the court considers whether it would materially inconvenience persons of ordinary, not fastidious, habits.

LEX POSTERIOR DEROGAT PRIORI (L)

A prior statute gives place to a latter.

LEX PROSPICIT, NON RESPICIT (L)

The law looks forward, not backward, i.e., statutes are not, as a rule, retrospective.

LEX REPROBAT MORAM   (L)

The law disapproves of delay.

LEX SCRIPTA   (L)

The written or statute law.

LEX SEMPER DABIT REMEDIUM   (L)

The law will always furnish a remedy.

LEX SUCCURRIT MINORIBUS   (L)

The law assists minors.

LEX TERRAE   (L)

The law of the land; the process of law.

LEX UNO ORE OMNES ALLOQUITUR   (L)

The law speaks to all in the same way.

LEY   (L)

(Fr., loi) Law.

LEZE MAJESTY   (L)

(Lez majes ti) Or laesae majestatis crimen, an offense against sovereign power; treason.

LIBEL   (L)

Defamatory writing; any published matter whic tends to degrade a person in the eyes of his neighbors, or to render him ridiculous, or to injure his property or business. It may be published by writing, effigy, picture, or the like. Cf. Slander. In admiralty, the plaintiff's written statement of his case, analogous to a complaint (q.v.).

LEBELLUS FAMOSUS   (L)

A libel; a defamatory writing, sign or picture.

LIBELOUS PER SE   (L)

Descriptive of various acts of libel (q.v.), which are actionable without proof of special damages. Usually, they are of three classes: 1) those inputting to the plaintiff criminal acts involving moral turpitude; 2) those imputing a contagious or offensive disease; and 3) those tending to injure plaintiff in his occupation or business.

LIBERATE   (L)

To set free.

LIBERTY   (L)

Freedom from restraint; self–determination. Authority to do something. A franchise.

LICENSE   (L)

Authority to act in some manner which would be wrongful or illegal to do, if authority were not granted. The authority may be pertinent to a public matter, e.g., the privilege of driving a motor vehicle on the public highways, or to a private matter,

e.g., the privilege of manufacturing a patented article. In public matters, licenses are often required in order to regulate the
activity.

LICENTIOUSNESS (L)

Ignoring moral restraints. Doing what one pleases without
regard to the rights of others.

LIEU (L)

In lieu of, in the place, or instead of.

LIMITATION (L)

A restriction; a thing which limits or restrains. Various
periods of time, fixed by different state and federal statutes,
called statutes of limitations, within which a lawsuit must be
commenced, and after the expiration of which, the claimant
will be forever barred from the right to bring the action. A
clause in a conveyance, or will, which declares how long the
estate transferred thereby shall continue, e.g., "heirs," or
"heirs of the body," are words of limitation which define the
nature of the estate conveyed.

LIMITED (L)

Restricted; circumscribed; not full.

LIMITED ACCESS HIGHWAY, OR FREEWAY (L)

A highway especially designed for through traffic, and over
which abutting property owners have no easement or right of
access, by reason of the fact that their property abuts on such
highway.

LINDBERG ACT (L)

An act forbidding the interstate transportation of kidnapped
persons.

LINE COMMAND (PA)

The exercise of authority delegated by the chief to his immediate subordinates and by them to their subordinates down the
lines of direct control to the lowest level.

LINE FUNCTIONS (PA)

Operations carried out in direct relation to the primary goal of
the organization.

LINES OF AUTHORITY (PA)

The logical flow of policy, orders, reports, and information;
the direction, up or down, being determined by the nature of
the communication.

LINE SPECTRUM (Cr's)

A type of emission spectrum showing a series of lines separated
by black areas. Each line represents a definite wavelength or
frequency.

LINE UP (PA)

A procedure of placing crime suspects with others, not believed

implicated in the crime, in a line or other position so that witnesses can view them for the purpose of making possible identification.

LIQUID   (Cr's)

A state of matter in which molecules are in contact with one
another but are not rigidly held in place.

LIQUIDATION   (L)

Ascertaining and fixing the value of something, e.g., a stock of
foods, or the amount of damages. Paying, settling and discharging an indebtedness or liability. Winding up the business
of a person or firm.

LIS   (L)

An action, or dispute.

LITIGANT   (L)

One engaged in a lawsuit as a party.

LITIGATION   (L)

A lawsuit, a contest in court.

LOAN–SHARKING   (L)

The lending of money at exorbitant interest rates.

LOCAL   (L)

Pertaining to a particular place or district.

LOCAL ACTION   (L)

A lawsuit which must be brought in the county or district
where the subject matter lies, or the cause of action arose, as
distinguished from transitory (q.v.).

LOCAL STATUTES   (L)

Legislative acts, the effect of which is limited to a particular
place, as distinguished from general statutes.

LODGER   (L)

One who occupies rooms in a house, general control of which
remains to the landlord.

LOMBROSIAN THEORY   (Cr'y)

A theory in criminology, set forth by Cesare Lombroso in the
late 19th century, holding that criminal behavior is the result
of biological, rather than social, psychological, or environmental
factors. Lombroso regarded criminals as being essentially
physiologically degenerate and animalistic, and believed that
criminal types could be detected through such measures as head
shape. This theory has no standing in modern research on
criminal behavior.

See also: Lombroso, Cesare.

LOMBROSO, CESARE (1836–1909)   (Cr'y)

Founder of the Positivistic school of criminology. His work was
instrumental in shifting the focus of criminology and penology
from the previous metaphysical, legal and juristic emphasis to a

potentially scientific foundation.

See also: Lombrosian Theory.

LONG ARM STATUTE   (L)

Various acts providing for personal jurisdiction, via substituted service of process, over nonresident persons or corporations which voluntarily go into a state, directly or by agent, or com-- municate with persons in the state, for limited purposes, in actions concerning claims relating to the performance or exe- cution of those purposes, e.g., transacting business in the state, contracting to supply services of goods in the state, or selling goods outside the state when the seller knows that the goods will be used or consumed in the state.

LOST PAPERS   (L)

Writings so mislaid that they cannot be found after diligent search. Secondary evidence thereof is generally admissible.

LOTTERY   (L)

A scheme for the distribution of prizes by lot, in which the elements of consideration, prize, and chance are present.

LOW ORDER EXPLOSIVE   (Cr's)

Explosive with a velocity of detonation less than 1000 meters per second. For example, black powder and smokeless powder.

LOWER NEPHRON NEPHROSIS   (Cr's)

Kidney condition seen in crushing injuries, in which the lower excretory tubules are plugged with pigmented casts.

LUCID INTERVAL   (L)

A period of sanity intervening between two attacks of insanity; a temporary cure or return of health.

LUCRI CAUSA   (L)

For the sake of gain; a term descriptive of the felonious in- tent with which property is taken.

LUES   (Cr's)

Syphilis, luetic, pertaining to lues.

LUMINAL   (Cr's)

Pertaining to the cavity of a tubular organ (e.g. blood vessel).

LUNATIC   (L)

A person of unsound mind; an insane person. Occasionally defined by various state statutes.

LYMPHOCYTES   (Cr's)

A variety of white blood corpuscules.

LYNCH LAW   (L)

Summary punishment of real or suspected criminals, without proper judicial authority.

MACHINE REST   (Cr's)

A rigid base to which a rifle is affixed, or upon which it rests, to assist in accurate testing.

MACROSCOPIC   (Cr's)

Pertaining to examination with the naked eye as distinguished from miscroscopic.

MAFIA   (Cr'y)

A form of organized and generally violent crime.

MAGAZINE   (Cr's)

A separate or integrated device wherein ammunition is held in position to be fed into the firing chamber of a firearm.

MAGISTRATE   (L)

A local official exercising summary judicial jurisdiction over violations of municipal ordinances or minor criminal cases.

MAGNA CARTA   (L)

A symbolic document, issued by King John in 1215 A.D., that marked the beginning of civil and constitutional rights in English speaking countries.

MAGNA CULPA DOLUS EST   (L)

Gross negligence is equivalent to fraud.

MAGNUM   (Cr's)

Cartridge of increased power than earlier standards for the same calibre, also firearms with the capacity to use magnum cartridges, manufactures sometimes use word for glamour, not the increased power.

MAINPERNABLE   (L)

An offense or person charged therewith, that may be allowed bail.

See also: Mainpernors.

MAINPERNORS   (L)

Formerly, persons to whom a man was delivered out of prison, on their becoming bound to produce him whenever required. Similar to a person who serves as bail (q.v.).

See also: Mainpernable.

MAINPRISE   (L)

An old term for bail (q.v.).

MAINTENANCE   (PA)

The service, repair, and maintenance, in good order, of police equipment and property.

MAINTENANCE WORK   (Cor)

The use of inmate labor related to the care and upkeep of the institution and the inmate population.

MAJOR NON POLICE FUNCTIONS   (PA)

A near--endless list of staff--type services provided by the police department as an adjunct to its main function. Most commonly accepted among the non police functions is the maintenance of detention facilities and services. Others include ambulance, towing, impounding, police fleet repair and maintenance, escort, traffic engineering, bail collecting, laboratory and similarily unrelated services.

MAL, MALA, OR MALUM   (L)
Bad; wrong; fraudulent. Used as a prefix.

MALADJUSTMENT   (Cr'y)
A condition or process involving the inability or unwillingness of an individual or group to conform to prevailing psycholog-- ical, social, or cultural standards -- either their own or those of an external system.

MALA FIDES   (L)
Bad faith, the opposite of bona fides.

MALA IN SE   (L)
Acts wrong in themselves, whether prohibited by human laws or not, as distinguished from mala prohibita.

MALA PRAXIS   (L)
Malpractice; bad or unskilled treatment by a physician, or other professional person, resulting in an injury to the person who employs him.

MALA PROHIBITA   (L)
Acts prohibited by human laws, but not necessarily mala in se, or wrong in themselves.

MALEFACTOR   (L)
A wrongdoer; one convicted of a crime.

MALEFICIA PROPOSITIS DISTINGUUNTUR   (L)
Evil deeds are distinguished from evil purposes.

MALFEASANCE   (L)
The commission of an unlawful act, particularly by a public official.

MALICE   (L)
The intent to do injury to another, without just cause or excuse.

MALICIOUS   (L)
See: Malice.

MALICIOUS ARREST   (L)
Imprisonment or prosecution, a malicious setting in motion of the law, without probable cause, whereby someone is wrong-- fully and maliciously accused of a criminal offense or a civil wrong, and by reason of which that person sustains damage.

MALICIOUS INJURIES   (L)
Injuries wantonly inflicted on person or property, without just cause, e.g., arson or destruction of property.

MALINGERER   (L)
One who feigns illness or disease; e.g., to escape military duty

or obtain charity.

MALITA PRAECOGITATA (L)
Malice aforethought.

MALPRACTICE (L)
The negligent, or otherwise improper, performance by a physician, attorney or other professional person, of duties devolved
and incumbent upon him as a result of professional relations
with a patient or client.

MANAGEMENT PLANS (PA)
Systematized projection of all operations involved in the organization and management of personnel and material and in the
procurement and disbursement of money.

MANDAMUS (L)
A writ (court order) requiring a government official to perform
a certain act.

MANDATARY (L)
One to whom a mandate or charge is given.

MANDATE (L)
A judicial command. A charge or commission. Occasionally,
a bailment (q.v.) of goods, without reward, to have something
done to them, not merely for safe custody.

MANDATORY RELEASE (Cor)
A type of release wherein accumulated time for good behavior
and work credits deducted from the sentence makes release
legally mandatory.

MANIA (L, Cr'y)
Various forms of mental disease, involving excitement.

MANIC–DEPRESSIVE PSYCHOSIS (Cr'y)
A psychosis characterized by alternation between extreme
emotional states of elation (mania) and depression. In the
manic phase there may be extreme excitement, hyperactivity,
delirium, or occasionally violence. The depressive phase may
involve sadness and feelings of inferiority, severe depression,
suicidal tendencies or occasionally stupor. Some patients alter-
nate between manic and normal states or between depressive
and normal states. Manic depressive psychosis has been shown
to vary by such characteristics as sex and ethnic group.

MANIFESTO (L)
A declaration of the reasons for the acts of one government
toward another, made by the nation's constituted authorities.

MANN ACT (L)
A federal law which prohibits interstate transportation of
women for immoral purposes.

MANSLAUGHTER (L)
The unlawful killing of another, without malice. It is either

voluntary, i.e., upon sudden heat, or under strong provocation, or involuntary, i.e., without intending the death of the per-- son, upon the commission of some other unlawful act.

MARITAL   (L)

Pertaining to marriage, e.g., marital rights, marital duties.

MARKSMAN   (L)

One who cannot write, and therefore makes only an X mark in executing instruments, another writing his name on each side of such mark.

MARSHAL   (L)

A federal officer, whose duty is to execute the process of the United States courts. His duties are similar to those of a sheriff. In some jurisdictions, an officer of a city or town, whose duties are analogous to those of a chief of police.

MARTIAL LAW   (L)

Temporary control of an area and the population thereof, im-- posed by a military commander under authority of his civilian chief. It may be imposed in the territory of an enemy in war, or in the home territory when normal authority is unable to function. When imposed in enemy territory, it must be exer-- cised in accordance with international law and the conventions of civilized warfare. When imposed in home territory, its justification is subject to judicial review.

See also: Military Law.

MASOCHISM AND SADISM   (Cr'y)

The sadist achieves sexual excitement by inflicting punishment, mental or physical, on another. The masochist, on the other hand, derives his pleasure from submitting to ill treatment at the hands of a sadist or another. In some persons both of these deviations are mingled.

MASS   (Cr'y)

An elementary grouping of people participating in some form of unstructured large group behavior.

MASTER'S TEST   (Cr's)

Recording of electrocardiogram while the patient performs a specific exercise to test the coronary circulation.

MATERIAL WITNESS, ARREST OF   (L)

A person cannot be arrested merely as a material witness until after the court or examining magistrate has required him, while in court, to give bail and he has failed to do so; or where such person is not in court and it is shown to be impracticable to secure his presence by subpoena.

MAXIM   (L)

An axiom; a general or leading principle.

MAXIMUM CUSTODY INSTITUTION   (Cor)

A penal institution with walls around the perimeter, cell blocks
with inside cell construction or back--to--back construction
with each cell facing a wall, armed guard towers, wall towers
and similar security measures.

MAXIMUM CUSTODY PRISONER   (Cor)

An inmate who must be locked up at all times and be accompa--
nied by an officer when moving from one place to another.

MAXIMUM SECURITY INSTITUTIONS   (Cor)

Mainly concerned with keeping inmates within the confines of
the facility.

See also: Maximum Custody Institution.

MAYHEM   (L)

At common law, the deprivation of a member of the body
proper for defense in a fight, e.g., an arm, leg, eye, or foretooth,
or of those parts, the loss of which abates a man's courage; but
not a jawtooth, ear, or nose, because they were supposed to be
of no use in fighting. Often defined by various state statutes,
which may make no distinction between one member and
another with regard to the offense of cutting or wounding.

MC CARRAN ACT   (L)

A federal law to protect the United States against certain un--
American and subversive activities, by requiring registration of
Communist organizations.

MEANDER   (L)

To wander or wind. Descriptive of the banks or course of a
stream.

MEDIA   (Cr's)

Middle layer of a blood vessel wall.

MEDIAL   (Cr's)

Pertaining to the middle, near the median plane.

MEDIASTINUM   (Cr's)

Connective tissue in the thoracic cavity separating it into right
and left halves.

MEDIUM CUSTODY INSTITUTION   (Cor)

Usually has a strong perimeter fence with guard towers, but
with generally less restriction inside the fences or compound.

MEDIUM CUSTODY PRISONER   (Cor)

An inmate living inside the walls who can work in gangs under
supervision outside the walls, alone inside the walls, sometimes
called an "inside trusty."

MEDIUM SECURITY INSTITUTIONS   (Cor)

Less elaborate physical restraint than in maximum security insti--
tutions, and therefore less expensive to construct.

See also: Medium Custody Institution.

MEDULLA   (Cr's)

Central part of an organ.

MEDULLA OBLONGATA (Cr's)

Rear part of the brain which connects with the spinal cord and contains the vital centers of respiration and heartbeat.

MELENA (Cr's)

Passage of black, tarry stools caused by digested blood.

MELIUS INQUIRENDUM (L)

Formerly, a writ for a second inquiry.

MEMBER (PA)

A term applied to all persons on the police department payroll including civilian employees.

MENINGES (Cr's)

The three membraneous coverings of the brain, pia, arachnoid and dura.

MENINGIOMA (Cr's)

Tumor of the Meninges.

MENINGITIS (Cr's)

Inflammation of the meninges.

MEN OF STRAW (L)

Formerly, those who frequented courts for the purpose of giv--ing false evidence. Worthless persons, those without means.

MENS REA (L)

Criminal, evil, guilty intent.

MENTAL CRUELTY (L)

Habitual behavior of such a cruel and inhuman manner as to indicate a settled aversion to a person's spouse, or to destroy permanently his or her peace or happiness.

MENTAL DISORDER (Cr'y)

A serious personality disorganization, mental illness, or psycho-sis manifested in deviation from social norms. A person with a mental disorder finds it difficult to adjust to his social environ--ment.

MENTAL ILLNESS (Cr'y)

A nonorganic, socio--psychological disorder wherein the indi--vidual is unable to protect his ego or social self sufficiently to participate in ordinary social life and obtain at least a minimal degree of social and psychological rewards.

MESAORTITIS (Cr's)

Usually syphylitic inflammation of the wall of the aorta.

MESENTERY (Cr's)

Membrane which supports the intestines within the abdomen.

MESODERMAL (Cr's)

Pertaining to the mesoderm which is the middle layer of the three primary germ layers of embryo.

MESSUAGE (L)

A dwelling house, with outbuildings, garden, and the curtilage (q.v.).

METAL BULLET POINT (Cr's)
Bullet having lead bearing and metal tip.

METAL–CASED BULLET (Cr's)
One with a jacket of metal completely encasing the nose.

METASTASIS (Cr's)
Transfer of a disease from one part of the body to another, specially in the case of malignant tumors.

METHADONE (Cr's)
Methadone hydrochloride. An addictive drug also known by the following trade names: Methadon, Amidone, Amidon, Dolophine, and Adanon. Its pharmacologic action is like that of morphine, except for its failure to produce a seditive action.

METHEMOGLOBIN (Cr's)
Pathologic form of hemoglobin unable to combine with oxygen, occurring following administration of certain drugs and chemi-- cals.

MICROCRYSTALLINE TESTS (Cr's)
Tests to identify specific substances by the color and morphol- ogy of the crystals formed when the substance is mixed with specific reagents.

MID–RANGE (Cr's)
The distance between short range and long range; pertaining to firearms.

MILEAGE (L)
Compensation allowed by law to witnesses, sheriffs, and other public officers, for expenses incurred while traveling on public business.

MILITARY LAW (L)
A system for the government of persons in military service; distinguished from martial law (q.v.), which affects all persons within the scope of military operations or occupation, whether they are in the service or not.
    See also: Martial Law.

MILLING (Cr'y)
A type of physical behavior found in an early stage of certain types of crowd formation, characterized by restless, random movement of the crowd's members. This uncoordinated move-- ment reflects the sensitivity of the members to each other and the diffuse interstimulation based upon a feeling of physical proximity and a sense of crisis.

MINATUR INNOCENTIBUS QUI PARCIT NOCENTIBUS (L)
He threatens the innocent who spares the guilty.

MINERAL (Cr's)
A naturally occurring crystalline solid.

141

MINIMUM CUSTODY INSTITUTION (Cor)

Frequently possesses a single fence or no fences, no towers, and no obvious security measures.

See also: Minimum Security Institution.

MINIMUM SECURITY INSTITUTIONS (Cor)

Usually operate without any guard posts or armed guards.

May not even have a fence denoting the area out–of–bounds to inmates.

See also: Minimum Custody Institution.

MINIMUM SECURITY PRISONER (Cor)

An inmate who can live outside the walls and work alone out--side the walls, generally referred to as a full trusty.

MINORITY (L)

Descriptive of a person or group of persons, who do not pre–dominate in numbers within the nation, electorate or other group to which they belong, e.g., Black persons or persons of Mexican descent in the United States. The status of a person who is of less than full age.

MISADVENTURE (L)

An accident or misfortune by which an injury occurs to another, without negligence and while performing a lawful act.

MISBEHAVIOR (L)

Improper or unlawful conduct; misconduct.

MISCARRIAGE (L)

A failure of justice. Abortion (q.v.).

MISCARRIAGE OF JUSTICE (L)

Prejudice to substantial rights of a party.

MISDEMEANOR (L)

Offenses less serious than felonies and generally punishable by fine or imprisonment otherwise than in penitentiary and for less than one year.

MISDIRECTION (L)

Judicial error in instructing or charging a trial jury.

MISFEASANCE (L)

The improper performance of some lawful act. A wrongful act.

MISFIRE (Cr's)

The failure of the priming mixture to explode when the primer has been struck an adequate blow by a firing pin or the failure of the exploding primer to ignite the powder.

MISNOMER (L)

The assigning of an incorrect name to a person in legal docu–ments or judicial proceedings.

MISPRISON OF FELONY (L)

Concealment of a felony committed by another without

previous concert with or subsequent assistance to the felon as would make the party concealing an accessory before or after the fact.

See also: Treason.

MISREPRESENTATION   (L)

A false statement constituting grounds for rescission of a con--tract or recovery of damages for losses caused thereby.

MISSING PERSON   (L)

A missing person is any minor reported missing or an adult who is: seriously affected mentally or physically, or absent under involuntary circumstances.

MISTAKE   (L)

An error in judgement or conduct; an act done or omitted, by reason of ignorance of law or facts, which a party would not have committed if he had rightly understood the law or facts.

MISTRIAL   (L)

An erroneous trial lacking some fundamental requisite, or at which an event supervenes, causing termination of proceedings because a fair verdict cannot be obtained thereby.

MITIGATING CIRCUMSTANCES   (L)

Such as do not constitute a justification or excuse of the offense in question but which, in fairness and mercy, may be con--sidered as extenuating or reducing the degree of moral culpa--bility. Those that affect basis for award of exemplary damages, or reduce actual damages by showing, not that they were never suffered, but that they have been partially extinguished. And in actions for libel and slander, circumstances bearing on defen--dant's liability for exemplary damages by reducing moral culpa--bility, or on liability for actual damages by showing partial extinguishment thereof.

MITIGATION   (L)

Reduction of damages or of punishment.

MITRAL VALVE   (Cr's)

Valve between the two left chambers of the heart.

MITTIMUS   (L)

A written court order directing the keeper of a prison to re-ceive and safely keep an offender. A form of process trans-ferring records from one court to another.

MIXED QUESTIONS OF LAW AND FACT   (L)

Cases wherein a jury finds the particular facts, the court decid--ing upon the legal result thereof.

MOB   (Cr'y)

A very active and emotionally aroused aggregation of people or crowd with a common purpose or interest that motivates them to acts of destruction, violence, or aggression.

MODUS OPERADI   (PA)
>   The manner of operation.

MOLECULE   (Cr's)
>   Two or more atoms held together by chemical bonds.

MOLESTATION   (L)
>   Annoyance of an individual with intent to control his actions. The abnormal, sexually motivated dusturbing of children.

MONOCHROMATIC LIGHT   (Cr's)
>   Light having a single wavelength or frequency.

MONOMANIA   (L)
>   Insanity (q.v.) related to a single subject, manifested by a single delusion of the mind.

MONOMER   (Cr's)
>   The basic unit of structure from which a polymer is constructed.

MOOT   (L)
>   (1) Descriptive of something not genuine or concrete; pre–tended. (2) A meeting to argue points of law as an exercise.

MOOT CASE OR MOOT POINT   (L)
>   An issue before a court which is not genuine, has already been disposed of, or the resolution of which cannot be implemented.

MOOT COURT   (L)
>   A court of academic exercise where pretended cases (q.v.) are argued and decided.

MORAL CERTAINTY   (L)
>   The degree of probability to induce a person to act in the ordi–nary affairs of life as if the thing were certain. The degree of assurance falling short of absolute certainty which leaves room for no reasonable doubt.

MORAL EVIDENCE   (L)
>   That kind of evidence which, without developing an absolute and necessary certainty, generates a high degree of probability founded upon analogy or induction, experience of the ordinary course of nature or the sequence of events, and the testimony of men.

MORAL TURPITUDE   (L)
>   An act of baseness, vileness or depravity, contrary to the rule of right and duty between human beings.

MORATORIUM   (L)
>   A lawful suspension of legal remedies against debtors during times of financial distress.

MORES   (Cr'y)
>   Those social norms which dictate moral standards of behavior to a group or society. Conformity is not optional, with non–conformity severely sanctioned. Singular: mos.

MORTIS CAUSA (L)

In prospect of death.

MORTUARY (L, Cr's)

A place where deceased persons are kept temporarily and pre--pared for interment. (2) Formerly, a gift left by a person at his death to his parish church.

MOS (Cr'y)

See: Mores.

MOSES, LAW OF (Cr'y)

An early written code (1500B.C.–900B.C.).

MOTION (L)

Applications by parties or their counsel to a court for a rule or order, either in the progress of a lawsuit, or summarily, e.g., a motion for a writ of habeas corpus. A motion may be made either ex parte (q.v.), or on notice to the other side, and when based on facts not found in the record, must be supported by an affidavit, a deposition or testimony in open court, that such facts are true.

MOTION DAY (L)

A court designated time specifically for the hearing of motions and other non--jury matters.

MOTIVE (L)

A specifically goal--oriented impulse to act in a certain manner stemming from "unconscious" sources not recognized by the individual. Human motives in any particular situation, while often predictable, may vary considerably, since it is not only the external situation that determines the motive, but also the internal meaning attributed to it by the individual in whom social and psychological processes are in constant flux. (There are ego--involved and hidden motives). Elements of motive may involve such items as gain, sex, revenge, anger, homicidal mania and sex perversion.

MOTOR VEHICLE (L)

Device for transporting persons or property upon public high--ways not including construction equipment, farm tractors, muscular powered conveyances, or conveyances propelled by electric power from overhead wires.

MULCT (L)

Occasionally, a fine of money, or a penalty.

MULTA NON VETAT LEX, QUAE TAMEN TACITE DAMNAVIT (L)

The law does not forbid many things which it has silently con--demned.

MULTIPLE–FACTOR APPROACH (Cr'y)

The theory that each criminal act entails different behaviors and cultural conditions; no single positive factor produces crime, though one factor might predominate in causing the specific criminal act of the particular offender.

MULTITUDE (L)

A large assembly of persons, although there is no consensus as to how many constitute a multitude.

MULTITUDO IMPERITORIUM PERDIT CURIAM (L)

A multitude of ignorant practitioners destroys a court.

MUNICIPAL (L)

Commonly, that which relates to a city; more generally, per-taining to a state or nation.

MUNICIPAL LAW (L)

Jurisprudence pertaining to a particular city, state, or nation, as distinguished from international law.

MURDER (L)

The malicious, intentional killing of another, with malice either express or implied; often divided into degrees, depending upon the amount of malice and deliberation exhibited by the mur-derer, and whether the act was committed in perpetration of some other crime; i.e., arson, rape, burglary, or robbery.

MUSHROOMING (Cr's)

Expansion and flattening of the point of a bullet on impact.

MUTE, STANDING (L)

A defendant who abstains from pleading to an indictment. Various rules of criminal procedure dictate that the court shall then enter a plea of not guilty.

MUTINY (L)

Unlawful resistance to a superior military or maritime officer. A disobedience of orders, accompanied by force, commotion, threats, or other violent disturbances.

MUZZLE ENERGY (Cr's)

Amount of energy of the bullet at the muzzle given in foot pounds.

MUZZLE FLASH (Cr's)

Flame appearing at muzzle of firearm caused by expulsion of burning powder in atmosphere.

MUZZLE VELOCITY (Cr's)

The speed, measured in feet per second, of a projectile exiting the barrel of a weapon.

MYCOTIC ANEURYSM (Cr's)

Small saccular dilatation of a blood vessel usually produced by growth of bacteria in the wall of the vessel.

MYOCARDIAL DEHYDROGENASE (Cr's)

The enzyme present in the heart muscle.

MYOCARDIUM (Cr's)

The heart muscle.

MYOGLOBIN   (Cr's)

Pigment which resembles hemoglobin and imparts the red color to muscle.

MYXEDEMA   (Cr's)

A condition which is caused by loss of adequate function of the thyroid gland.

NAKED (L)

Incomplete; not clothed with power.

NALLINE TEST (Cr's)

A test used to determine whether or not a person is using nar--cotics.

NARCOTIC (Cr's)

The term "narcotic," "naracotics," or "narcotic drugs" means opium, coa leaves (cocaine), isonipecaine (demoerol), amidone, isoamidone, kito–bemidone or any compound, manufacture, salt, derivative or preparation thereof. The term also includes opiates.

NARCOTICS ADDICTION (Cr'y)

Continued use of narcotics in ever–increasing amounts and upon which there is a physical dependency.

NARRATIO (L)

A count; a declaration.

NASCITURUS (L)

Not yet born.

NATURA APPETIT PERFECTUM, ITA ET LEX (L)

Nature aspires to perfection; so does the law.

NATURAL (L)

According to nature; not artificial.

NATURAL AND PROBABLE CONSEQUENCES (L)

Those effects or results which a person of average competence and knowledge, in the situation of a person whose conduct is in question, having the same opportunities of observation, is expected to foresee as likely to follow on such conduct.

NATURAL–BORN CITIZENS (L)

Persons born within the jurisdiction of a national government, i.e., its territorial limits. Those born to citizens in temporary foreign residence.

NATURAL CHILD (L)

The child of one's body, not necessarily illegitimate. Occa-sionally, equivalent to bastard.

NATURALIZATION (L)

The legal act of investing aliens with the privileges and obliga--tions of a citizen (q.v.).

NATURAL LAW (L)

A body of transcendental, permanent principles discoverable by "right reason" and supposed to govern man's activities; in this context man--made ("positive") law is proper only to the extent it is based on Natural Law.

NE ADMITTAS (L)

Do not admit.

NEAR–GROUP (Cr'y)

The middle range of group existence between less definite mobs and stable organization.

NECESSITAS QUOD COGIT, DEFENDIT   (L)

Necessity defends what it compels, e.g., acts necesary for self-preservation.

NECESSITAS SUB LEGE NON CONTINETUR, QUIA QUID
ALIAS NON EST LICITUM NECESSITAS FACIT
LICITUM   (L)

Necessity is not limited by law, since what otherwise is not lawful, necessity makes lawful.

NECESSITAS VINCIT LEGEM   (L)

Necessity overcomes law.

NECESSITY   (L)

Pressing need; overruling power; compulsion; irresistible force. Depends upon the context in which it is used and the facts to which it is applied.

NECROPHILISM   (Cr'y)

Sexual desire concentrated on dead bodies.

NECROSIS   (Cr's)

Tissue death.

NE DISTURBA PAS   (L)

The defendant did not obstruct.

NE EXEAT, OR NE EXEAT REPUBLICA   (L)

A prerogative writ, issued by a court, to prevent a defendant from going away and evading the jurisdiction.

NEGATIVISM   (Cr'y)

An attitude of noncooperation, nonconformity, and/or pessi-mism.

NEGLIGENCE   (L)

Failure to use ordinary care, under particular factual circum-stances revealed by evidence in a lawsuit.

NEGLIGENCE, CONCURRENT   (L)

Injury caused by concurrent, independent, carelessness of two or more persons.

NEGLIGENCE, CONTRIBUTORY   (L)

An act or omission amounting to want of ordinary care on part of complaining party, which, concurrent with defendant's negli-gence, is proximate cause of injury.

NEGLIGENCE, CRIMINAL   (L)

An act or omission which an ordinarily careful and prudent man would refrain from or do respectively, under like circumstances, by reason of which another person is endangered in life or bodily safety; the word "ordinary" being synonymous with "reasonable" in this connection.

NEGLIGENCE, DEGREES OF   (L)

There are degrees of care, and failure to exercise proper degree of care is "negligence," but there are no degrees of negligence.

NEGLIGENCE, GROSS (L)

The intentional failure to perform a manifest duty in reckless disregard of the consequences as affecting the life of property of another; such a gross want of care and regard for the rights of others as to justify the presumption of willfullness and wan–tonness.

NEGLIGENCE, ORDINARY (L)

The omission of that degree of care which a man of common prudence usually takes of his own concerns. Failure to exercise care of an ordinarily prudent person in same situation. A want of that care and prudence that the great majority of mankind exercise under the same or similar circumstances.

NEGLIGENCE, PASSIVE (L)

Negligence which permits defects, obstacles, or pitfalls to exist upon premises causing dangers to arise from physical conditions of land itself.

NEGLIGENCE PER SE (L)

Negligence (q.v.) of itself or as a matter of law, e.g., the viola--tion of a statute passed for the protection of the public.

NEGLIGENCE, SIMPLE, SLIGHT (L)

Negligence (q.v.) neither gross nor wanton; merely a failure to exercise that degree of care which those of extraordinary pru--dence are accustomed to use.

NEGLIGENCE, WANTON (L)

Conscious indifference to the probable injurious consequences of reckless act or omission, where the party is without actual intent to injure.

NEGLIGENCE, WILLFUL (L)

Occasionally, a higher or more aggravated form of negligence than "gross;" a willful determination not to perform a known duty, or a reckless disregard of the safety or the rights of others, as manifested by the conscious and intentional omission of the care proper under the circumstances.

NEGOTIABLE INSTRUMENT (L)

A written promise or request for the payment of a certain sum.

NEMINEM LAEDIT QUI JURE SUO UTITUR (L)

He who stands on his own rights injures no one.

NEMO DE DOMO SUA EXTRAHI POTEST (L)

No one can be dragged out of his own house. Every man's house is his castle.

NEMO DEBET ALIENA JACTURA LOCUPLETARI (L)

No one ought to gain by another's loss.

NEMO DEBET BIS PUNIRI PRO UNO DELICTO (L)

No one ought to be punished twice for the same offense.

NEMO DEBET ESSE JUDEX IN PROPRIA CAUSA (L)

No one should be judge in his own cause.

NEMO EST SUPRA LEGES (L)

No one is above the law.

NEMO PRAESUMITUR MALUS (L)

No one is presumed to be bad.

NEMO TENETUR EDERE INSTRUMENTA CONTRA SE (L)

No one is obliged to produce instruments which tell against himself.

NEMO TENETUR SEIPSUM ACCUSARE (L)

No one is bound to incriminate himself.

NEOPLASM (Cr's)

Tumor.

NE UNQUES (L)

Never.

NE UNQUES ACCOUPLE (L)

Never lawfully married.

NEURAL (Cr's)

Pertaining to nerves or the nervous system.

NEUROSES (Cr'y)

A group of mild personality disorders or chronic emotional difficulties; less serious than psychosis and considered to be functional in character rather than organic.

NEUTRALIZATION THEORY (Cr'y)

A theory formulated by Gresham Sykes and David Matza, which suggests that "good" people are released from the influ--ence of anticriminal norms as they find rationalization which permit them to preserve a favorable self--image in spite of their criminal activity.

NEUTRON (Cr's)

A particle having no electric charge, which along with the pro--ton, is a basic unit in the structure of the nucleus of an atom.

NEUTRON ACTIVATION ANALYSIS (Cr's)

A procedure for detecting the presence and amounts of chemi-cal elements in a substance even when present in extremely small quantities. Radioactive materials are used in the test.

NEWLY DISCOVERED EVIDENCE (L)

Proof which could not have been discovered with reasonable diligence and produced at the trial; not newly recollected evi-dence.

NEW MATTER (L)

Various facts not previously alleged in the pleadings, by either party to a lawsuit.

NEW TRIAL (L)

A rehearing of a lawsuit, before another jury, granted by the court on motion of the party dissatisfied with the result of a previous trial, upon a proper showing that substantial justice requires it.

NEXT FRIEND (L)

One who, without having been regularly appointed guardian, brings suit and acts for an infant or other person who is under a legal disability. The next friend is usually a relative, and is responsible for the propriety of the proceedings and the court costs.

NIENT COMPRISE (L)

Not included.

NIENT CULPABLE (L)

Not guilty; a plea to a criminal charge or an allegation of tort.

NIGHTTIME (L)

The period between senset and sunrise lacking sufficient natural light to readily discern objects otherwise normally observable.

NIHIL HABET (L)

He has nothing; a return made by the sheriff, when he has not been able to take anything on an execution (q.v.).

NIHIL HABET FORUM EX SCENA (L)

The court has nothing to do with what is not before it.

NISI (L)

A decree, rule or order of the court is described as nisi, when it is not to be of force unless the party against whom it is made fails within a certain time to show cause against it, i.e., a good reason why it should not be made.

NISI PRIUS (L)

Unless before; formerly, words in an English writ, directing the sheriff to summon jurors. In the United States, the term is descriptive of the trial of civil cases before a single judge, with a jury; a trial court; a court of first instance.

NO KNOCK LAW (L)

A law which empowers a police officer to enter a home or other place, with a suitable court order, without knocking or announc-ing the identity, when to do so would imperil the safety of the officer or when evidence might be easily and quickly destroyed or disposed of.

NOLENS VOLENS (L)

Whether willing or unwilling.

NOLLE PROSEQUI (L)

In practice, a formal entry upon the record, by plaintiff in a civil suit, or the prosecuting officer in a criminal action, by which he declares that he "will no further prosecute" the case, either as to some of the counts or some of the defendants, or or altogether.

NOLO CONTENDERE (L)

I will not contest it. The name of a plea in a criminal action, having the same legal effect as a plea of guilty, so far as regards all proceedings on the indictment, and on which the defendant may be sentenced.

NOMINAL (L)

Existing in name only; unimportant.

NON COMPOS MENTIS (L)

Descriptive of a person who is not of sound mind, e.g., a lunatic, idiot or drunken person.

NON CULPABILIS (L)

Not guilty.

NON DECIPITUR QUI SCIT SE DECIPI (L)

He is not deceived who knows himself to be deceived.

NON EST INVEN'TUS (L)

Not found; a sheriff's return, when the defendant is not found in his territorial jurisdiction.

NON EST REGULA QUIN FALLAT (L)

There is no rule which may not fail, i.e., every rule has its excep--tions.

NON FACIAS MALUM UT INDE VENIAT MONUM (L)

You are not to do evil that good may come of it.

NON OBSTANTE VEREDICTO (L)

Notwithstanding the verdict. A type of judgement which is entered by the court, for legal cause, despite a contrary or dif--ferent verdict rendered by the jury. Abbreviated N.O.V.

NONACCESS (L)

Nonexistence of sexual intercourse between husband and wife.

NONAGE (L)

Not of full age; infancy.

NONCOMFORMITY (Cr'y)

Behavior perceived as divergent from social expectations in a particular situation.

NONJUSTICIABLE (L)

Matters which courts consider unsuitable for judicial determina-tion.

NONRESIDENT (L)

One not living within some geographical area.

NORM CONTAINMENT THEORY (Cr'y)

Individuals retain norms and values at a differential rate. The extent of retention is influenced by behavior patterns, environ--mental situation, peer groups, delinquent subcultures, and indi--vidual socialization. This differential rate of norm containment relates to a differential susceptibility to delinquent and criminal responses to pressure and stresses of society.

NORMS (Cr'y)

Standards by which human acts are approved or condemned; prescriptions or proscriptions for human behavior.

NOTARY PUBLIC (L)

A public office authorized to authenticate and certify documents such as deeds, contracts, affidavits with his signature and seal.

NOT GUILTY (L)

General denial of an accusation, requiring the prosecutor to prove every material fact alleged. Formerly, the general issue in actions of trespass, trover, and other actions founded on tort. The verdict of acquittal.

NOTICE (L)

Information given to a person of some act done, or about to be done; knowledge. It may be written, or oral, but written notice is preferable as avoiding disputes as to its terms. A person has notice of a fact when he has actual knowledge of it, or he has received a notice or notification of it.

NOTICE IN PAIS (L)

Information received other than from the record or writing.

NOTORIOUS (L)

Well known; obvious; apparent. Occasionally, not requiring proof.

NOXIOUS (Cr'y, Cr's)

Harmful.

NUCLEUS (Cr's)

The core of an atom in which the protons and neutrons exist.

NUISANCE (L)

Various activities which annoy, harm, inconvenience or damage other persons, under the particular facts and circumstances proven in a lawsuit or criminal prosecution. It may be (a) private, as where one uses his property so as to damage another's or to disturb his quiet enjoyment of it; or (b) public, or common, where the whole community is annoyed or inconvenienced by the offensive acts, e.g., where a person obstructs a highway, or carries on a business that fills the air with noxious and offensive fumes.

NULLITY OF MARRIAGE (L)

A state of facts regarding an ostensible marriage, which renders it cancelable, void or voidable, at the will of one of the parties to it.

NULLIUS FILIUS (L)

A son of nobody. A bastard.

NUMBERS OPERATION (Cr'y)

Lotteries, policy or bolita, in which the player normally bets on a three–digit number selected from some predetermined source such as the volume of money bet at a racetrack. The player seeks to increase his investment 500–600 times.

NUPTIAS NON CONCUBITUS SED CONSENSUS FACIT   (L)

Not cohabitation but consent makes the marriage.

NYMPHOMANIA   (Cr'y)

A condition of very strong sexual desire in females.

OATH (L)

Various solemn affirmations, declarations or promises, made under a sense of responsibility to God, for the truth of what is stated, or the faithful performance of what is undertaken. Oaths are judicial, i.e., made in the course of judicial proceedings, or extrajudicial, i.e., voluntary or outside of judicial proceedings, evidentiary, i.e., relating to past facts, or promissory, i.e., relating to the future performance of acts or duties, e.g., those of a judge, director or other official.

OATH PURGATORY (L)

A solemn affirmation, declaration or promise, made by one in contempt of court, concerning facts tending to excuse the default.

OBITER DICTUM (L)

Judicial statements not immediately necessary for the decision in a case and distinguished from the holding; the principle on which the decision rests, also called the ratio decidendi or rule of the decision.

OBJECTION (L)

Resistance or protestation on legal grounds.

OBLIGATION (L)

Various undertakings or events binding a person, unusually to do or not do a certain act. A perfect obligation: one which can be enforced by the law. A bond. The operative part of a bond.

OBSCENE (L)

Language, literature and other forms of communication calculated to promote corruption of sexual morals.

OBSTRUCTION OF JUSTICE (L)

The intentional hindering of or obstructing an arrest, conviction and/or punishment of accused persons, including all proper and necessary proceedings for administering justice.

O'CLOCK (Cr's)

To illustrate, face the target with watch in hand, and with back of watch toward target. A shot in the line of figure XII would be a 12 o'clock shot; one in the line of III, a 3 o'clock shot, etc.

OCULOMOTOR NERVE (Cr's)

Nerve supplying the muscles which moves the eyes.

OFF DUTY (PA)

A period of time when the officer is not working and is free from specified routine duties.

OFFENSE (L)

A crime or misdemeanor; a breach of criminal law. Used as a "genus," the term comprehends every crime and misdemeanor; as a "species," it signifies a crime not indictable, but punishable summarily or by forfeiture of a penalty.

OFFENSE, CONTINUING (L)

A transaction or series of acts set in motion by a single im--pulse, and manipulated by an unintermittent force, regardless of time--span.

OFFENSE, CRIMINAL (L)

Misdemeanors and felonies; an offense subjecting the offender to indictment.

OFFENSE, QUASI (L)

One imputed to an individual responsible for its injurious consequences; not by actual commission, but because the per--petrator is presumed to have acted under his commands.

OFFER (L)

A proposed act, the proposition of which becomes an obliga--tion, or contract, if undonditionally accepted by the person to whom it is made, before it is withdrawn.

OFFICE (L)

A position of appointment entailing particular rights and duties. The room or place in which an officer transacts public business, and keeps those papers, records, and documents committed to his care.

OFFICE OR DESK (PA)

Within a division, personnel may be divided into offices or desks to designate a post or location in order to facilitate specialization of assignment.

OFFICER (L)

One, elected or appointed, who performs an agency function for a public entity, e.g., nation, state, county, city or court, or for a private corporation. If a public officer, he will usually have specific duties assigned to him by law.

OFFICER, POLICE (PA)

All sworn personnel of a police department who posses the power of arrest.

OFFICIAL (L)

Pertaining to a public charge or office. An officer (q.v.).

OLFACTORY NERVE (Cr's)

Nerve of smell.

OLIGOSPERMIA (Cr's)

A condition describing an abnormally low sperm count.

OMISSION (L)

The neglect to perform what the law requires.

OMNIA PRAESUMUNTUR RITE ET SOLEMNITER ESSE ACTA DONEC PROBEUTR IN CONTRARIUM (L)

All things are presumed to have been done properly and with due formalities, until it be proved to the contrary.

ON DUTY (PA)

When an officer is actively engaged in the performance of his responsibilities.

ONUS (L)

Burden, responsibility.

OPEN (L)

To commence, e.g., the trial of a case. The duty to open a case rests with the party having the affirmative of the issue, or against whom judgement must be rendered if no proof is offered. To make public, e.g., sealed dispositions, verdicts, or orders. To vacate, or subject to re-examination, e.g., judgements or public bids.

OPEN COURT - (L)

Court proceeding held in a public place, to which all persons who conduct themselves properly have free access. Opposed to court in chambers.

OPENING STATEMENT (L)

An informative and nonargumentative recital to a judge and jury, concerning counsel's case and the facts which he intends to establish in support thereof, given before any evidence is offered in a trial.

OPERATIONAL PLANS (PA)

Preparation and development of techniques and programs that assist in accomplishment of the primary police task.

OPIATE (Cr's)

Any drug found to have an addiction--forming or addiction--sustaining liability similar to morphine or cocaine. (2) Deriva--tive of opium.

OPINION (L)

An inference or conclusion, formed or entertained by a witness, as opposed to facts directly seen, heard or perceived by him. Usually not competent testimony. A judge's statement of the reasons for the decision which the court pronounces. An attor--ney's statement, usually in writing, of what he believes the law to be, as to a particular question, or state of facts, or proposed line of conduct, about which a client asks his advice.

OPPRESSION (L)

The abuse of authority by a public officer. To repress by the cruel or unjust use of authority.

ORAL (L)

Delivered by word of mouth; verbal.

ORBIT (Cr's)

Bony socket of the eye.

ORDEAL (Cr'y, L)

Formerly, a method of criminal trial founded on superstition.

It was of four kinds, i.e., by combat, by fire, by hot water, and by cold water.

ORDER   (L)

A mandate or direction by an individual or by judicial authority. Court orders as distinguished from judgements (q.v.); decisions or directions concerning summary or interlocutory matters. In commercial paper transactions, a direction to pay; more than an authorization or request. It must identify the party to pay with reasonable certainty.

ORDER, POLICE   (PA)

An instruction given by a ranking officer to an subordinate; or, by a police officer to a civilian in line with the duties of the former.

ORDINANCE   (L)

A law, statute, or legislative enactment; particularly, the legislative enactments or statutes of a municipal corporation.

ORDINARY   (L)

Occasionally, a judge with limited jurisdiction; e.g., probate, and administration and supervision of estates.

ORGANIC COMPOUND   (Cr's)

Substance composed of carbon and hydropan, and, often, smaller amounts of oxygen, nitrogen, chlorine, phosphorus, or other elements.

ORGANIZED CRIME   (L, Cr'y)

The combination of two or more persons for the purpose of establishing, in a geographic area, a monopoly or virtual monopoly in a criminal activity of a type that provides a continuing financial profit, using gangster techniques and corruption to accomplish their aim.

ORGANIZING   (PA)

The activity of developing structure and preparing for action.

ORIGINAL   (L)

First; primary; not derived from any other source, or authority, e.g., original jurisdiction. An authentic instrument, as distinguished from a copy.

ORIGINAL JURISDICTION   (L)

The authority to hear a case in the first instance, rather than on appeal from another lower court. Most of the Supreme Court's cases come from appellate rather than original jurisdiction.

ORPHAN   (L)

A minor who has lost both parents.

OSTIUM   (Cr's)

Opening.

OUST   (L)

Ouster, to dispossess; dispossession.

OUTLAW   (Cr'y, L)
   One deprived of the benefits and the protection of law.
OUT OF COURT   (L)
   Not before the court, e.g., a settlement between the parties
   made out of court. The situation of a plaintiff who has
   been nonsuited or is otherwise unable to maintain his lawsuit.
OUT OF THE STATE   (L)
   A person who is a nonresident (q.v.) of the state or is tempo–
   rarily outside of the state and beyond the reach of its process.
OVERT   (L)
   Visible, open, public.
OXIDATION   (Cr's)
   The combination of oxygen with other substances to produce
   new products.
OXIDIZING AGENT   (Cr's)
   A substance that supplies oxygen to a chemical reaction.
OVUM   (Cr's)
   The female reproductive cell; egg.
OYEZ   (L)
   Occasionally, hear ye, usually pronounced: Oh, yea!

PACCHIONIAN GRANULATIONS (Cr's)

Small elevations of arachnoid tissue concerned with regulation of the amount of circulating cerebrospinal fluid.

PACTUM (L)

An agreement.

PAIN AND SUFFERING (L)

Various kinds of distress and discomfort, e.g., aches, hurts and soreness, for which a court or jury may award damages.

PANCREAS (Cr's)

A gland which secretes digestive juices and insulin and is located behind the stomach.

PANCREATITIS (Cr's)

Inflammation of the pancreas.

PANDER (L)

To pimp.

PANEL (L)

A division, or portion, or the members of a court, having the authority and powers of the entire court. Those persons summoned to act as jurors at a particular term of court, or for the trial of a particular action.

PAPER BOOK (L)

An appendix to an appellate court brief; an abstract of the evidence and pleadings necessary to the full understanding of a case.

PAPER MONEY (L)

The promissory notes of the government, which pass as money.

PAPERS (L)

Various documents, pleadings, court orders and judgements, motions, notices, exhibits, instruments and records.

PAPILLARY MUSCLE (Cr's)

Muscle within a heart chamber which moves the heart valve.

PARAMOUR (L)

An illegal or illicit lover.

PARDON (L)

An act of grace, proceeding from the power intrusted with the execution of the laws, which exempts the individual on whom it is bestowed from the punishment the law inflicts for a crime he has committed. It implies guilt and does not proceed on the theory of innocence of the person pardoned.

PARDON, ABSOLUTE AND UNCONDITIONAL (L)

Freeing of a criminal without condition. That which reaches both the punishment prescribed for the offense and the guilt of the offender. It obliterates in legal contemplation the offense itself. It goes no further than to restore the accused to his civil rights and remit the penalty imposed for the particular offense

of which he was convicted in so far as it remains unpaid.
See also: Pardon, Full.
PARDON, CONDITIONAL   (L)
One to which a condition is annexed, performance of which is necessary to the validity of the pardon; not becoming operative until the grantee has performed some specific act, or where it becomes void when come specific event transpires. One granted on the condition that it shall only endure until the voluntary doing of some act by the person pardoned, or that it shall be revoked by a subsequent act on his part, as he shall leave the state and never return.
PARDON, FULL   (L)
One freely and unconditionally absolving a party from all legal consequences, direct and collateral, of crime and conviction.
See also: Pardon, absolute and unconditional.
PARDON, GENERAL   (L)
One granted to all of the person participating in a given criminal or treasonable offense (generally political).
PARDON, PARTIAL   (L)
Remission from only a portion of punishment or absolution from only a portion of the legal consequences of a crime.
PARENCHYMA   (Cr's)
Functional tissue of an organ.
PARENS PATRIAE   (L)
A doctrine by which the government supervises children and other persons who are under a legal disability. It often takes the form of supervision which is analogous to that of a parent.
PARENT   (L)
The lawful father or mother of a person.
PARENTICIDE   (L)
One who murders a parent; the act of doing so.
PARFOCAL   (Cr's)
Construction of a microscope such that when an image is focused with one objective in position, the other objective can be rotated into place and the field will remain in focus.
PARI DELICTO   (L)
In equal fault; guilty to the same extent.
PARIETAL REGION OF BRAIN   (Cr's)
Related to the upper position portion of the brain.
PARISH   (L)
In Louisiana, a civil division, corresponding to the county in other states.
PARKING   (L)
The storing or stationing of automobiles or other vehicles.

PAROL (L)

By word of mouth.

PAROLE (Cor)

A method of prisoner release on the basis of individual response and progress within the correctional institution, providing the necessary controls and guidance while serving the remainder of their sentences within the free community.

PAROLE CLINIC (Cor)

Part of the correctional process serving the needs of released correctional clients. It also may provide more intensive services outside and make sentence or comitment to an institution un-- necessary for many offenders.

PAROLE RATIONALE (Cor)

Each criminal law violator should have a carefully planned, highly individualized program if he is to successfully return to life outside the correctional institution. Successful reentry into society is often made more difficult by the effects of institutional life and by the attitude of the community to which the criminal law violator returns.

PAROLE REVOCATION (Cor)

Recommendation by the parole officer to the parole board that a parolee be returned to prison.

PAROXYSM (Cr's)

Sudden attack of a disease.

PARRICIDE, OR PATRICIDE (L)

One who kills his father; the act of doing so.

PARTICEPS CRIMINIS (L)

A partner in crime.

PARTY (L)

One who takes part in a legal transaction, e.g., a person with an immediate interest in an agreement or deed, or a plaintiff or a defendant in a lawsuit. As distinct from third party, a person who has engaged in a transaction or made an agreement.

PASSIVE (L)

Inactive or permitted.

PAT DOWN (PA)

A search of a suspect's outer clothing to check for weapons.

PATHOLOGICAL DRINKING (Cr'y)

A form addictive or nonaddictive alcoholism which disrupts one's social or economic life.

PATHOMETER (Cr's)

An instrument commonly known as a lie detector, a polygraph.

PATROL OPERATIONS (PA)

Police officers moving about within prescribed areas, to repress criminal activity, regulate conduct, and perform a number of services to the public.

PATRONAGE (L)

Government appointments awarded primarily on a basis other than merit, most frequently on the basis of loyalty and service to a political party, or on the basis of friendship.

PATTERN (Cr's)

The distribution of shot after leaving the muzzle.

PATTERN AREA (Cr's)

That part of a fingerprint containing the ridges necessary to determine classification; the working area of classification.

PAUPER, OR INDIGENT PERSON (L)

An economically poor, destitute or helpless person; one who is unable to provide for and maintain himself or his family from his income or his other resources.

PAWN BROKER (Cr'y, L)

A person who takes articles as security on loans with interest.

PEACE (L)

Public order; freedom from war, violence, or public disturbance.

PEACE BOND (L)

A bond (q.v.) for good behavior; a bail (q.v.) in a reasonable sum, conditioned on the defendant keeping the peace and on his good behavior for a fixed period of time, e.g., one year, which may be required by a court, if there are reasonable grounds to believe that the release of a defendant would endanger persons or property. Regulated by various state statutes and rules of criminal procedure.

PEDDLER (L)

One who carries merchandise from place to place and sells it or offers to sell it.

PEDOPHILIA (Cr'y)

The seduction of female children by adult males.

PEER (L)

A person considered equal.

PENAL (L, Cor)

Pertaining to or respecting punishment.

PENAL ACTION (L)

A lawsuit to recover a statutory penalty.

PENAL BILL (L)

Formerly, a bond to do a certain act, or in default thereof, pay a certain sum of money by way of penalty.

PENAL COLONY (Cor)

Exportation of criminals to sparsely peopled lands. Russia used Siberia, Spain and Portugal used Africa, France sent hers to South America and England to North America.

PENAL LAWS, OR PENAL STATUTES (L)

Legislative acts prohibiting particular behavior, and imposing a penalty for the commission thereof.

PENALTY (L)

Punishment. The consequence imposed upon the perpetrator, for violation of a penal law or personal right.

PENITENTIARY (L, Cor)

A prison or place of punishment wherein convicts sentenced to confinement and hard labor are confined by authority of law.

PENNSYLVANIA SYSTEM (Cor)

A penitentiary system, adopted by Eastern State Penitentiary, when it opened in 1829, advocating complete silence and separation of prisoners. The Quakers were convinced that prisoners could be redeemed in the sight of God and man if placed in solitude to pray, meditate upon their sins, and reconstruct their lives.

PENOLOGY (Cor, Cr'y)

The branch of criminology concerned with government policies and practices in dealing with persons convicted of crimes.

PEPTIC ULCER (Cr's)

Ulcer of the stomach or the first segment of the small intestine.

PERCENTAGE OF PATTERN (Cr's)

Number of pellet marks in a thirty–inch circle, over a forty–yard range, divided by number of pellets in the load.

PER CURIAM (L)

By the court.

PER DIEM (L)

By the day.

PEREMPTORY (L)

Absolute; final; admitting of no excuse for nonperformance, e.g., an order or mandamus.

PERFORMANCE (L)

The act of doing something, especially something required by a contract or condition, which relieves a person from all further liability thereunder.

PERICARDIAL SPACE (Cr's)

Space within the heart sac.

PERICARDIUM (Cr's)

Heart sac.

PERIL (L)

Danger; risk; that which threatens or causes a loss, e.g., of the subject of insurance.

PERINEUM (Cr's)

The area between the anus and the posterior part of the external genitalia.

PERIODIC TABLE (Cr's)

Chart of elements arranged according to their atomic numbers. Vertical rows are called groups or families, horizontal rows are called series.

PERIOSTEUM (Cr's)

Membrane of tissue which covers all bones except at the articular surfaces.

PERITONEUM (Cr's)

Membrane which lines the abdominal cavity and surrounds all abdominal organs.

PERITONITIS (Cr's)

Inflammation of the peritoneum.

PERIVASCULAR (Cr's)

Around blood vessels.

PERIVASCULAR INFILTRATION (Cr's)

Inflammatory cells infiltrating the tissue around a blood vessel.

PERJURY (L)

A false statement under oath or affirmation, wilfully made in regard to a material matter of fact.

PERMISSIVE (L)

Suffered, or allowed. That which permits, allowing freedom, lenient.

PERPETUATING TESTIMONY (L)

A court proceeding to give, take and record in writing, the testimony of a party or a witness to be used in a lawsuit not yet commenced, when by reason of, e.g., the witness's age, or infirmity, or going abroad, the testimony is likely to be lost. Authorized by various state statutes and rules of civil procedure and by Fed. R. Civ. P. 27

PER SE (L)

By itself.

PERSON (L)

A human being or a corporation. An individual or an organization.

PERSONA DESIGNATA (L)

A person described as an individual, as distinguished from one described merely as a member of a class.

PERSONAL (L)

Appertaining to a person, or to the person.

PERSONAL INJURY (L)

A hurt or wrong, either to the physical body or the reputation of a person, or to both.

PERSONALITY (Cr'y)

Habitual patterns and qualities of behavior of any individual as expressed by physical and mental activities and attitudes, distinctive individual qualities of a person considered collectively.

PERSONATION   (L)

Pretending to be another person, whether real or fictitious.

PERSONNEL ADMINISTRATION   (PA)

A management function concerned with the human resources of an organization.

PERSONNEL ORDERS   (PA)

Orders giving force and effect to personnel actions, e.g., ap--pointments, assignments, transfers, promotions and disciplinary measures.

PERSUASION   (L)

Influencing another by request, argument, or representation. When carried to such an extent as to deprive the person influ--enced of freedom of will, it is a ground for setting aside a will or other instrument made in pursuance thereof.

PER TOTAM CURIAM   (L)

By the full court.

PETECHIA   (Cr's)

Spot--like hemorrhage.

PETITION   (L)

A request made to a public official or public body with author--ity to act concerning it. Under some codes of civil procedure, the written statement of the plaintiff's case which initiates a lawsuit.

PETITION FOR REHEARING   (L)

A request to a court, by a party adversely affected by a final decision in a particular appeal or lawsuit, that the court recon--sider its earlier decision, upon particular grounds, e.g., the court has overlooked a material fact in the record or a controlling statute or decision.

PETTY, OR PETIT   (L)

Small; trifling; of little importance.

PHAGOCYTOSIS   (Cr's)

Destruction of particulati matter by special cells known as phagocytes. Some white blood corpuscles are phagocytes.

PHARYNX   (Cr's)

Throat.

PHENOTYPE   (Cr's)

Physical manifestation of a genetic trait such as shape, color and blood type.

PHILOSOPHY OF LAW ENFORCEMENT   (Cr'y, PA)

A philosophy encompassing three points:

1) A greater concern for the preservation of individual liberty than the pursuit of justice.

2) Americans have confidence in law to a greater extent than most peoples.

3) Selective enforcement of laws is desired in order to maintain a reasonable amount of law and order.

PHIMOS   (Cr's)

Lightness of the foreskin so that it cannot draw back over the glans.

PHLEBOTHROMBOSIS   (Cr's)

Presence of a clot in the vein.

PHOBIA   (Cr'y)

Abnormal, illogical fear.

PHOTON   (Cr's)

A small packet of electromagnetic radiation energy. Each photon contains a unit of energy equal to the product of Plank's constant and the frequency of radiation $E = hf$.

PHYSICAL DEPENDENCE   (Cr'y)

Physiological need for a drug that has been brought about by its regular use. Dependence is characterized by withdrawal sickness when administration of the drug is abruptly stopped.

PHYSICAL EVIDENCE   (L, Cr's, PA)

Any physical thing found at the scene of a crime, or elsewhere, having relevance to the crime and its investigation.

PHYSICAL PROPERTY   (Cr's)

Describes the behavior of a substance without reference to any other substance.

PICKETING   (L)

An attempt to influence someone by patrolling a particular area, usually with placards or signs. When peaceful, a legal form of communication.

PIECE--PRICE SYSTEM   (Cor, Cr'y)

A system of prisoner employment used in the late 1700's at the Walnut Street Jail in Pennsylvania. Under this system, a private contractor furnished the raw material and received the finished product, and the work was done in the prison for an agreed price.

PILFERER   (L)

One who unlawfully takes merchandise for personal gain.

PILLORY   (Cor, Cr'y)

An early form of sentence whereby the extremities, including the head, hands and feet of the live convicted criminal were placed in a wooden frame, often on public display, for a period of time as a method of punishment.

PLAIN ARCH, FINGERPRINTS   (Cr's)

A series of ridges entering from one side of a pattern, flowing without interruption across the finger, and terminating at the outer side after a slight rise in the outer. There are no recurving ridges in the true arch.

PLAIN WHORL, FINGERPRINTS (Cr's)

A pattern in which one or more ridges appear to revolve around a center point, called the core, often making a complete circuit.

PLAIN VIEW (L, PA)

An exception to the general requirement of a valid search war--rant to legitimize a search or seizure.

PLAINT (L)

Formerly, a written statement of a cause of action, analogous to a complaint (q.v.) or a petition (q.v.), used to initiate a law--suit.

PLAINTIFF (L)

One who initiates a lawsuit.

PLANE--POLARIZED LIGHT (Cr'y)

Light confined to a single plane of vibration.

PLANNING AND RESEARCH (PA)

A process for developing predetermined courses of action which offer the greatest potential for obtaining desired goals.

PLASMA (Cr's)

A variety of white blood corpuscles.

PLASTIC PRINTS, FINGERPRINTS (Cr's)

Actual impressions formed by pressing the friction ridges into a plastic material. Melted candle wax, putty, tar, and soap are typical of these materials. Ordinarily these prints require no development.

PLATOON (PA)

Personnel assigned to one work shift. Ordinarily commanded by a lieutenant, the platoon may serve an entire city or a dis--trict thereof.

PLEA (L)

A defendant's formal response to the charge in an indictment, or to a civil lawsuit.

PLEAD (L)

To answer the opposing party's plea in an action. To file a pleading in court. To make a plea, e.g., of not guilty. Occa-sionally, to argue a cause in court.

PLEADER (L)

One who files a pleading.
See: Plead.

PLENA ET CELERIS JUSTITIA FIAT PARTIBUS (L)

Let full and speedy justice be done to the parties.

PLEOMORPHIC (Cr's)

Occurring in various distinct forms.

PLURALITY (L)

A greater number; a larger number of votes cast for one candi-
date than any other; less than a majority.

PLUS PECCAT AUCTOR QUAM ACTOR   (L)

The instigator of a crime offends more than the doer of it.

POACHING   (L)

Unlawfully taking or destroying game.

POISON   (Cr's, L)

A substance which, when introduced into the body in small
quantities, causes a harmful or deadly effect.

POLICE   (L, PA)

That branch of governmental administration appointed by a
state, county or city to care for various portions of the public
safety, e.g., prevent crimes and protect the public, investigate
crimes and allegations thereof, make arrests, patrol the streets
and highways and maintain public order.

POLICE COURT   (L)

A municipal tribunal which tries those accused of violating
local ordinances, or acts as a preliminary examination and
commitment of those accused of graver offenses; essentially
equivalent to the criminal court of a justice of the peace in rural
communities.

POLICE HAZARDS   (PA)

Those situations or conditions having the potential to induce
incidents requiring some kind of police response.

POLICE LABORATORY DUTIES   (Cr's, PA)

Reconstruction of the crime and identification of the criminal
by scientific examination of physical evidence.

THE POLICE MISSION   (PA)

Maintenance of social order within carefully prescribed ethical
and constitutional restrictions.

POLICE POWER   (L, PA)

The authority of federal and state legislatures to enact laws
regulating and restraining private rights and occupations for the
promotion of public health, safety, welfare and order.

POLICY   (PA)

The broad general plan or principle underlying methods of procedure or the conduct of a department's affairs affecting all
levels of personnel and influencing all aspects of performance.

POLITICAL EXECUTIVE   (PA)

Those institutions formally responsible for governing a political
community, i.e., for applying binding decisions formulated,
to a greater or lesser extent, by the executive institutions
themselves.

POLITICAL JUSTICE   (L, PA)

The use of judicial process for the purpose of gaining, upholding, enlarging, limiting, or destroying political power or influence. It may accompany or confirm political or military action or it may be a substitute for such action.

POLITICAL MACHINE   (PA)

A group composed of professional politicians whose principal objective is the acquisition, maintenance, and enlargement of political power.

POLITICAL OFFENSE   (L, Cr'y)

An offense against public security committed for the purpose of changing the form of government, or the persons in office, or altering the laws by illegal means.

POLITICAL ORDER   (L, Cr'y)

Indicative of concentration of constitutions, whether written or not, and on constitutionalism, or principles of order for government.

POLYANDRY   (L)

The state of a woman who has several husbands.

POLYGAMY   (L)

Plurality of wives or husbands.

POLYMER   (Cr's)

A substance composed of a large number of atoms. These atoms are usually arranged in repeating units or monomers.

POLYMORPHISM   (Cr's)

The occurrence in a population of two or more common alleles producing a variety of phenotypes. For example, blood types are examples of polymorphism.

PORENCEPHALY   (Cr's)

The presence of a cyst or centry in the brain which establishes communication between the subarachnoid space and the ven--tricle system.

PORNOGRAPHY   (L)

Visual forms of communication intended to arouse sexual desire or create sexual excitement. Works having as their object material gain via appeal to sexual curiosity and appetite.

POSITIVE LAW   (L)

Definite rules of human conduct with appropriate sanctions for their enforcement, both prescribed by a determinate human superior or sovereign.

POSSE COMITATIS   (L)

The power of a county, which includes all able--bodied men therein, who may be called on by the sheriff to assist him in preserving the peace.

POSSESSIO   (L)

Detention or possession.

POST   (PA)

A fixed point or location to which an officer is assigned for duty, such as an intersection or crosswalk for traffic duty; a spot or location for general guard duty, observation and surveillance or for the apprehension of a person wanted for, or about to commit, a crime; or a designated desk or office.

POSTERIOR   (Cr's)

Rear, back.

POSTHUMOUS CHILD   (L)

One born after his or her father's death, or removed from the body of a dead mother.

POST–MORTEM   (L, Cr's)

After death. (2) An examination of a human body after death.

POST--MORTEM LIVIDITY   (Cr's)

The dark blue discoloration observable on the parts of a body nearest the ground. The blood settles, due to its own weight, into the lowest parts of the body. This coloring appears approximately two to six hours after death.

POST NATAL   (Cr's)

Occurring after birth.

POUND   (L)

An enclosure wherein stray or unclaimed animals are placed. A place where distrained goods are kept.

POWDER CHARGE   (Cr's)

The amount of powder used in a load.

POWDERS, GUN   (Cr's)

Powders used in loading are of three types; black; semismoke-less, and smokeless. Smokeless powders are divided into two types: "bulk," meaning the charge corresponds, or nearly so, in bulk to the charge of black powder; "dense" meaning it is denser and of much less bulk. Single–base: Powder containing nitrocellullose as the only explosive ingredient. Double–base: Powder containing nitrocellullose and nitroglycerin as the prin-ciple explosive ingredients.

POWER, IMPLIED   (L)

Such as are necessary to make available and carry into effect powers expressly granted or conferred, and therefore must be presumed to have been within the intent of the constitutional or legislative grant.

POWER, INHERENT   (L)

Those enjoyed by possessors of natural right, without having been received from another; e.g., the powers of a people to establish a form of government, of a father to control his children. Some are regulated and restricted in their legal exer--cise, but are not technically considered in the law as powers.

PRACTICE COURT   (L)

Course of study in legal education, in which law students engage in pretended trials.

See also: Moot.

PRACTICE OF LAW   (L)

Any service rendered, involving legal knowledge or legal advice,
e.g., representation, counsel, advocacy, or drafting of instruments, which is rendered in respect to the rights, duties, obligations, liabilities or business affairs of someone requiring the
services. Often defined by various rules of court, and occasionally by various state statutes.

PREAMBLE   (L).

Introduction or preface. Introduction of a legislative resolution or act, which states its intent, and the mischiefs to be
remedied.

PRECEDENT   (L)

An adjudged case or court decision furnishing an example or
authority for an identical or similar case afterwards arising or
a similar question of law.

PRECEPT   (L)

A command given by a person in authority.

PRECINCT   (PA)

(1) A police district. (2) A minor political subdivision of a
county or city.

PRECIPITIN   (Cr's)

An antibody that reacts with its corresponding antigen to form
a precipitati.

PREGNANCY   (L)

The condition of a woman who is with child.

PREJUDICE   (L)

An unsubstantiated prejudgement of an individual or group,
favorable or unfavorable in character, tending toward action in
a consonant direction.

PREJUDICIAL ERROR   (L)

Error (q.v.) committed during trial of sufficient importance to
be grounds for new trial, or reversal on appeal.

PRELIMINARY   (L)

Something which precedes, e.g., something which is intorduc-
tory or preparatory.

PRELIMINARY HEARING   (L)

Usually held in a lower court; a testing of the evidence against
the defendant.

PRELIMINARY INVESTIGATION   (PA, Cr's)

That conducted to the point at which postponement of further
investigation does not jeopardize its successful completion.

PREMEDITATION   (L)

A design or intention, formed to commit a crime or do an act, before it is done.

PREMISES   (L)

Land and its appurtenances.

PREPONDERANCE OF EVIDENCE   (L)

(1) The greater weight of evidence, in merit and worth. (2) Sufficient evidence to overcome doubt or speculation.

PREROGATIVE   (L)

The special powers and privileges of the government.

PREROGATIVE WRITS   (L)

Orders or process, the issuance of which is descretionary with the court, as opposed to writs of right. They are the writs of procedendo, mandamus, prohibition, quo warranto, habeas corpus, corpus, and certiorari, which are extraordinary remedies.

PRESCRIBE   (L)

To order or direct; to lay down rules.

PRESENCE OF AN OFFICER, OFFENSE COMMITTED IN   (L)

An offense within rules authorizing arrest without a warrant, wherein an officer sees an act constituting it, though at distance, or when circumstances within his observation give probable cause for belief that defendant has committed offense, or when he hears disturbance created by offense and proceeds at once to scene, or if offense is continuing, or has not been fully consummated when arrest is made.

PRESENTENCE INVESTIGATION   (Cr'y, Cor)

Performed by the probation officer to learn the family and social background of the offender and to assess his strengths and weaknesses with a view toward working out a treatment program.

PRESENTMENT   (L)

A written statement by a grand jury, made of their own knowledge or from statements of witnesses, and without a bill indictment being presented by the prosecuting officer, accusing a person of having committed an offense against the law.

PRESENTS   (L)

A document, legal instrument or other writing.

PRESERVATIVE   (Cr's)

A substance added to blood in order to inhibit the growth of micro organisms. Sodium fluoride is a common preservative.

PRESIDENT'S COMMISSION ON LAW ENFORCEMENT AND
    ADMINISTRATION OF JUSTICE   (Cor, Cr'y, L, PA)

A study, in 1966, of the entire system of criminal justice.

PRESUMPTION   (L)

A conclusion, or inference, drawn from the proven existence

of some fact or group of facts. Presumptions may be either
(a) juris et de jure (of law and by the principles of law), such
as the presumption of incapacity in a minor to act, which are
conclusive and irrebuttable; (b) juris (of law), which may be
disproved, or rebutted, by evidence; or (c) judicis, or facti,
i.e., presumptions of fact, drawn by a judge from the evidence.

PRESUMPTION OF INNOCENCE   (L)
The conclusion drawn by law favoring one brought to trial on
criminal charges, requiring acquittal unless guilt is established
by sufficient evidence.

PRESUMPTIVE   (L)
Descriptive of something inferred or presumed.

PRE--TRIAL CONFERENCE, OR PRE–TRIAL HEARING   (L)
A preliminary meeting between judge and counsel for the par--
ties of a lawsuit, at the discretion of the court, to consider any
matters that may aid in disposition of the case.

PREVARICATION   (L)
Equivocation; deceitfully seeming to undertake a thing, with
the purpose of defeating or destroying it.

PREVENTION OF CRIMINALITY   (PA)
The process of eliminating hazards or diminishing their effec–
tiveness by taking the police into sectors of the community
where criminal tendencies are bred and motivated, seeking to
reduce the causes of crime.

PRIMA FACIE   (L)
At first sight; on the first appearance; on the face of it; so
far as can be judged from the first disclosure; presumably; a fact
presumed to be true unless disproved by some evidence to the
contrary.

PRIMA FACIE EVIDENCE   (L)
Proof of a fact or collection thereof, creating a presumption of
existence of other facts, or from which some conclusion may
be legally drawn, but which may be discredited or overcome by
other relevant proof.

PRIMARY   (L)
First, or principal.

PRIMARY EVIDENCE   (L)
The best possible evidence, affording the greatest certainty of
the fact in question. E.G., a written instrument is itself the best
possible evidence of its existence and its contents.

PRIMARY LINE ELEMENT   (PA)
The patrol force of a police department.

PRIMARY OBLIGATION   (L)
A duty, or responsibility; correlative of a primary right (q.v.).

PRIMARY PURPOSE OF PATROL   (PA)

Elimination of opportunity, or belief in the opportunity, for successful misconduct.

PRIMARY RIGHT (L)

A privilege, the breach of which gives rise to a secondary right, e.g., the breach of the primary right of driving on the highways free from negligent interference by other persons, gives rise to the secondary right of damages.

PRIMER (Cr's)

A metallic cup charged with an explosive composition. A sharp blow striking the primer ignites the charge.

PRINCIPAL (L)

The leading, or most important; the original; a person, firm or corporation from whom an agent derives his authority; a person who is first responsible, and for whose fulfillment of an obligation a surety becomes bound; the chief, or actual, perpetrator of a crime, as distinguished from the accessory, who may assist him; the important part of an estate, as distinguished from incidents, or accessories; a sum of money loaned, as distinguished from the interest paid for its use.

PRINCIPAL CHALLENGE (L)

Challenge (q.v.) of a juror for cause.

PRINCIPLE OF LAW (L)

A rule; a doctrine; an abstract generalization concerning legal consequences to be assigned as the result of facts. Courts decide unique factual disputes, and in doing so, either apply former generalizations or generate new ones.

PRIOR TEMPORE, POTIOR JURE (L)

First in time, strongest in law.

PRISON (Cor)

A public building or other place for the confinement or safe custody of persons, as lawful punishment or otherwise in the administration of justice.

PRISONER (Cor, L)

One held in confinement against his will, usually to answer a criminal charge, or as punishment for a crime of which he has been convicted.

PRISONER EMPLOYMENT, SYSTEMS OF (Cor)

Many types of inmate work used in corrections; the piece-price, contract, lease, state account, state use, and public works and ways systems, have been or are now part of correctional programs.

PRISONIZATION (Cor)

The automaton–like behavior of long–term prisoners devoid of initiative, living on a day–to–day basis, responding to simple diversions of routine and blocking of both past and future.

PRIVILEGE (L)

An exceptional right, or exemption either personal, or attached to a person or office.

PRIVILEGE FROM ARREST (L)

One who has the privilege may have the arrest voided, that is, set aside.

PRIVILEGIUM NON VALET CONTRA REMPUBLICAM (L)

A privilege avails not against the interest of the public.

PROBABLE CAUSE (L)

A reasonable ground of suspicion supported by circumstances sufficiently strong in themselves to warrant a cautious man to believe the accused guilty.

PROBATE (L)

Proof to a court having jurisdiction, that an instrument, offered as the last will and testament of a deceased person, is proper. It is then received, filed and recorded, and said to be admitted to probate or probated.

PROBATE COURT (L)

Various state courts having jurisdiction in the matter of proving wills, appointing executors and administrators and supervising the administration of estates.

PROBATION (Cor)

A judicial function placing a convicted offender or juvenile delinquent under court supervision; usually by means of a probation officer or agent.

PRO BONO PUBLICO (L)

For the public, or general good.

PROCENDO (L)

A prerogative writ, addressed by a superior court to an inferior court, directing the latter to proceed forthwith to judgement.

PROCEDURAL LAW (L)

A branch of law prescribing, in detail, methods to be used to determine and enforce the rights and duties of persons toward each other under substantive law.

PROCEDURAL PLANS (PA)

Inclusive of every procedure outlined and adopted as the standard method of action to be followed by all members of the department under specified conditions. Procedural plans include report regulations, record division operations, dispatching procedures, and procedures for stopping, questioning, searching, handcuffing, and transporting persons.

PROCESS (L)

The means whereby a court enforces obedience to its orders. Process is termed (a) original, when it is intended to compel the appearance of the defendant; (b) mesne, when issued pending suit to secure the attendance of jurors and witnesses; and (c) final, when issued to enforce execution of a judgement.

In patent law, the art or method by which any particular result is produced, e.g., the smelting of ores or the vulcanizing of rubber.

PROCLAMATION   (L)

A public announcement by authority of a chief executive. The declaration of a bailiff (q.v.), made by authority of the court, of what is about to be done.

PROFESSIONAL AUTO THIEF   (Cr'y)

One who steals cars for monetary gain; usually belonging to, or employed by, an auto larceny ring.

PROFESSIONAL THIEF   (Cr'y)

One who pursues thievery as a profession.

PROHIBITION   (L)

Formerly, national laws prohibiting the manufacture and sale of intoxicating liquors in the United States.

PROHIBITION, WRIT OF   (L)

An order or mandate from a superior court, preventing an inferior court from taking cognizance of, or determining, a matter outside its jurisdiction.

PROLICIDE   (L)

The destruction of human offspring; it includes foeticide and infanticide.

PROLIXITY   (L)

A long and unnecessary statement of facts in a pleading of affi–davit.

PROMOTION   (PA)

The movement upward from one classification or rank to one with higher pay and more responsibility and prestige.

PROOF   (L)

The effect of evidence; the establishment of a fact by evidence.

PROOF BEYOND A REASONABLE DOUBT   (L)

Such proof as precludes every reasonable hypothesis except that which it tends to support and which is wholly consistent with the defendant's guilt and inconsistent with any other rational conclusion.

PROOF MARKS   (Cr's)

Distinctive stamp placed upon firearms by manufacturers, indi–cating arm will withstand pressure generated by firing.

PROPAGANDA   (Cr'y)

A deliberate and guided attempt to induce people to accept a given view, sentiment, or value.

PROPER   (L)

Genuine, suitable or correct.   Occasionally, that which is

one's own.

PROPERTY MANAGEMENT (PA)

Care of department--owned property and property temporarily in police custody, ie., lost or stolen property.

PROPTER AFFECTUM (L)

Formerly, a challenge to a juror, on account of some defect or incapacity.

PROPTER DEFECTUM (L)

Challenge to a juror on the basis of a defect or incapacity.

PROPTER DELICTUM (L)

Formerly, a challenge to a juror, on account of crime.

PROROGATION (L)

A putting off to another time, or postponement.

PROSECUTE (L)

To follow up; to carry on an action or other judicial proceed-- ing; to institute legal proceedings against, or conduct criminal proceedings in court against. To "prosecute" an action is not merely to commence it, but includes following it to an ultimate conclusion.

PROSECUTOR (L)

One who brings legal action against another, in the name of the government. A public prosecutor is an officer appointed or elected to conduct all prosecutions in behalf of the government A private prosecutor is an individual who, not holding office, conducts an accusation against another. Occasionally, an aggrieved person will employ a private attorney to serve as such a prosecutor.

PROSTITUTION (L)

Primarily, a criminal act of rendering sexual service through the use of the female body in exchange for monetary gain.

PRO TEM, OR PRO TEMPORE (L)

For the time being.

PROTEINS (Cr's)

Polymers of amino acids that play basic roles in the structures and functions of living things.

PROTEST (L)

A solemn declaration of opinion, usually of dissent. An express reservation of self-defense against the effects of an admission implied from an act. In commercial paper trans- actions, a certificate of dishonor, made under the hand and seal of a United States consul, or vide consul or a notary public, or other person authorized to certify dishonor by the law of the place where dishonor occurs. It may be made upon information satisfactory to such person. A document drawn by the

master of a ship, and formally attested, stating the circum--
stances under which damage has happened to the ship, or her
cargo.

PROTONS   (Cr's)
A positively charged particle that is one of the basic structures
in the nucleus of an atom.

PROXIMATE CAUSE   (L)
That which produces a result, which otherwise could not occur.
An original event, in natural, unbroken sequence, producing a particular result, without which the result would not have
occurred.

PSYCHOGENIC THEORIES   (Cr'y)
Theories of crime causation ascriptive to the criminal of a
different intensity of attitudes, opinions, feelings, and/or po--
tentials than the noncriminal.

PSYCHOLOGICAL DEPENDENCE   (Cr'y, Cr's)
The conditioned use of a drug caused by underlying emotional
needs.

PSYCHONEUROSIS   (Cr'y)
Neurosis based on emotional conflict.

PSYCHOPATHIC PERSONALITY   (Cr'y)
A personality type generally lacking in ethical character mor--
ality, emotional stability, and a sense of responsibility; the
psychopath may appear intelligent and even normal at
frist glance.

PSYCHOSIS   (Cr'y)
A severe mental or personality disorder manifesting loss of
contact with reality, commonly known as insanity. Usually
requires hospitalization because of inability to participate in
ordinary social life. The cause may be classified as either
organic or functional. Paranoia, schizophrenia, and manic de--
pressive psychosis are examples of psychoses.

PUBERTY   (L)
The age of fourteen in males and twelve in females. The
state of physical development when it is first possible to beget
or bear children.

PUBLIC   (L)
A form of elementary collective behavior consisting of people
divided over a particular issue. The people as a whole; community at large.

PUBLIC INFORMATION OFFICER   (PA)
The officer whose mission is to gain public support for police
policies and win citizen cooperation in department programs to
facilitate accomplishment of the police task.

PUBLIC LAW   (L)

As a field of inquiry in political science, embraces the study of all political or governmental legal phenomena.

PUBLIC WORKS AND WAYS SYSTEM   (Cor)

A system of prisoner employment currently in use whereby inmates provide labor for construction and maintenance of public facilities.

PUMP   (Cr's)

Repeating rifle of shotgun in which the mechanism is activated manually by means of a slide.

PUNCH JOBS   (Cr's)

Safe burglary by which the dial is knocked off with a sledge hammer, the spindle is punched back with a center punch and mallet, and the small sockets broken, allowing release of the lock.

PUNISHMENT, CRUEL AND UNUSUAL   (L)

Such degree of punishment amounting to torture or barbarity, or any cruel and degrading punishment not known to the com-- mon law; also, any punishment so disproportionate to the offense as to shock the moral sense of the community.

PUNISHMENT, CUMULATIVE   (L)

Increased punishment inflicted for a second or third conviction of the same offense under the statutes relating to habitual criminals. To be distinguished from a "cumulative sentence."

PUNISHMENT, IN CRIMINAL LAW   (L)

Any negative sanction inflicted upon a person by legal authority, judgement and sentence of a court, for an offense committed, or legal duty omitted; a deprivation of property of some right. Exclusive of civil penalty redounding to the bene-- fit of an individual, such as forfeiture of interest.

PUNISHMENT, INFAMOUS   (L)

Punishment by imprisonment, as in a penitentiary. Particularly, imprisonment at hard labor.

PUNITIVE POWER   (L)

The power and authority to inflict punishment upon those having committed actions inherently evil and injurious to the public, or statutory law.

PURPURA   (Cr's)

Patchy hemorrhages in the skin and mucous membranes.

PURPOSE OF ORGANIZATION   (PA)

To arrange and utilize the total resources of personnel and material in such a way as to make and expedite attainment of specified objectives an efficient, effective, economical and har-- monious operation.

PURSUIT OF HAPPINESS   (L)

The constitutional right to personal freedom, freedom of con-- tract, exemption from oppression or invidious discrimination, the right to follow one's individual preference in the choice of an occupation and the application of his energies, liberty of conscience, and the right to enjoy the domestic relations and the privileges of the family and the hom.

PUTATIVE   (L)

Alleged, supposed.

PYELONEPHRITIS   (Cr's)

Inflammation of the kidney and its pelves.

PYROLYSIS   (Cr's)

The decomposition of organic matter by heat.

PYROMANIAC   (Cr'y, L)

A pathological fire setter.

QUACUMQUE VIA   (L)

Whichever way it is taken.

QUAE COMMUNI LEGI DEROGANT STRICTE INTERPRE-
TANTUR   (L)

Those things which derogate from the common law are to be strictly construed.

QUAE CONTRA RATIONEM JURIS INTRODUCTA SUNT, NON
DEBENT TRAHI IN CONSEQUENTIAM   (L)

Things introduced contrary to the spirit of the law ought not to be drawn into a precedent.

QUAERE   (L)

Inquire; meaning that the question or proposition, to which the word is appended, is a doubtful one.

QUALIFICATION   (L)

Anything which makes one fit or eligible for an office or posi- tion, or to exercise a franchise, such as voting. (2) A limita- tion; diminution.

QUALIFIED   (L)

Limited, restricted, modified. Competent, suited.

QUALIFY   (L)

To take an oath of office, to which one has been appointed or elected, and to execute any necessary bond.

QUANDO ALIQUID PROHIBETUR EX DIRECTO, PROHIBETUR
ET PER OBLIQUUM   (L)

When a thing is forbidden to be done directly, it is also for- bidden to be done directly.

QUARANTINE   (L)

Enforced detention authorized by statute to prevent the spread of contagious disease.

QUARE CLAUSUM FREGIT   (L)

Trespass (q.v.), consisting of an unauthorized entry on the land of another.

QUASH   (L)

To annul or suppress, e.g., an indictment, conviction, or order.

QUASI   (L)

As if; almost. Often used to indicate significant similarity or likeness to the word that follows, while denoting that the word that follows must be considered in a flexible sense.

QUASI CRIMES   (L)

All offenses not crimes or misdemeanors, but which are in the nature of crimes -- a class of offenses against the public; not declared crimes, but wrongs against the general or local public which should properly be repressed or punished by forfeitures and penalties.

QUASI-JUDICIAL   (L)

Resembling judicial action or procedure; applies to the action of an administrative body with limited powers to hold hearings and make decisions affecting the rights of specified persons under the law.

QUESTION   (L)

An interrogatory. An issue to be decided; a question of law or fact.

QUI BENE INTERROGAT, BENE DOCET   (L)

He who interrogates well, teaches well.

QUI DESTRUIT MEDIUM, DESTRUIT FINEM   (L)

He who destroys the means destroys the end.

QUID PRO QUO   (L)

Something for something; a consideration.

QUIETUS   (L)

Freed, or acquitted; a written discharge or release given to a public officer when he faithfully accounts for public funds collected, turning them over to the public treasury.

QUI FACIT PER ALIUM FACIT PER SE   (L)

He who acts through another, acts by or for himself; the doctrine of respondent superior in the law of agency.

QUI JURE SUO UTITUR, NEMINI FACIT INJURIAM   (L)

He who uses his legal rights harms no one.

QUI NON IMPROBAT, APPROBAT   (L)

He who does not disapprove, approves.

QUI TACET, CONSENTIRE VIDETUR   (L)

He who is silent is understood to consent.

QUITTANCE   (L)

An acquittance or release.

QUORUM   (L)

The minimum number of members, e.g., directors on a board of directors, or members of a legislative body, necessary to be present, in order to constitute a meeting capable of transacting business.

QUO WARRANTO   (L)

By what right or authority. A proceeding requiring a person to show by what right he exercized any office or liberty.

RACIST (Cr'y)

One who believes that one or more race is superior to others.

RACKET (Cr'y)

An organized commercial activity that is illegal and not fully institutionalized, although it may be informally supported by a significant part of the population. Examples are gambling, bootlegging, and prostitution.

RADIAL LOOPS, FINGERPRINTS (Cr's)

A flow of ridges starting and terminating in the direction of the thumb of the same hand on which they are found.

RADICALISM (Cr'y)

A nonconformist approach to social and political problems characterized by extreme dissatisfaction with the status quo and a call to change society as quickly as possible and by vigorous means. The extreme leftist and rightist are considered radicals. Both desire to make fundamental changes in society and its leadership, although they would each change certain things.

RADIOACTIVITY (Cr's)

The particle and/or gamma ray radiation emitted by the unstable nucleus of some isotopes.

RAID (PA)

A surprise invasion of a building or area; a small scale attack of a limited territory.

RANGE (Cr's)

Maximum distance a bullet will travel, e.g., maximum range at muzzle elevation between 29° and 35°, .22 long rifle with 40 grains of powder — 1500 yds.; .45 ACP with 234 grains of powder — 1640 yards; .30 cal. MI with 152 grains of powder — 3500 yards; also, distance that a bullet traveled from muzzle to target.

RANKING OFFICER (PA)

The officer having the highest grade of rank, or earliest date of appointment where differentiation of rank does not exist, unless otherwise ordered by the chief. The officer of highest rank is in command and should be held responsible.

RAPE (L)

The act of sexual intercourse between male and female, by force and against the will of the latter. Often defined by various state statutes.

RATIONES (L)

Formerly, the pleadings in a lawsuit.

RAVISH (L)

See: Rape.

RAVISHMENT (L)

Occasionally, the taking of a wife from her husband, or a ward from his guardian.

REACTION TIME   (PA, L)
   The elapsed time between the initiation of an action and the
   required response.
READY, WILLING AND ABLE   (L)
   Descriptive of one who, without cash in hand, is able to com-
   mand the necessary funds to complete his obligations under a
   contract within the time allowed.
REAL EVIDENCE   (L)
   Tangible objects introduced at a trial proving or disproving a
   fact in issue. Evidence which speaks for itself.
REAL IMAGE   (Cr's)
   An image formed by the actual convergence of light rays upon
   a screen.
REAL THINGS   (L)
   Substantial and immovable property including all rights and
   profits annexed to, or issuing out of, them.
REAM   (Cr's)
   To enlarge bore to specific diameter by removing metal with
   reamer.
REASONABLE CARE, OR ORDINARY CARE   (L)
   The conduct of a reasonable, prudent person under similar
   circumstances.
REASONABLE CERTAINTY, OR REASONABLE MEDICAL
      CERTAINTY   (L)
   The quality of proof necessary to authorize recovery for per-
   manent personal injuries; a qualified medical opinion, based
   on reasonable probability, taking the fact of damages out of
   the area of speculation.
REASONABLE DOUBT   (L)
   The state of mind of jurors, in which, after the comparison and
   consideration of all the evidence, they cannot say that they feel
   an abiding conviction, to a moral certainty, of the truth of a
   criminal charge against a defendant.
REASONABLE TIME   (L)
   Any time fixed by agreement; not manifestly unreasonable,
   depending on the nature, purpose and circumstances of such
   action as is required.
REBUTTER   (L)
   Under older forms of pleading, the response of a defendant to
   a plaintiff's surrejoinder.
REBUTTING EVIDENCE, OR REBUTTAL EVIDENCE   (L)
   Proof given by one party in a lawsuit, to explain or disprove
   evidence produced by the other party.
RECALL   (L)
   Retirement of a popularly elected official, before expiration of
   his term, resulting from a subsequent vote of the people.

RECAPTION (L)

Self-help; the right of a person, who has been deprived of his goods, wife or child by another, to retake them, provided he does so without a breach of the peace.

RECAPTURE (L)

The recovery by force of property captured by an enemy.

RECEIVING STOLEN GOODS (L)

The offense of knowingly accepting, buying or concealing goods and chattels illegally obtained by another.

RECEPTION CLASSIFICATION CENTER (Cor)

A correctional institution under a single administrator where psychologists, psychiatrists, physicians, dentists, social workers, counselors, teachers, and chaplains work as a team to ascertain each offender's attitudes and limitations in an effort to work out a rehabilitation program for each.

RECIDIVISM (Cr'y)

Repeated return to criminal behavior, especially following imprisonment. Recidivists are sometimes called "repeaters" or habitual criminals.

RECKLESS DRIVING (L)

Offenses pertaining to operation of a motor vehicle in such a manner as to indicate a wilful disregard for the lives or safety of others.

RECLAIM (L)

To demand again; to claim anew, or repossess. To put waste or wild lands, or lands injured by incursions of rivers or the sea, in a cultivated and fruitful condition.

RECOGNITION (L)

Express or implied acknowledgment that an act done for a person, by another, was done by authority of the former.

RECOGNIZANCE, OR RECOGNIZANCE BOND (L)

An obligation, or acknowledgment of a debt, in a court of law, under the condition the debt shall be void on performance of a stipulated undertaking, e.g., to appear before the proper court, to keep the peace, or to pay the debt, interest and costs that the plaintiff may recover.

RECOIL (Cr's)

Movement of a firearm in the opposite direction of discharge.

RECORD (L)

A written memorial of actions of a legislature or court. The copy of a deed or other instrument relating to real property, officially preserved in a public office.

RECORDER (L)

In some jurisdictions, a public officer having charge of the records of deeds, instruments relating to real property, and other legal instruments required by law to be recorded.

RECORDS TASKS (PA)

The operations necessary to maintain, in logical order, facts relating to crime, criminals, and other police matters.

RECOVERY (L)

The obtaining of an object or money via a lawsuit.

RECRIMINATION (L)

A legal defense for divorce, establishing that the complaining party is equally as guilty of misconduct as the defendant. In such case, the court has discretion to deny divorce for that reason.

RECURRENT INSANITY (L)

Insanity (q.v.) of temporary character and returning from time to time.

REDUCTIO AD ABSURDUM (L)

The method of disproving an argument by showing that it leads to an absurd consequence.

RE--EXAMINATION (L)

A second interrogation following and relating to cross--examination.

REFEREE (L)

One to whom something in question is referred for arbitration. An administrative officer appointed to hear and determine claims and disputes, e.g., in workmen's compensation cases.

REFERENCE (L)

Submission of a controversy to a referee (q.v.). The proceedings before a referee.

REFERENDUM (L)

The practice of referring measures passed by the legislature to the voters for approval or rejection. A popular election held pursuant to such practice.

REFORMATION, OR RECTIFICATION (L)

The correction of a written instrument, via lawsuit, showing it to express the true agreement or intention of the parties.

REFORM MOVEMENT (Cr'y)

A specific social movement aimed at effecting social changes by working through the established system.

REFRACTION (Cr's)

The bending of a light wave as it passes from one medium to another.

REFRACTIVE INDEX (Cr's)

The ratio of the speed of light in a vacuum to its speed in a given substance.

REFRESH THE MEMORY, OR REFRESH THE RECOLLECTION (L)

To refer a witness to something, while he is testifying, to bring facts within his recall.

REGISTER   (L)

A book in which facts of a public or quasi public character, e.g., marriages, births, or deaths, are officially recorded.

REGISTRAR   (L)

A public or private officer, whose business is to keep various official or corporate records.

REGRESS   (L)

A going back; re–entry.

REGULAR ON ITS FACE   (L)

Descriptive of process from a court having authority to issue it, and which is legal in form, containing nothing to apprise any-one that it is issued without authority.

REHABILITATION   (Cor, Cr'y)

The process whereby an individual loses the desire and intent to commit criminal acts and accepts the behavior standards of society.

REHEARING   (L)

A second trial of a lawsuit, after judgment has been pronounced. A second consideration or argument in a court of appeal. Usually authorized in only a few enumerated instances, pursu-ant to various rules of court, or rules of civil procedure.

REJOINDER   (L)

Formerly, a common law pleading.

RELATIVE   (L)

One who would, by legal descent, receive the property of a deceased person, in case of intestacy.

RELEVANCY   (L)

The connection between a fact tendered in evidence and the issue to be proved.

RELICT   (L)

A surviving spouse.

RELIEF   (L)

Redress or assistance, granted by a court to a person, on account of wrongs which another has done to the former. (2) Formerly, payment which a tenant made to the lord, on coming into possession of an estate.

RELINQUISHMENT   (L)

Forsaking or abandonment of something, e.g., a claim in a lawsuit.

REMAND   (L)

To recommit a person to jail or prison. To send a lawsuit back to the same court from which it came, for trial or other action.

REMISSION   (L)

Release or discharge of a debt or fine. Pardon of an offense or crime.

REMITTITUR (L)

In some jurisdictions, a form of decision made by appellate courts, in which a lawsuit is disposed of on appeal by ordering a new trial, unless a party agrees to accept a specific lesser amount of damages, than that awarded in the trial court.

REMOVAL OF CAUSE (L)

Change of venue; transfer of a lawsuit from one state court to another, or from a state court to a federal court.

RENDITION (L)

The return of fugitive from justice to the state in which he is accused of having committed a crime, by the order of the governor of the state to which the fugitive has gone.

RENOUNCE (L)

To reject or give up something.

REPATRIATION (L)

Recovery of a person's rights as a citizen, e.g., return of a civilian or soldier, captured during war, to his own nation.

REPEAL (L)

To annul or set aside a legislative act by another legislative act. Repeals may be express, i.e., declared by direct language in the new act, or implied, i.e., when the new act contains provisions contrary to, or irreconcilable with, those of the former act.

REPLEADER (L)

To plead again. Formerly a procedure when the pleadings in a lawsuit failed to raise a definite issue.

REPORT (PA)

A written communication, or verbal report confirmed by written communication; usually rendered before reporting off duty.

REPORTER (L)

A court official responsible for recording trial proceedings, including questions propounded, and answers made. A court official responsible for compiling, indexing, and publishing opinions of an appellate court.

REPORT REVIEW PROCESS (PA)

A process established to provide a means for scheduled review and control of all reports and held responsible for maintaining departmental standards for writing and filing reports and for prompt disposition of cases.

REPORTS, OR REPORTS OF CASES (L)

Books in which precedent court opinions are recorded having been judicially argued and determined. Occasionally called Reporters.

REPRESSION OF CRIME (PA)

In addition to adequate patrol, a continuous effort is made toward eliminating or reducing hazards, thereby reducing criminal opportunity.

REPRIEVE (L)

Withdrawal for a specific period of time of execution of a sentence. Usually granted to allow a convicted person to prepare and present information in his own behalf.

REPRISAL (L)

The revengeful taking or doing of one thing, in satisfaction for another. Occasionally between nations when no other means of obtaining redress are available.

REPUBLICAN FORM OF GOVERNMENT (L)

Government by popular representation. E.g., the United States shall guarantee to every state in the union a republican form of government. U.S. Const., Art. IV, Sec. IV.

REPUGNANT (L)

That which is inconsistent with, or incompatible with, something else.

REPUTATION (L)

The opinion of one's character, generally entertained by those who know him best.

REQUEST (L)

A demand or notice of a desire, on the part of one of the parties to a contract, that the other should perform his part.

REQUISITION (L)

(1) A formal demand for something which one has a right to receive. (2) The demand made by the governor of one state, on the governor of another state, for the return of a fugitive from justice.

RESCIND (L)

To abrogate a contract.

RES COMMUNES (L)

Things which cannot be appropriated to the exclusive use of an individual, e.g., light, air, and flowing water.

RES GESTAE (L)

All of the things done, including words spoken, in the course of a transaction or event.

RESIDENCE (L)

A permanent place of abode, or for carrying on business.

RESIGNATION (L)

The act of voluntarily declining to serve longer in an office, and renouncing its rights and privileges.

RES JUDICATA (L)

A matter upon which a competent court of law has passed judgment and which it will therefore not re-examine.

RESOLUTION (L)

Expression of intent or opinion by a legislative assembly. Annulment of a contract, by consent of the parties, or by decision of a competent court.

RESORT, COURT OF LAST (L)

A tribunal from which there is no further appeal.

RESPITE (L)

Temporary suspension of execution of a sentence. The grant of additional time, by creditors to a debtor, within which to pay his debts.

RESPONDENT (L)

A party against whom a motion is filed in the course of a lawsuit; analogous to a defendant or an appellee.

RESTITUTION (L)

The restoration of property, or a right, to one unjustly deprived of it. A writ of restitution is the process by which a successful appellant may recover something of which he has been deprived under a prior judgment.

RESTRAINING ORDER (L)

A temporary court directive preserving the status quo pending a full hearing, entered in a lawsuit, without notice if necessary, on a summary showing of necessity to prevent immediate and irreparable injury.

RETAINER (L)

Employment of an attorney, by a client, to give professional services. The fee paid for such employment. Occasionally, the right of an executor or administrator to pay his own debt out of the assets of his testator, in priority to all other debts of equal degree.

RETORSION (L)

Retaliation against the citizens of a nation, by another nation, because of similar treatment of its citizens by the former.

RETRACT (L)

To withdraw, e.g., a damaging statement, or an offer before acceptance.

RETRAXIT (L)

Formerly, a proceeding analogous to a nolle prosequi (q.v.), except that it barred any future action.

RETREATISM (Cr'y)

A form of deviant behavior in which the individual rejects the culturally defined goals of success and the institutionalized means of attaining them. Retreatism is a mode of adaptation

to the frustration of being unable to attain culturally valued g
goals. Examples of retreatism may be found in the behavior of
psychotics, hobos, alcoholics, and drug addicts.

RETROACTIVE STATUTE   (L)

A legislative act imposing a new or additional burden, duty,
obligation or liability concerning a past transaction or event.

RETROPERITONEUM   (Cr's)

Behind the peritoneum. The kidneys, adrenals, aorta, and vena
cava are in the retroperitoneal area.

RETURN   (L)

An indorsement or report by an officer, recording the manner
in which he executed the process or order of a court.

RETURN DAY   (L)

The date named in a court order or fixed by statute, by which
an officer must report the manner in which he executed the
order or process.

REVERSE   (L)

To set aside a judgment, order, or other decision, on appeal or
by the same court, and enter a contrary or different order or
decision.

REVIEW   (L)

A second examination of a determination, e.g., an appeal or a
writ of certiorari.

REVIVAL   (L)

The restoration or revitalization of something having lost its
legal significance due to intervening facts or the passage of
time, e.g., a will or a lawsuit.

REVIVE   (L)

To give new life to a right of action once barred, e.g., by
acknowledging or promising to pay a debt barred by the statute
of limitation, or barred by a discharge in bankruptcy. To
restore, to its original force, a dormant judgment.

REVOCATION   (L)

The recalling or withdrawing of a grant, e.g., an unaccepted
offer, a gift by will, or an agency. The making void of a
deed, will or other instrument. A will may often be revoked by
another will, by burning or other act done with the intention
of revoking, by the disposition of the property during the
testator's lifetime, or by marriage. The revocation of wills is
usually regulated by various state statutes.

REVOLUTIONARY MOVEMENT   (Cr'y)

A specific social movement seeking to reverse the social order —
one whose purpose is not to improve but to destroy and replace.

REVOLVER (Cr's)

A firearm with a cylinder of several chambers so arranged as to revolve on an axis and be discharged successively by the same lock.

RICOCHET (Cr's)

A glancing shot, rebounding from a flat surface.

RIDER (L)

An unrelated enactment or provision included in a proposed legislative measure.

RIDGE CHARACTERISTICS (Cr's)

Ridge endings, bifurcations, enclosures, and other ridge details, which must match in two fingerprints in order for their common origin to be established. Also called minutiae.

RIFLING (Cr's)

Grooves cut into the bore to impart rotary motion to projectiles.

RIFLING BROACH (Cr's)

A tool for cutting the rifling in barrels in one operation.

RIFLING PITCH (Cr's)

The angle at which the rifling spiral is cut in relation to the axis of the bore. Usually expressed as one turn in inches.

RIGHT (L)

A legitimate or socially recognized moral or legal justification for an individual to be allowed specified behavior or to demand specified behavior of others with regard to himself.

RIGHTS, CIVIL (L)

Rights belonging to every citizen of a state or country, or, in a wider sense, to all its inhabitants, and not connected with the organization or administration or government. E.g., the rights of property, marriage, protection by the laws, freedom of contract, trial by jury, etc. Rights appertaining to a person in virtue of his citizenship in a state or community. Rights capable of being enforced or redressed in civil action. Certain rights secured to citizens of the United States by the thirteenth and fourteenth amendments to the Constitution, and by various acts of Congress made in pursuance thereof.

RIGHTS, NATURAL (L)

Rights which grow from the nature of man and depend upon personality, as distinguished from such as are created by law and depend upon civilized society. Those rights plainly assured by natural law. Those which, by fair deduction from the present physical, moral, social, and religious characteristics of man, he must be invested with, and which he ought to have realized for him in a jurial society, in order to fulfill the ends to which his nature calls him.

RIGHTS, PERSONAL   (L)

The right of personal security, comprising those of life, limb, body, health, reputation, and the right of personal liberty.

RIGHTS, POLITICAL   (L)

The power to participate, directly or indirectly, in the establishment or administration of government. The right of citizenship, suffrage, petition, and to hold public office.

RIGHT TO COUNSEL   (L)

The right to be represented by an attorney and, in certain circumstances, have an attorney appointed by the court.

RIGHT TO SUMMON   (PA, L)

A peace officer has the right to summon and require the assistance of as many bystanders as may be necessary to enable him to perform his duty in making an arrest, or preventing or suppressing a breach of the peace.

RIGOR MORTIS   (Cr's)

The stiffening beginning at the head and gradually spreading down over the whole body, two to six hours after death. After eight to twenty hours (in most cases two to twelve) the rigor is complete, disappearing after two to three days, although in some cases lasting until the fifth day.

RIM   (Cr's)

Flanged portion of cartridge case for certain types of rifles and revolvers. Permits extraction.

RIM–FIRE   (Cr's)

A cartridge fired by a blow on the rim of the cartridge-head. A rim-fire rifle or pistol is one that fires a rim-fire cartridge.

RIOT   (L)

A tumultuous disturbance of the peace by three or more persons, assembled of their own authority. Often defined by various state statutes.

RISK   (L)

A danger or hazard, e.g., death, fire, or perils of the sea.

ROBBERY   (L)

The taking of any thing of value from another in his presence and against his will, either by force or fear of violence.

ROLLS, OR ROLL   (L)

Formerly, a court record entered on parchment which could be rolled up; hence, any records of a court or office.

ROUT   (L)

A lesser form of riot (q.v.), in which the purpose is not carried out.

ROUTE   (PA)

A length of street or streets, designated for patrol purposes. A route is most frequently used for the assignment of traffic officers, although it is sometimes used for the assignment of foot patrolmen.

ROUTINE PREVENTIVE PATROL (PA)

Patrol directed primarily at diminishing less tangible hazards not readily isolated and identified.

RULE (L)

An order of a court or other competent legal authority. A principle of law.

RULE DAY (L)

A particular day or days of the month, regularly set aside by a court, for the purpose of announcing decisions. Often held concurrently with motion day (q.v.).

RULE OF CONTROL (COMMAND) (PA)

He who gives an order must ascertain that it has been properly executed.

RULE OF LAW (L)

A doctrine of the supremacy of law. The rights of persons under the law are protected from arbitrary acts of the government by regular courts of justice.

RULES OF COURT (L)

Various orders established by a court for the purpose of regulating the conduct of the business of the court. E.g., licensing for the practice of law, civil procedure, criminal procedure and appellate procedure.

RUN (L)

To pass by; to take effect. E.g., statutes of limitation run against a claim, when the time has passed within which it can be enforced, by actions at law.

SABOTAGE (L)

Intentional damage to machinery or otherwise injuring the property of an employer, or of a nation at war.

SADISM AND MASOCHISM (Cr'y)

The sadist achieves sexual excitement by inflicting punishment, mental or physical, on another. The masochist, on the other hand, derives his pleasure from submitting to ill treatment at the hands of a sadist or another. In some persons both of these deviations are mingled.

SAFE–CONDUCT (L)

A permit enabling an enemy subject to travel to a particular place for a particular purpose.

SAFETY (Cr's)

A device designed to lock the trigger or firing mechanism of a firearm to prevent accidental discharge.

SAFETY FUSE (Cr's)

A cord containing a core of black powder. It is used to carry a flame at a uniform rate to an explosive charge.

SALUS POPULI (OR RESPUBLICAE) SUPREMA LEX (L)

The safety of the community (or state) is the highest law.

SAMPLE (L)

A small quantity of a substance or merchandise, exhibited as a fair specimen of the whole. In sales transactions, an object actually drawn from the bulk of goods which is the subject matter of the sale. Any sample or model which is made part of the basis of a bargain creates an express warranty that the whole of the goods shall conform to the sample or model.

SANCTION (Cr'y, L)

The power of enforcing a statute, or inflicting a penalty for its violation. Consent. A penalty or reward directed at a person or group to discourage or encourage specified behavior.

SANCTION, LEGAL (Cr'y)

A sanction that is part of a formalized code of justice backed by some form of authority.

SANCTION, NEGATIVE (Cr'y)

A sanction intended to punish rather than reward.

SANCTION, ORGANIZED (Cr'y)

A sanction carried out by recognized, traditional procedure by the whole community or by its representatives.

SANE (L)

Descriptive of a person having sufficient judgment, intelligence, reason and mental power to observe and know the difference between right and wrong, or one who, having such, has sufficient will power to refrain from doing the wrong.

SANS (L)
Without.
SCANDAL (L)
A libelous statement or action. In pleading, unnecessary al-
legations reflecting cruelly on the moral character of an indi-
vidual, or stating anything in repulsive language which detracts
from the dignity of the court.
SCIENTER (L)
Knowingly, wilfully. An element in crime and some civil
wrongs, descriptive of the perpetrator's guilty knowledge.
SCINTILLA OF EVIDENCE (L)
The slightest bit of evidence tending to support a material issue
in a lawsuit. In some jurisdictions, only such an amount of
evidence is necessary in a civil action to justify a jury verdict.
SCIRE DEBES CUM QUO CONTRAHIS (L)
You ought to know with whom you are dealing.
SCIRE ET SCIRE DEBERE AEQUIPARANTUR IN LEGE (L)
Knowledge, and the duty to know, are held for the same in
law, i.e., the law considers a person cognizant of that which he
ought to know.
SCIRE FACIAS (L)
Cause to know. In some jurisdictions, a judicial writ
founded on some record, and requiring the person against whom
it is brought to show cause why the party bringing it should not
have advantage of such record, or why the record should not be
annulled and vacated.
SCIRE FECI (L)
The sheriff's return on a scire facias, that he has given notice to
the party against whom it was issued.
SCRIBERE EST AGERE (L)
To write is to act, e.g., an overt act of treason may consist of
writing.
SCROLL (L)
Formerly, a mark made with a pen, intended to take the place
of a seal.
SEAL (L)
An impression on wax, paper, or other substance capable of
being impressed, made for the purpose of authenticating the
document to which it is attached. The metal die, or other
instrument, with which the impression is made.
SEAR (Cr's)
A part so designed as to release the firing mechanism upon
pressure being applied to trigger.

SEARCH (L)

An exploration or inspection of a person's house, premises, vehicle, or person, by a public officer, e.g., a policeman, for the purpose of discovering evidence of crime, or one accused of a crime. A prying into hidden places for that which is concealed — not to observe that which is open to view.

SEARCH AND SEIZURE, CRITERIA FOR (L, PA)

Reliable probable cause. Particularity of warrant. Facts of the warrant stated under oath. Legal entry into the premises to secure evidence.

SEARCH WARRANT (L)

A written court order, specifying the place of search and the things looked for, directing that they should be brought before the court when found.

SECONDARY LINE ELEMENT (PA)

Specialized elements of patrol resources to handle aspects of traffic, criminal and other investigations, and other field-related responsibilities.

SECRETOR (Cr's)

An individual who secretes his/her blood type antigen in body fluids. Approximately 80 percent of the population are secretors.

SECTION (L)

Division, e.g., of a legislative act, a statute, or book, less than a chapter, and greater than a clause. A subdivision of a township (q.v.) under United States survey, one mile square, and containing six hundred and forty acres.

SECTION (PA)

Functional units within a division calling for additional specialization, and consequently further classification according to duties. Such extensive subdivision is found in large departments.

SECTOR (PA)

An area containing two or more beats, routes or posts. The squad of officers assigned to a sector is headed by a sergeant.

SEDITION (L)

Publications, utterances, or other activities, short of overt acts of treason, deemed encouragement to resistance of laws or disrespect for government.

SEDUCTION (L)

The offense of a person deceitfully inducing another into an unlawful act of sexual intercourse. Often defined by various state statutes.

SEIZURE (L)

The act of taking possession of property, e.g., for a violation of law or by virtue of an execution.

SELECTIVE ENFORCEMENT   (PA)
    The application of enforcement effort against certain types of
    crimes or violations prevalent in particular areas and/or times.
SELF–DEFENSE   (L)
    The protection of one's person and property from injury; to
    defend oneself when attacked, repel force by force, and even
    commit homicide in resistance of an attempted felony, e.g.,
    murder, rape, robbery or burglary.
SELF INCRIMINATION   (L)
    Implication of oneself in crime or wrongdoing.
SELF–SERVING   (L)
    Descriptive of statements made in the interest of the person
    making them.
SEMI–AUTOMATIC   (Cr's)
    Firearm which fires, extracts, ejects and reloads once for each
    pull of the trigger.
SENILE ATROPHY OF ORGANS   (Cr's)
    Shrinkage of organs in old age.
SENILITY   (L)
    The effects of old age on the mind.
SENSITIVITY TRAINING   (Cor)
    A treatment process which includes a wide experiential range in
    human relations that increase awareness — group dynamics,
    organizational development, and verbal and nonverbal experien-
    ces. To experience what certain other types of people ex-
    perience.
SENSUS VERBORUM EST ANIMA LEGIS   (L)
    The meaning of words is the soul of the law.
SENTENCE   (L)
    A formally pronounced judgment of punishment in a criminal
    proceeding.
SENTENCE, CUMULATIVE   (L)
    Separate sentences (each additional to the other) imposed on a
    defendant convicted upon an indictment containing several
    counts, each of such counts charging a distinct offense, or who
    is under conviction at the same time for several distinct offen-
    ses; one of such sentences being made to begin at the expiration
    of another.
SENTENCES TO RUN CONCURRENTLY   (L)
    Merely means that accused is given privileges of serving each
    day as a portion of each sentence.
SEPARATION   (L)
    The living apart of husband and wife, in pursuance of a mutual
    agreement.

SEPTUM PELLUCIDUM   (Cr's)
>Dividing brain tissue between the lateral ventricles.

SEQUESTER   (L)
>To separate or set apart.

SERGEANT--AT--ARMS   (L)
>An officer appointed by a legislative body to carry out its orders, analogous to a bailiff or a sheriff.

SEROLOGY   (Cr's)
>A study of the reactions and properties of serum.

SERUM   (Cr's)
>The liquid that separates from the blood when a clot is formed.

SERVICE   (L)
>The act of bringing notice of a judicial proceedings to the attention of the person affected by it, e.g., by delivering to him a copy of a written summons or notice.

SERVICES CALLED FOR   (PA)
>The actions normally taken in dealing with incidents. Services given by the police which the public requests, e.g., unlock a car.

SESSION   (L)
>A term; the sitting of a court or legislature for the transaction of business.

SEVER   (L)
>To divide, e.g., a joint tenancy is severed when one joint tenant conveys his share to a stranger. To remove, e.g., growing crops or fixtures. Defendants sever their defenses when they plead independently.

SHADOWING   (PA)
>The act of following a person without that person's knowledge. Also, tailing.

SHAKEDOWN   (Cor)
>A search of cell blocks or dormitories.

SHAM PLEADING   (L)
>A written pleading (q.v.), in good form, but patently false and in bad faith.

SHELL   (Cr's)
>Brass, gilding metal, or other suitable material, drawn and shaped to chambers of firearms. Priming mixture is contained in the rim cavity to permit ignition at any point where the rim is struck by the blow of the firing pin.

SHERIFF   (L)
>The chief law enforcement officer of a county whose duties include keeping the peace, making arrests, execution of court process, and performance of such other duties as may be prescribed by state statute. Formerly called shire-reeve in England.

SHIRE (L)

A geographical division in England, analogous to a county in the United States.

SHOCKING POWER (Cr's)

The energy expended by a projectile on impact resulting from a combination of momentum and penetration.

SHOT (Cr's)

Lead allow spherical pellets in a selection of "sizes" or diameters and designed to pass through the bore and choke, striking the target with a pattern of uniform density.

SHOTGUN (Cr's)

Smooth bore shoulder firearm designed to fire shells containing numerous pellets as projectiles.

SHUNTING (PA)

The asking of a question relative to digression from the original line of questioning; preferable to interrupting the subject since the "shunt" appears to rise out of an interest in what the subject is saying.

SHYSTER (L)

A derogatory term for a person who carries on a business, or practices law, dishonestly.

SICK LEAVE (PA)

The period during which an officer is excused from active duty by reason of illness or injury.

SICKLE CELL DISEASE (Cr's)

A disease of the blood in which the red blood corpuscles become crescent-shaped and disintegrate.

SIGHT (Cr's)

Any of a variety of devices, mechanical or optical, designed to assist in aiming a firearm.

SIGHT ELEVATION (Cr's)

The height or adjustment to which a rear sight is set to zero the firearm in at any specific range.

SIGNATURE (L)

The name or mark of a person, subscribed or printed by himself, or by his direction.

SIMPLE (L)

Plain; unconditional; not under seal, nor of record; not combined with anything else.

SIMPLE WHORLS, FINGERPRINTS (Cr's)

Whorls having two deltas and the core consisting of circles, ellipses, or spirals turning to the right or left.

SINE QUA NON (L)

An indispensable thing, a necessity.

SISTER (L)

A woman with the same parentage as another, or, having one common parent only, she is called a half sister.

SITUATIONAL DEVIATION (Cr'y)

A consequence of the stress or pressure of a particular situation.

SKID ROW (Cr'y)

An area found in large cities predominantly inhabited by homeless men and characterized by a concentration of prostitutes, alcoholics, thieves, flophouses, striptease joints, and rescue missions. It is an area of physical deterioration where the demoralized poor who are mentally or physically ill find cheap rent and partial escape from middle class ridicule and censure. The term was used often by classical ecologists.

SKILLED WITNESS (L)

One who is allowed to give evidence on matters of opinion and abstract fact, because of knowledge, training, and experience not acquired by ordinary persons.

SKIN WORKER (Cr'y)

A commercial shoplifter who specializes in the theft of furs.

SLANDER (L)

The malicious defamation of a person's reputation, profession, or business, by spoken words.

SLEUTH (PA)

An undercover investigator.

SLIDE (Cr's)

Reciprocating part that unlocks the barrel from breech block. The operating rod in slide action guns.

SLUM (Cr'y)

A residential area inhabited primarily by poor, often demoralized families, and characterized by substandard, unsanitary conditions, overcrowding, and usually social disorganization.

SMITH ACT (L)

An act to prohibit certain subversive activities; to amend certain provisions of law with respect to the admission and deportation of aliens; and to require the fingerprinting and registration of aliens.

SMOKELESS POWDER (Cr's)

An explosive consisting of nitrocellulose.

SMUDGING (Cr's)

Burning powder produces smoke and powder which is deposited on nearby objects when the gun has been held at a distance of from two to eighteen inches. The result is a dirty, grimy smudge at entrance, the size of which is a function of the caliber of bullet, type of powder used, and the firing distance.

SMUGGLING   (L)

The knowing and intentional importing or exporting of prohibited articles, or of defrauding the revenue by importing or
exporting goods, without paying duty on them.

SOCIAL CONTROL   (Cr'y)

Formal and informal methods that hold individuals to the expected norms of behavior in any society, i.e., mores, folkways,
customs, taboos, codes, and laws.

SOCIAL CONTROL, NEGATIVE   (Cr'y)

Social control that depends on punishment or fear of punishment, ranging from laws (threatening death, imprisonment, or
fines) to folkways, the violation of which brings ridicule, social
disapproval, or rejection.

SOCIAL CONTROL, POSITIVE   (Cr'y)

Social control that depends on positive motivation of the individual to conform. This may be effected simply through the
promise of rewards, ranging from tangible material benefits to
social approval.

SOCIAL GROUP WORK   (Cr'y)

In social work, the technique of sponsoring and working with
voluntary social groups, such as clubs and gangs, in order to
develop socially desirable qualities.

SOCIAL IMPERATIVE   (Cr'y)

Any of several basic requirements of social organization that
provide for the resolution of problems inherent in interpersonal
relationships. These are requirements that must be met by all
forms of social organization if the organization is to persist.

SOCIAL PATHOLOGY   (Cr'y)

Any "diseased" condition of society, such as crime, vice, or
alcoholism; this term was used by early sociologists, but is ob-
solescent today.

SOCIAL PERCEPTION   (Cr'y)

The entire range of judgment, interpretation, and impression
involved in virtually all human relations.

SOCIAL PROBLEM   (Cr'y)

Any undesirable condition or situation judged by an influential
number of persons within a community to be intolerable and to
require group action toward constructive reform. Examples are
juvenile delinquency, drug addition, crime, prostitution, divorce,
chronic unemployment, poverty, and mental illness.

SOCIAL STIGMA   (Cr'y)

An undesirable differentness of an individual that disqualifies
him from full social acceptance. It is an attribute or stereotype
that departs negatively from the expectations of others. The
individual with social deformities (hangman, ex-convict,

prostitute) or physical deformities (amputated body parts, scars) is not accorded the respect given to "normal" individuals.

SOCIAL WORK (Cr'y)

A specialized professional field concerned with the application of sociological and psychological principles to the solution of specific community problems and the alleviation of individual distress. Specific areas dealt with include poverty, unemployment, youth guidance and organization, recreation, delinquency, family disorganization, health, drug addiction, and mental illness.

SOCIAL WORK APPROACH (Cr'y)

Belief that change in the correctional client can be accomplished through casework, group work, and community organization. The emphasis is more toward adjustment with the environment than on depth psychotherapy.

SOCIOGENIC THEORIES (Cr'y)

Theories of crime causation that consider man as a social being who learns behavior from any number of the segment of his society or culture.

SOCIOGRAPHY (Cr'y)

The detailed quantitative description of a specified problem of social relations within a delimited spatial environment, for example, a detailed description of crime and the distribution of crime rates in a particular area.

SOCIOLOGICAL JURISPRUDENCE (Cr'y)

The philosophy that law should be developed in terms of its effect on a variety of interests in society.

SOCIOLOGY, APPLIED (Cr'y)

The application of sociological principles and insights to the analysis and understanding of a concrete social situation or system of social relationships. Applied sociology is not to be confused with either social work or social reform.

SOCIOLOGY, OCCUPATIONAL (Cr'y)

The application of principles of sociology to the analysis of professions and occupations. The study of career patterns is a part of occupational sociology.

SOCIOLOGY OF LAW (Cr'y)

The study of the legal institution in terms of sociological concepts.

SOCIOPATH (Cr'y)

A person who tends to act in an antisocial way.

SODOMY (L)

Refers to the sexual relationship between the male penis and the rectum of a male or female. The term, however, is used in a legal sense to cover almost any sexual act, whether in the form of sexual stimulation by the use of the mouth or tongue or actual intercourse through anus or with an animal, bird, or dead body, which is unnatural or is defined as a crime against nature.

See also: Buggery.

SOFT—POINT BULLET (Cr's)

A semi-metal-encased bullet with a lead tip which mushrooms on impact, thereby increasing shocking power and tissue destruction.

SOLAR PLEXUS (Cr's)

Network of nerve tissue behind the stomach.

SOLICITOR (L)

An attorney at law.

SOLICITOR GENERAL (L)

An officer of the United States Department of Justice, who determines which lawsuits involving the federal government will be appealed, and who briefs and argues all cases before the United States Supreme Court, in which the federal government is a party.

SOLID (Cr's)

A state of matter in which the molecules are held closely together in a rigid state.

SOLITARY CONFINEMENT (L, Cor)

The separate confinement of a prisoner, with only occasional access of any other person, and that only at the discretion of the jailer; in a stricter sense, complete isolation of a prisoner from all human society, and his confinement in a cell so arranged as to deny all direct intercourse with and sight of any human being, and all employment or instruction.

SOLVENT (L)

The condition of a person who has sufficient money or property, or both, with which to pay his debts in full.

SOMATIC (Cr'y)

Pertaining to the body.

SOUND JUDICIAL DISCRETION (L)

Discretion exercised on full and fair consideration of the facts presented to the judge by the well-known and established mode of procedure with regard to what is right and equitable under the circumstances.

SOURCES OF THE LAW (L)

The origins from which particular positive laws derive their authority and coercive force. Such are constitutions, treaties, statutes, usages, and customs. In another sense, the authoritative or reliable works, records, documents, edicts, etc., to which we are to look for an understanding of what constitutes the law.

SOVEREIGNTY (L)

A legal attribute of a state entitling it to make decisions respecting matters within its jurisdiction free of external restraint or coercion.

SPAN OF CONTROL (PA)

The organizational responsibility of one man to direct, coordinate, and control immediate subordinates.

SPEAKING DEMURRER (L)

A demurrer (q.v.) alleging new matter in addition to that contained in the pleading to which the demurrer is filed.

SPECIAL (L)

Distinctive; relative to a particular act, thing or person; opposed to general.

SPECIAL AGENT (L)

A representative whose authority is confined to a particular or individual instance.

SPECIAL ASSUMPSIT (L)

An action of assumpsit brought on express contract.

SPECIAL DUTY (PA)

Service requiring an officer to be excused from the performance of regular duties.

SPECIAL ISSUE (L)

In a pleading, denial of some particular material allegation, and in effect, denying right of action, though not traversing the whole declaration.

SPECIAL MATTERS (L)

In court pleadings, allegations concerning capacity, fraud, mistake, condition of the mind, conditions precedent, official documents or acts, judgments, time and place, and special damage.

SPECIAL ORDERS (PA)

Self-cancelling orders issued by the chief of police providing specific direction applicable to a specific circumstance or situation of a temporary nature, and ordinarily not affecting the entire department.

SPECIAL OWNER (L)

One who has the care, control, custody, management or use of property without attendant title.

SPECIAL PLEADING (L)

Allegations of new matter, avoiding the effect of previous allegations of the other party, as distinguished from a direct denial of them.

SPECIAL SESSION (L)

An extra sitting of a court, grand jury or legislative body, held at a time other than that regularly scheduled for its sittings.

SPECIAL VERDICT (L)

The finding by a trial jury of particular facts in a lawsuit, usually to answer questions submitted, leaving to the court the application of the law to the facts thus found.

SPECIMEN (Cr's)

An item of physical evidence.

SPERM (Cr's)

The male reproductive cell.

SPITE FENCE (L)

A barrier erected by a landowner, the sole purpose being to shut off light and air from the windows of buildings on the adjoining premises.

SPLIT SENTENCE (L)

Penalty of fine and imprisonment imposed, and imprisonment suspended while the fine is enforced.

SPOLIATION (L)

The mutilation, or destruction of something, e.g., the erasure or alteration of a writing.

SPOLIATUS DEBET ANTE OMNIA RESTITUI (L)

A person who has been robbed ought, first of all, to have his goods restored.

SPONTANEOUS COMBUSTION (Cr's)

A fire caused by a natural heat producing process in the presence of sufficient air and fuel.

SPONTANEOUS EXCLAMATION (L)

An utterance concerning circumstances of a startling nature by an individual under conditions of excitement, shock or surprise, warranting inference of spontaneity not the product of deliberation or design.

SPOT MAPS (PA)

Maps which indicate locations of police hazards.

SPRING GUN (Cr's)

A booby trap; a firearm set as a trap and discharged upon contact with a hidden wire or cord.

SPURIOUS (L)

Not genuine, fictitious.

SQUATTER (L)

One who settles on public lands, or the private lands of others, without legal authority.

SQUIB, SQUIB LOAD (Cr's)

A defective powder charge producing an extremely weak combustion.

STABIT PRAESUMPTIO DONEC PROBETUR IN CONTRARIUM (L)

A presumption stands until the contrary is proved.

STAFF INSPECTION   (PA)

Inspection to determine whether a job has been satisfactorily completed. The staff inspection unit has no line or command authority and merely observes, evaluates and reports its subsequent findings.

STAFF OR DELEGATED SUPERVISION   (PA)

Responsibility of command of an element given or delegated to the supervisor of another, perhaps unrelated, element. Essentially, such responsibility extends only to normal operations, i.e., matters of attendance, attention to duties, personal conduct, and adherence to prescribed work procedures. It does not give license to changes of established policy and procedure under normal conditions.

STAFF SERVICES   (PA)

Services essentially oriented to people and management, e.g., recruitment, selection, training, promotion, planning and research, community relations, and public information services, budget development and control, and inspectional services.

STAR CHAMBER   (L)

A court originally having jurisdiction in cases where ordinary justice was so obstructed by one party, through writs, combination of maintenance, or overawing influence that no inferior court would find its process obeyed. The court consisted of the Privy Council, the common-law judges and (it seems) all peers of Parliament. In the reign of Henry VIII, and his successors, the jurisdiction of the court was illegally extended to such a degree (especially in punishing disobedience to the king's arbitrary proclamations) that it became odious to the nation, and was abolished.

STARE DECISIS   (L)

Literally, "to stand on the decision"; precedent. To follow past decisions to the extent that situations in those cases are congruent with the situation now before the court.

STARE DECISIS, ET NON QUIETA MOVERE   (L)

Adhere to precedents and do not unsettle things established.

STATE ACCOUNT SYSTEM   (Cor)

A current system of prisoner employment at various prisons whereby goods produced in prison are sold on the open market.

STATE'S EVIDENCE   (L)

Evidence given by an accomplice against his confederates in crime in the hope of mitigation of his own sentence.

STATE USE SYSTEM   (Cor)

A current system of prisoner employment at various prisons whereby goods produced in prisons are used by other state agencies, frequently schools and jails.

STATEWAY   (Cr'y)

A social norm that has been enacted into law. The term is seldom used today.

STATISTICAL STUDIES   (Cr'y)

The most common criminological approach. An attempt to develop crime categories in order to establish correlations between arrests and/or convictions and other specific physical and social variables.

STATUS   (L)

The condition of a person, or thing, in the eyes of the law.

STATUS QUO   (L)

The existing state of things at any given date.

STATUTE   (L)

A law enacted, for prospective application, by the legislature of a nation or state. It may be (a) declaratory, i.e., one which does not alter existing law, as opposed to remedial or amending; (b) enabling, i.e., a removing restrictions, as opposed to disabling. Statutes may also be either public, or private, the latter including those having special application to particular persons or places.

STATUTE, CRIMINAL   (L)

A legislative act relating to crime or its punishment.

STATUTE OF LIMITATIONS   (L)

A statute fixing the period during which existing claims may be collected, judgments enforced, or crimes prosecuted and which, after lapse of the prescribed period, serves as a legal bar to such actions.

STATUTES AT LARGE   (L)

Laws enacted by Congress for prospective application, originally compiled in chronological order of enactment and subsequently reorganized into the United States Code.

STATUTORY   (L)

Created by, or depending upon, statute, as distinguished from equitable or common-law rules.

STATUTORY CONSTRUCTION   (L)

Court determination of the meaning of a statute (q.v.) relative to a particular factual dispute before it.

STATUTORY RAPE   (L)

Carnal knowledge of a minor female (12–17 years) not involving force or violence and ultimately dependent upon female cooperation.

STAY–AD–INTERIM   (L)

A stoppage of proceedings during the meantime.

STAY OF EXECUTION (L)

Delay in issuance of execution (q.v.), or suspension of authority to levy one already issued, until a future time; generally allowed in cases of appeal, or proceedings in error, on the filing of a sufficient bond for satisfaction of judgment, or decree, if affirmed.

See also: Cess'et execu'tio.

STAY OF PROCEEDINGS (L)

Suspension of a lawsuit, e.g., where plaintiff is wholly incapacitated from suing, or ought not to be allowed to plead; or pending appeal, or where there is an action pending elsewhere to determine the same question, or one which should be first determined, or until the plaintiff, if a nonresident, shall furnish security for costs.

See also: Cess'et process'us.

STEALING (L)

See: Larceny.

STENOSIS (Cr's)

Narrowing.

STEP LENGTH (Cr's)

The distance between centers of two successive heelprints. It depends upon the size of the walker, the habits of the walker, and the speed of the walk.

STET PROCESSUS (L)

An order of the court to stay proceedings.

STIMULANT (Cr's)

A substance taken to increase alertness or activity.

STINT (L)

Limit.

STIPULATION (L)

An agreement, bargain, proviso, or condition, e.g., an agreement between opposing litigants that certain facts are true.
In admiralty practice, recognizance in the nature of bail, for appearance of a defendant.

STOKES–ADAMS SYNDROME (Cr's)

Sudden onset of unconsciousness, often associated with heart block.

STOP AND FRISK (PA, L)

A law operative in many states and upheld by the U.S. Supreme Court in Terry V. Ohio, authorizing a police officer to pat down a person who is suspected of having committed, is committing or is about to commit a crime and the officer's life or limb is endangered.

STRANDING (L)

The running of a ship on shore, accidentally or voluntarily. When accidental, or done voluntarily to avoid a worse fate, the loss is one within the terms of an ordinary policy of marine insurance.

STRANGER (L)

One neither a party (q.v.), nor in privity with a party, in a legal transaction.

STRATEGIC INTELLIGENCE (PA)

Intelligence concerned with anticipating and thwarting major moves of highly movile, influential, interstate criminal organizations.

STRAW MAN (L)

One who is only a nominal party to a transaction.

STRESS (Cr'y)

Any unpleasant and disturbing emotional experience due to frustration (expressed, for example, in anger, anxiety, confusion, discomfort, etc.). Stress often results from an alteration of or interference with an individual's usual pattern of behavior.

STRICTISSIMI JURIS (L)

Of the most strict law, i.e., to be most strictly applied.

STRIKE (L)

An organized refusal of workmen to work, for the purpose of generating economic pressure to cause an employer to grant improved wages or working conditions.

STRIKING ENERGY (Cr's)

The energy impact measured in foot-pounds.

STRUCK JURY (L)

A trial jury obtained by striking names from a list of potential jurors furnished by the court, or a proper officer thereof.

STUDY OF TRAITS (Cr'y)

A methodological approach to the understanding of criminals which attempts to compare one or more of their conditions or characteristics with those of non-criminal equivalents.

SUBCULTURE (Cr'y)

The culture of an identifiable segment of a society. A subculture is part of the total culture of a society but it differs from the larger culture in certain respects — for example, in language, customs, values, or social norms. It is agreed that ethnic groups have subcultures but writers also refer to the subcultures of occupations, adolescents, criminals, social classes, etc.

SUBDURAL (Cr's)

Situated beneath the dura.

SUBDURAL SPACE (Cr's)

Space between brain and dura matter.

SUBGALEAL (Cr's)

Situated beneath the scalp.

SUBJECT MATTER (L)

The object under discussion or consideration, or in dispute.

SUBMISSION (L)

A yielding. The agreement or court decision by which matters in dispute are referred to someone, e.g., a judge, jury, referee, or arbitrator, for decision.

SUBORNATION (L)

The offense of procuring another person to commit a crime, e.g., perjury.

SUBPOENA (L)

A court order or writ, commanding attendance in court, under penalty for failure to do so. A "subpoena ad testificandum" is personally served upon a witness to compel him to attend a trial, or deposition, and give evidence. A "subpoena duces tecum" is personally served upon a person who has in his possession a book, instrument, or tangible item, the production of which in evidence is desired, commanding him to bring it with him, and produce it at the trial or deposition.

SUBSEQUENT (L)

Following after. A condition subsequent is a condition which, if not performed, defeats or diverts a right or estate existing or vested.

SUBSTANTIAL EVIDENCE (L)

More than a mere scintilla (q.v.); such relevant evidence as reasonably might be accepted as adequate to support a conclusion.

SUBSTANTIVE EVIDENCE (L)

That adduced for the purpose of proving a fact in issue, as opposed to evidence given for the purpose of discrediting a witness or of corroborating his testimony.

SUBSTANTIVE LAW (L)

That part of law creating, defining, and regulating rights, as opposed to "adjective or remedial law," which prescribes methods of enforcing the rights or obtaining redress for their invasion.

SUBSTITUTE (L)

One put in place of another; an object put in place of another. To put on in the place of another.

SUBVERSION (L)

The undermining by various means, normally clandestine, of the loyalty of part or all of a population toward either betrayal or overthrow of its government.

SUBVERSIVE INTELLIGENCE (PA)

Intelligence relative to assembling, analyzing, and disseminating information about individuals or groups whose interest is the overthrow of existing governmental process by covert subversion or overt revolution.

SUCCESSION (Cr'y)

The complete takeover of a neighborhood by newly arriving members of a group.

SUCCESSOR (L)

One who replaces another, e.g., in public office, as heir to particular property, or as the subsequent owner of particular property.

SUDDEN PASSION (L)

In manslaughter, an intense and vehement emotional excitement, leading to violent and aggressive action, e.g., rage, hatred, furious resentment or terror.

SUE (L)

To initiate a civil lawsuit or civil action.

SUI JURIS (L)

Of his own right.

SUICIDE (L)

The voluntary and intentional destruction of one's self.

SUIT (L)

A lawsuit or civil action.

SULCUS (Cr's)

Shallow furrow on the surface of the brain, separating adjacent convolutions.

SUMERIAN CODES (Cr'y, L)

Ancient laws written c. 3500 B.C.

SUMMARY (L)

Short; speedy; unceremonious; opposed to plenary, or regular.

SUMMARY JUDGEMENT (L)

Decision of a court concerning merits of a lawsuit, rendered on the motion of a party, when the pleadings, depositions, answers to interrogatories and admissions on file, together with any affidavits, show there is no genuine issue of material fact, and the party who made the motion is entitled to judgment as a matter of law.

SUMMARY JURISDICTION (L)

Authority of a court to make an order without further preliminaries; e.g., committing for trial.

SUMMING UP (L)

The trial argument made by counsel at the close of evidence. In some jurisdictions, a concise review of evidence in a trial, made by a judge, in charging a jury.

SUMMONS   (L)

A court order, or writ, commanding the party therein named to appear in court on, or before, a specified date, and defend the complain in an action commenced against him.

SUNDAY LAW OR BLUE LAW   (L)

A legislative act requiring cessation from labor and business on the Sabbath.

SUPERIOR COURT   (L)

A court of record or general trial superior to a justice of the peace or magistrate's court. An intermediate court between the general trial court and the highest appellate court.

SUPERIOR OFFICER   (PA)

One having supervisory responsibilities, either temporarily or permanently, over officers of lower rank.

SUPERSEDEAS   (L)

A court order or writ by which proceedings are stayed.

SUPERVISION   (PA)

The guidance of subordinate persons toward accomplishment of goals established by planning, within prescribed policy guidelines and in accordance with established procedures.

SUPPRESSION VERI   (L)

L., a wilful concealment of material facts.

SUPPURATION   (Cr's)

Formation of pus.

SUPRA PROTEST   (L)

After protest.

SUPREME COURT   (L)

A court of high power and extensive jurisdiction, existing in most states; in some, the official style of the chief appellate court or court of last resort. In others (such as New York), a court of general original jurisdiction, possessing also (in New York) some appellate jurisdiction, but not the court of last resort.

SURETY   (L)

One who undertakes to become responsible for the debt of another; one who binds himself for the performance of some act of another.

SURPLUSAGE   (L)

In court pleadings the allegation of unnecessary matter, which may be ordered stricken by the court. Upon motion made by a party, the court may order stricken from any pleading any insufficient defense, or any redundant, immaterial, impertinent, or scandalous matter.

SURRENDER (L)

To relinquish or forego; to yield up an estate for life, or years, e.g., a lease, so that it merges in the fee or reversion. It may occur by deed or by operation of law.

SURVEILLANCE (PA)

The covert observation of places, persons and vehicles for purposes of obtaining information concerning identities or activities of the subjects.

SURVEY OF RELEASE PROCEDURES (Cor)

A Works Progress Administration survey, published in 1939–40, concentrating on probation, parole, pardon, executive clemency, goodtime deductions, prisons, and expiration of sentence.

SURVIVOR (L)

One of two or more persons, who lives longer than the other, or others. In England, and in some of the United States, when one of two or more joint tenants survives the other, or others, he becomes vested with the whole estate by virtue of the right of survivorship.

SUSPECT (Cr's, L, PA)

One whose guilt is considered on reasonable grounds to be a practical possibility.

SUSPENDED SENTENCE (L)

Suspension of imposition of legal sanction or suspension of execution thereof.

SUSPENSION (L)

An interruption, stay or delay. Concerning estates or rights, a temporary extinguishment which may be followed by a revival.

SUSPENSION OF OFFICERS (PA)

Temporary denial of an officer's privilege of performing his duties in consequence of violation of department regulations; either the first step in the disciplinary process or the penalty assessed. The suspended officer ordinarily does not receive pay.

SUTHERLAND, EDWIN H. (Cr'y)

Twentieth century criminologist, who presented the first important modern theory of crime in 1937, when he offered his theory of differential association. The theory maintains that one learns delinquent behavior from his associates.

SWINDLER (L, Cry)

One who defrauds others by cheating and deception or through fraudulent schemes.

SYNCOPE (Cr's)

Fainting, temporary loss of consciousness.

SYNDICALISM, CRIMINAL (L, Cr'y)

Any doctrine or precept advocating, teaching, or aiding and abetting the commission of crime, sabotage, or unlawful acts of force and violence or unlawful methods of terrorism, as a means of accomplishing a change in industrial ownership, or control, or effecting any political change.

SYSTOLE   (Cr's)

Contraction of the heart causing expulsion of blood.

TACHYCARDIA (Cr's)

Excessive rapidity of the heart beat.

TACIT (L)

Inferred, silent, implied from silence.

TACK (L)

To add or append. A lease.

TACTICAL INTELLIGENCE (PA)

Tactical intelligence is closely allied with predatory crime and modus operandi analysis.

TACTICAL PLANS (PA)

Plans restricted to methods of action to be taken at designated locations and under specific situations; e.g., action to be taken in the event of a jail emergency or when a report is received that a robbery is in progress at a specified location.

TAKE–DOWN SYSTEM OR TAKE--DOWN RIFLE (Cr's)

A firearm employing a barrel which can readily be taken from the action for compactness in carrying the arm.

TALES, OR TALESMAN (L)

Jurors summoned to fill vacancies existing in the regular panel.

TALES DE CIRCUMSTANTIBUS (L)

Jurors selected from bystanders.

TANGIBLE (L)

Descriptive of something which may be felt or touched; corporeal.

TATTOOING (Cr's)

The embedding of burning powder and particles of molten metal into the skin of the victim, upon discharge of a firearm, in a pattern around the entrance wound.

TAX EVASION (L)

A deceit, consisting of a breach of law, by which the revenue laws' application to a particular taxpayer is frustrated. (2) To not pay taxes rightfully due the government.

TEAM TREATMENT (Cor)

A group of three persons, generally a counselor, a custodial officer, and a school teacher assigned to each individual prisoner.

TEGMENTUM (Cr's)

Roof, covering, coating.

TEMPORAL (Cr's)

Pertaining to the temple.

TEMPORARY INJUNCTION (L)

An injunction (q.v.), effective until trial of a lawsuit for which it was issued.

TENANT (L)

One holding or possessing real property, e.g., a lessee.

TENOR (L)

The meaning and intent of a written document, as opposed to its actual words. Occasionally, a correct copy.

TENTED ARCHES, FINGERPRINTS (Cr's)

Tented arches are modifications of simple arches, also devoid of real deltas, where one line goes straight in the center of the pattern with other lines grouped in pointed angles around this axis.

TENTORIUM (Cr's)

Fold of dure forming a partition between the cerebrum and cerebellum.

TENURE (L)

Any of various ways in which a person holds and retains property or an office.

TERMINUS A QUO (L)

The starting point.

TERMINUS AD QUEM (L)

The destination.

TERRITORY (L)

The portion of a nation subject to a particular jurisdiction, e.g., municipal, judicial, or military. A division of land belonging to the federal government, which is not within the boundaries of any particular state, and which is governed by United States officers.

TERRORISM (PA, Cr'y)

The use of terror for coercion.

TEST CASE (L)

A case brought forward to test the validity of a new piece of legislation. Financial support is often provided by a group.

TESTE (L)

The witnessing part of a writ, warrant, or other process indicating by whose authority it is issued.

TESTES PONDERANTUR NON NUMERANTUR (L)

Witnesses are weighed, not numbered, i.e., the mere number of the witnesses brought forward to prove any fact is not so important as their credibility and judgment.

TESTIMONY (L)

Oral evidence given by a witness under oath or affirmation.

THALAMUS (Cr's)

Large mass of grey matter serving as sensory relay station in the cerebral hemisphere.

THEFT (L)

See: Larceny.

THEORY OF OPPORTUNITY   (Cr'y)

Criminologists Richard F. Cloward and Lloyd E. Ohlin's theory that legitimate goals are available to middle and upper class youth but the means by which they are attained are not available to lower class youth. Delinquency results from associations with other have-nots who devise illegitimate means to achieve these goals.

THEORY OF RELATIVITY   (Cr'y)

A theory of crime causation formulated by Richard D. Knudten. The theory in shortened form, suggests that the definition, character, and incidence of delinquency and crime are relative to the cultural, social, smallgroup, and personality factors which produce and shape them.

THERAPEUTIC ABORTION   (L)

A cessation of pregnancy to preserve the mother's health or save her life.

THIRD DEGREE   (L, PA)

Various illegal methods attributed to police in the extorting of confessions from accused persons.

THIRD PARTY   (L)

One who is a stranger (q.v.) to a transaction, contract or proceeding.

THOROUGHFARE   (L)

A street or way open at both ends and free from obstruction.

THROMBOANGIITIS OBLITERANS   (Cr's)

Inflamation of a blood vessel associated with obstruction of the vessel by a clot.

THROMBOEMBOLISM   (Cr's)

Embolism of blood clot which has broken loose from its site of formation and is blocking a blood vessel.

THROMBOGENESIS   (Cr's)

Development of a thrombus.

THROMBOSIS   (Cr's)

Coagulation of blood in the circulatory system, forming a clot that obstructs circulation.

THROUGH OFFICIAL CHANNELS   (PA)

Through the hands of the superior officers in the chain of command.

THREE MILE LIMIT   (L)

An imaginary boundary, three miles from a nation's shoreline, marking the limit of control over ocean waters.

TIME   (L)

A measure of duration, e.g., days, months, or years. The particular minute, hour, or day, when an act is done, or a crime committed.

TIPSTAFF (L)

An English, and occasionally an American, officer of a court, whose duty it is to arrest persons guilty of contempt, and to take charge of prisoners.

TITHING (L)

Formerly, an English subdivision containing ten families, forming part of a hundred.

TITRATION (Cr's)

The analytical operation of adding a reagent until a reaction is complete, and then measuring the volume so added.

TOLL (L)

A payment for passage, e.g., over a road or ferry. To stop, delay, or suspend, e.g., the running of the statute of limitations. To bar, or take away, e.g., a writ of entry.

TOOL CONTROL (Cor)

Check system with receipts for the tools available in the prison shop and a classification system for differential storage of tools.

TORT (L)

Various, legally recognized, private injuries or wrongs, not arising as the result of a breach of contract.

TORTFEASOR (L)

One who commits a tort (q.v.); a wrongdoer; a trespasser.

TORTIOUS (L)

Wrongful; descriptive of an act which generates a tort (q.v.).

TORTURE (L)

The act of intentionally inflicting protracted bodily pain, or the pain produced thereby.

TOTAL DISABILITY (L)

In life insurance policies, such physical inability as will render the insured unable to perform all substantial and material acts, necessary to the prosecution of his business or occupation, in the customary or usual manner.

TO WIT (L)

To know; that is to say; namely.

TOWN (L)

A civil division less than a county; a small collection of houses; a village. Occasionally defined by various state statutes concerning municipal corporations.

TOWNSHIP (L)

A division of federal public lands into tracts of six miles square, containing thirty-six sections (q.v.), of six hundred and forty acres each. In some jurisdictions, a subdivision of a county.

TOXICOLOGY (Cr's)

The science of poisons; their effects, antidotes and recognition.

TRACHEOBRONCHIAL TREE (Cr's)

Pertaining to the airway and its major branches.

TRACING EVIDENCE (Cr's)

Articles which assist in locating a suspect, e.g., laundry marks.

TRAFFIC-ACCIDENT INVESTIGATION (PA)

The application of investigative methods and principles to the field of traffic accidents.

TRAFFIC CONTROL (PA)

The prevention of accidents and congestion.

TRAFFIC DIRECTION (PA)

The directing of drivers and pedestrian relative to how and where they may or may not move or stand at a particular place, especially during periods of congestion or in emergencies, and securing their compliance with the instructions.

TRAFFIC ENGINEERING (PA)

One of the police traffic-control tools. The design of roadway facilities to lessen frequency of accidents and amount of congestion thus facilitating safe, rapid movement.

TRAFFIC LAW ENFORCEMENT (PA)

All acts or operations relative to prevention of traffic law violations; observing, detecting, and taking appropriate action against motorists and pedestrians who commit violations.

TRAFFIC RECORDS (PA)

Records which enable the police to evaluate accomplishments by individuals and organization units to appraise the effectiveness of their traffic-control program.

TRAINING SCHOOL (Cor)

Juvenile institutions for long-term commitment and change of relatively delinquent youths into law abiding citizens.

TRAJECTORY (Cr's)

The curve which a bullet describes in flight relative to its momentum and gravitational force.

TRANSCRIPT (L)

A copy, especially an official copy.

TRANSFER (L)

To pass from one person to another; to convey.

TRANSFER OF RESPONSIBILITY FOR THE PERFORMANCE OF CERTAIN ACTIVITIES (PA)

Under some circumstances there is an actual part-time transfer of responsibility for and conduct of certain activities from one element to another. If, for example, a particular activity must be carried on around-the-clock that would occupy only a portion of one person's time during one watch, responsibility for it may be transferred to another element for the period of that watch, and the activity will be performed by the receiving element.

TRANSPORTATION (L)

Various means of moving persons or goods from one place to another. The punishment of sending a convicted criminal beyond the seas, or into exile.

TRANSPORTATION THIEF (Cr'y)

A criminal who steals automobiles for use in the commission of other crimes, e.g., robberies. Also, intoxicated persons and others who find themselves in need of transportation and steal an automobile.

TRANSVESTISM (Cr'y, L)

Adopting the dress, manner, and sometimes the sexual role of the opposite sex. The male transvestite supposedly feels inwardly that nature has made a mistake and that he is really a woman, and vice versa.

TRAUMA, OR TRAUMATIC INJURY (L)

A physical hurt, or injury, produced by violence.

TRAVERSE (L)

In older forms of pleading, denial of some matter of fact alleged. A traverse is either general, denying all that was alleged in the last pleading of the adverse party, or special, meeting the exact words of that portion of the pleading which it is intended to deny.

TREASON (L)

A federal crime involving the provision of aid and comfort to an enemy, or levying war on the United States. Conviction necessitates testimony of two witnesses to the same overt act, or confession in open court (U.S. Const. Art. III, Sec. III).

TREASURER OF THE UNITED STATES (L)

A federal officer whose duty is to receive and keep the moneys of the United States; to disburse them only on warrants drawn by the Secretary of the Treasury, and countersigned by the proper officer; to take receipts, and to keep and render accurate accounts to the comptroller.

TREATMENT, CORRECTIONAL (Cor)

Institutional programs which bring socializing influences to bear on the inmate population.

TREATY (L)

A written agreement between nations. Relating to the United States, it may be made by the President, by and with the advice and consent of the Senate, two-thirds of those present concurring. U.S. Const., Art. II, Sec. II.

TRESPASS (L)

Any transgression of the law, less than treason, felony, or misprision of either. Especially, trespass "quare clausum fregit," i.e., entry on another's close, or land without lawful authority. (3) Trespass on the case, or Case, is a general name for torts which formerly had no special writ or remedy.

TRESPASSER (L)

A person who commits a trespass (q.v.).

See: Trespass.

TRESPASSER AB INITIO (L)

In some jurisdictions, a person who, having lawfully entered, does something he is not entitled to do; his trespass or wrong then relates back, and he is a trespasser from the beginning.

TRIAL (L)

The examination of the issues in a civil or criminal lawsuit by an authorized tribunal; the presentation and decision of the issues of law or fact in an action. It may be by a judge or judges, with or without a jury (q.v.).

TRIAL BY COURT (L)

A judicial tribunal having original jurisdiction or power to hear and decide cases or controversies in the first instance.

TRIAL BY JURY (L)

A trial in which issues of fact are determined by the verdict of a jury of twelve persons duly selected, impaneled, and sworn.

TRIBADISM (Cr'y)

Mutual friction between women; a common and most effective method of achieving sexual excitement among female homosexuals.

TRIBUNAL (L)

A court. The place in which a session of court is held.

TRICUSPID VALVE (Cr's)

Valve between the right chambers of the heart.

TRIGGER PULL (Cr's)

The applied force necessary to release a firearm's firing mechanism. Referred to as a one-pound pull or two-pound pull, i.e., requiring a force of one or two pounds to release the trigger.

TRIORS, OR TRIERS (L)

In some jurisdictions, persons appointed by the court to decide on challenges (q.v.) to a jury.

TROVER, OR TROVER AND CONVERSION (L)

Formerly, a special form of trespass (q.v.) on the case, based on the finding (actual or fictitious) by the defendant of goods lost by the plaintiff.

TRUANCY (Cr'y, L)

The offense of a child absenting himself from school without acceptable excuse.

TRUE BILL (L)

An indictment or bill or indictment; the endorsement which the grand jury (q.v.) makes upon a bill of indictment when, having heard the evidence, they are satisfied there is a prima facie case against the accused.

TRUE OWNER   (L)

One who, at the time of the taking, had superior right of possession, i.e., the organization as against the custodian of the funds or as against a member; the estate as against a trustee.

TRUST   (L)

A right of property, real or personal, held by one party for the benefit of another.

TURPIS CAUSA   (L)

A base or immoral consideration, on which no contract or lawsuit can be founded.

TUTOR   (L)

The guardian (q.v.) of an infant.

TWELVE TABLES   (L)

The earliest codification (451--450, B.C.) of Roman law; this codification influenced Roman law for centuries. The Justinian Code of the fifth century A.D. was composed of much of the Twelve Tables.

TWIN LOOPS, FINGERPRINTS   (Cr's)

Two loops opening at different sides.

TWIST   (Cr's)

The angle of pitch or rate of turning of rifling in a pistol or rifle barrel.

TWO–ISSUE RULE   (L)

In some jurisdictions, if a case presents two separate issues, and if one issue, complete in itself as a cause of action or defense, is submitted to the jury free from error, and the jury returns a general verdict and there is nothing to indicate upon which issue the general verdict is grounded, the issue which presents the claimed error may be disregarded. This rule does not apply where one of the issues submitted to the jury is entirely unsupported by the evidence.

TWO–WAY MIRROR   (Cr's, PA)

A plain mirror on one side which permits a person on the other side to see through unobserved.

TYPE LINES, FINGERPRINTS   (Cr's)

The innermost ridges which start as parallel lines, diverge, and bound the pattern area, defining the working area of classification. They may not be continuous and may even be absent.

TYPOLOGY   (PA, Cr'y)

Classification scheme based on types.

UBI JUS, IBI REMEDIUM   (L)
Where there is a right, there is a remedy.

UBI JUS INCERTUM, IBI JUS NULLUM   (L)
Where the law is uncertain, there is no law.

**UBI LEX SPECIALIS, ET RATIO EJUS GENERALIS, GENERA-
.LITER ACCIPIENDA EST   (L)**
Where the law is special and the reason of it is general, it ought
to be taken as being general.

**UBI NON EST PRINCIPALIS, NON POTEST ESSE ACCESSORIUS
(L)**
Where there is no principal there can be no accessory.

ULTIMATE FACTS   (L)
The final, resulting certainty reached, by logical reasoning, from
the detailed, probative facts. Distinguished from evidence and
legal conclusions.

ULTIMATUM   (L)
A final offer, especially by either of the parties in a diplomatic
negotiation.

ULTRA VIRES   (L)
Beyond, outside of, in excess of powers.

UMPIRE   (L)
A referee; one who decides a question in dispute; especially one
chosen by arbitrators to finally determine a point on which they
are unable to agree.

UNCERTAINTY   (L)
Vagueness, indefiniteness. A gift by will is void for uncertainty,
if it is impossible to ascertain the testator's intention with regard to it.

UNCRIMPED   (Cr's)
Ammunition that is not crimped.

UNDEVELOPED LEADS   (Cr's)
A possible source of pertinent information which appears
necessary in bringing the investigation to a logical conclusion,
but which has not been researched.

UNDISCLOSED PRINCIPAL   (L)
One whose agent acts without disclosing the fact of his agency,
and without the third party's knowledge of the existence of the
principal.

UNDUE INFLUENCE   (L)
Improper persuasion resulting in an act otherwise than according to one's free will.

UNIDENTIFIED PERSON   (Cr's)
One physically or mentally affected to a degree or in a manner
requiring attention by police and who cannot be readily identified, or whose friends or relatives cannot be immediately located.

UNIFORM ACTS, OR UNIFORM LAWS   (L)
Various proposals for legislation to be consistently adopted by
all of the legislatures of the states of the United States, made
by the National Conference of Commissioners on Uniform
State Laws.
UNIFORM CODE OF MILITARY JUSTICE   (L)
Chapter 47 of an act to revise, codify and enact into law, titles
10 and 32 of the United States Code, concerning punishment
for offenses committed by military personnel.
UNIFORM CRIME REPORTS   (PA)
Bulletins issued by the Federal Bureau of Investigation containing statistical data on crime systematically and regularly collected from police agencies all over the United States. These reports are used as a source for the study of comparative rates of
crime among various regions and cities of the U.S.
UNINSURED MOTORIST   (L)
The owner or operator of an uninsured motor vehicle, of doubtful financial responsibility, or whose identity cannot be determined, who has caused personal injury or death resulting from
ownership, maintenance or use of a motor vehicle.
UNITED STATES COURT OF APPEALS   (L)
Formerly, Circuit Court of Appeals, United States courts of
any of eleven circuits or judicial divisions of the United States,
including the District of Columbia, second in rank to the Supreme Court and having appellate jurisdiction over decisions of
U.S. District courts, except where a direct review may be had by
the Supreme Court.
UNITED STATES MAGISTRATES   (L)
Judicial officers appointed by United States District courts to
perform the duties formerly performed by United States Commissioners (q.v.) and to render assistance to the Court, e.g., by
serving as special masters in civil actions, conducting pretrial
or discovery proceedings, and preliminary review of applications
for post-trial relief made by individuals convicted of criminal
offenses.
UNITED STATES OF AMERICA   (L)
The continguous states bounded on the North by Canada and
the Great Lakes, and on the south by Mexico and the Gulf of
Mexico, and extending from the Atlantic to the Pacific Ocean,
and the states of Alaska and Hawaii; united under one national
government, having a national constitution adopted in 1787,
and amended from time to time since. At present there are
50 states.
UNITY   (L)
Oneness; agreement in particulars.

UNIVERSAL (L)

Unlimited; without exception; relating to the whole, or all.

UNLAWFUL (L)

Contrary to law; illegal.

UNLAWFUL ASSEMBLY (L)

A gathering of three or more persons intent on committing a crime by force. A generic term comprehending, among other things, riot and affray. Often defined by various state statutes.

UNMARKED CAR (PA)

A vehicle which is not marked to identify it as belonging to a law enforcement agency.

UN NE DOIT PRISE ADVANTAGE DE SON TORT DEMESNE (L)

One ought not to take advantage of his own wrong.

UNSOUND MIND (L)

A generic term for a defective, impaired or diseased intellect, including lunacy and idiocy. Often defined by various state statutes.

UNWRITTEN LAW (L)

All that portion of the law, observed and administered in the courts, not enacted or promulgated in the form of a statute or ordinance, including unenacted portions of the common law, general and particular customs having the force of law, and rules, principles, and maxims established by judicial precedents or successive like decisions of the courts. The supposed rule that murder of the paramour or seducer of one's wife or daughter, respectively, is legally excusable.

USAGE (L)

Practice long continued.

USURPATION (L)

The taking and holding of property, or public office, without right.

USURY (L)

An unconscionable or exorbitant rate of interest; an excessive and illegal requirement of compensation for forbearance on a debt (interest).

UTERINE (L)

Born of the same mother.

UTTER (L)

To offer; to publish; to attempt to pass a forged document or counterfeit coin as genuine.

VACANT (L)

Empty; not occupied.

VACATION (L)

The period between one term of court and another.

VACUOLE (Cr's)

Space or cavity in the protoplasm of a cell.

VAGABOND, OR VAGRANT (L)

A wanderer; an idle person who, being able to maintain himself by lawful labor, either refuses to work, or resorts to unlawful practices, e.g., begging, to gain a living.

VALSALVA MANEUVER (Cr's)

Increase of the pressure within the lungs by forcible exhalation against a closed glottis.

VALUER (L)

One who appraises property.

VALVULAR LESION (Cr's)

Disease of a heart's valve or valves.

VARIABLE CHOKE (Cr's)

An adjustable device attached to the muzzle of a shotgun to control the pattern of the shot.

VARIANCE (L)

Under some codes of civil practice, a disagreement between successive pleadings by the same party. A disagreement between statements in pleadings and the evidence adduced in proof thereof.

VASA VASORUM (Cr's)

Small nutrient blood vessels which supply the walls of larger blood vessels.

VASOCONSTRICTION (Cr's)

Constriction of the blood vessels.

VASODILATATION (Cr's)

Dilatation of the blood vessels.

VEHICLE (L)

Every contrivance or means capable of transportation on land, water, or in the air. Occasionally defined by various state and federal statutes.

VEIN (Cr's)

A blood vessel that transports blood toward the heart.

VELOCITY (Cr's)

The speed of a projectile in flight, usually measured in feet-per-second.

VENA CAVA (Cr's)

Largest vein in the body by which blood is returned to the heart.

VENIRE FACIAS (L)

A writ to the sheriff to summon a jury.

VENIRE FACIAS AD RESPONDENDUM (L)

A writ of summons to answer an indictment for misdemeanor.

VENIRE FACIAS DE NOVO (L)

A writ to summon a jury for a new trial.

VENTILATED RIB (Cr's)

A raised usually matted, sighting surface separated from the barrel so as to eliminate heat waves in the line of sight.

VENTRICULAR FIBRILLATION (Cr's)

Incoordinated, extremely irregular heart beat.

VENUE OR VISNE, CHANGE OF (L)

The neighborhood; the county in which a particular lawsuit should be tried; the county from which the jury is taken for the trial of a lawsuit. Often regulated by various state and federal statutes. Change of venue: the sending of a lawsuit to be tried before a jury of another community, e.g., when circumstances render it impossible to have an impartial trial in the county where the cause of action arose.

VERBA ITA SUNT INTELLIGENDA, UT RES MAGIC VALEAT QUAM PEREAT (L)

Words are to be so understood that the object may be carried out rather than fail.

VERBAL (L)

By word of mouth, oral (q.v.).

VERDICT (L)

Latin; "veredictum"; a true declaration. In practice; the formal and unanimous decision or finding made by a jury, impaneled and sworn for trial of a cause, and reported to the court (and accepted by it), upon matters or questions duly submitted upon the trial. A declaration of truth as to matters of fact submitted to the jury. The definitive answer given by a jury concerning matters of fact committed to the jury for deliberation and determination.

VERDICT, ADVERSE (L)

Where a party, appealing from an allowance of damages by commissioners, recovers a verdict in his favor, but for a less amount of damages than had been originally allowed, such verdict is "adverse" to him, within the meaning of his undertaking to pay costs if the verdict should be adverse to him.

VERDICT, CHANCE (L)

A verdict determined by hazard or lot; not by deliberate understanding and agreement.

VERDICT, COMPROMISE (L)

One the result of improper compromise of vital principles, not by justifiable concession to views.

VERDICT CONTRARY TO LAW (L)

A verdict contrary to the principles of law as applied to facts the jury as called upon to try and to principles of law governing the cause.

VERDICT, FALSE (L)

One opposed to the principles of right and justice; an untrue verdict.

VERDICT OF NOT GUILTY (L)

A verdict of "not proven" in a particular trial; not a verdict of innocence, hence, not conclusive against the state in favor of a person other than the defendant actually acquitted.

VERIFICATION (L)

The affidavit of a party, e.g., in a court pleading, or of his agent or attorney, that certain statements of fact, e.g., the allegations of a pleading, are true.

VERITAS HABENDA EST IN JURATORE; JUSTITIA ET JUDICIUM IN JUDICE (L)

Truth is the thing that is needed and wanted in a juror, justice and judgement, in a judge.

VERITAS NIHIL VERETUR NISI ABSCONDI (L)

Truth fears nothing but concealment.

VERITAS NIMIUM ALTERCANDO AMITTITUR (L)

By too much altercation truth is lost.

VERTEX (Cr's)

Crown of the head.

VERTIGO (Cr's)

Dizziness.

VETO (L)

Refusal of an executive officer, whose assent is necessary to validate an act passed by a legislative body, to concur therein. The veto power is given to the President of the United States, U.S. Const., Art. I, Sec. VII, and to the governors of many of the states.

VEXATA QUAESTIO (L)

L., an undetermined point which has often been discussed.

VEXATIOUS (L)

Annoying; harassing; oppressive.

VEXATIOUS SUIT (L)

A lawsuit initiated without probable cause, to annoy or oppress.

VIA (L)

By way of.

VIABILITY (L)

Capability of living after birth.

VIABLE INFANT (L)

An infant fulfilling the criteria of normal formation and an intrauterine, seven month gestation period.

VICARIOUS LIABILITY (L)

The imputation of liability upon one person for the actions of another.

VICE (Cr'y, PA)

Disapproved behavior violating an important social norm within society; illegal activities considered personally or socially harmful, e.g., prostitution, gambling, and narcotic traffic.

VICE CONTROL (PA)

Enforcement of statutes relative to prostitution, obscenity, and illegal liquor, gambling and narcotics.

VICE PRESIDENT OF THE UNITED STATES (L)

The second officer in point of rank in the United States. He is elected at the same time and for the same term as the president. He is president of the Senate, but has no vote unless the Senate is equally divided. In case of the removal from office, death, resignation, or inability of the President, the duties of the President devolve on the Vice–President.

VICE AREA (Cr'y)

An urban area where there is a concentration of prostitutes, drug addicts, alcoholics, and other social deviants. It is an area of physical deterioration and is often part of a zone in transition. It is also characterized by a high crime rate, a lack of community organization, a high rate of personal disorganization, and the prevalence of a wide variety of social problems. (2) An area in which vice activities take place.

VICE VERSA (L)

Reversing the order; on the contrary.

VICINAGE (L)

Neighborhood; proximity.

VICTIMLESS CRIMES (Cr'y, L)

Crime without an official victim, such as prostitution or homosexuality.

VIDUITY (L)

Widowhood.

VI ET ARMIS (L)

With force and arms.

VIEW (L)

An inspection of property mentioned in evidence in a trial, or of a site where a crime has been committed, by the jury or persons called viewers, under court order.

VIGILANTE   (Cr'y, PA)
>A member of a group which undertakes to enforce the law and/
or maintain morals, without legal authority for such actions.

VIOLATION   (L)
>An act in contravention of statutory provisions or administrative
regulations. An act contrary to another's right, committed
with force. A rape.

VIOLENCE   (L)
>Illegal physical force used against private rights or public
liberty; assault or intimidation by display of force.

VIRTUAL IMAGE   (Cr's)
>In image that cannot be seen directly. It can only be seen by a
viewer looking through a lens.

VISA   (L)
>Recognition by one nation of the validity of a passport issued
by another nation; concurrence by one nation in the request
implied by issuance of a passport by another nation.

VISCUS   (Cr's)
>Any large internal organ.

VISIBLE PRINTS, FINGERPRINTS   (Cr's)
>Deposits of visible substances or stains left by soiled fingers.
Blood and dirt are the most common substances.

VITAL STATISTICS   (L)
>Public records of births, diseases, marriages and deaths.

VOCATIONAL REHABILITATION ACT OF 1920   (Cor, L)
>Federal law authorizing creation of a federal vocational
rehabilitation agency to fund state vocational rehabilitation
programs for worthy persons with physical, emotional, and
personality disorders. An amendment provides for the
rehabilitation of persons handicapped by cultural, economic
and social disadvantages.

VOICE PRINT   (Cr's)
>A spectrographic record of the energy output produced by the
sound of words or sounds made by a person when speaking.

VOID   (L)
>Empty, having no legal force, ineffectual, unenforceable.

VOIDABLE   (L)
>Capable of being later annulled.

VOIR DIRE   (L)
>The preliminary examination of a prospective juror, to deter-
mine his or her qualifications to serve as a juror. Occasionally, preliminary examination of a witness to determine his or
her competency to speak the truth.

VOLSTEAD ACT (L)

The legislative act passed by Congress and later repealed, regulating traffic in intoxicating liquors under U.S. Const., Amend. XVIII.

VOLUNTARY (L)

Acting without compulsion; done by design.

VOLUNTARY MANSLAUGHTER (L)

An unlawful killing committed in the heat of sudden passion caused by adequate provocation even though there was intent to kill or commit great bodily harm.

VOLUNTAS IN DELICTIS, NON EXITUS SPECTATUR (L)

In crimes the intention, and not the consequence is looked to.

VOLUNTEER (L)

One who injects himself into affairs of no legal or moral concern to him, or which do not affect his interests. One who receives a gift, promise, or conveyance, without giving valuable consideration thereof. One who offers his services to his country in time of war.

VOYEUR (Cr'y)

"Looker" or "viewer." A "Peeping Tom." Voyeurism: the derivation of sexual excitement and satisfaction from viewing the genitalia or naked body of another.

WAD (Cr's)

A yielding material, usually felt, placed over the powder of a shot shell to contain the powder, separate it from the shot and control the gas blast.

WAGER (L)

A bet; a promise by a person to pay a sum of money to another in case a certain thing does or does not happen.

WAIFS (L)

(1) Goods found, but unclaimed. (2) Goods stolen, but waived or thrown away by the thief in his flight.

WAIVE (L)

To forego; to decline to take advantage of, e.g., a legal right or an omission or irregularity.

WAIVER (L)

A positive act by which a legal right is relinquished.

WALKING LINE (Cr's)

An imaginary line which, in normal and ideal walking, fuses with the direction line and runs along the inner sides of both heelprints. The walking line, however, is often irregular, varying with each step because of the manner of putting down the foot.

WALKING PICTURE (Cr's)

The whole ensemble of footprints left by the walker.

WALNUT STREET JAIL (Cr'y)

A Pennsylvania jail established in 1790. It was the first use of separate facilities for men and women. Cells were constructed to provide solitary confinement in order to eliminate moral contamination from other prisoners and to force the prisoner to meditate on the evil of his ways.

WANTON MISCONDUCT (L)

Such behavior as manifests a disposition to perversity under such circumstances and conditions that the party doing the act, or failing to act, is conscious that his conduct will, in all common probability, result in injury.

WARD (L)

An infant under guardianship (q.v.). A subdivision of a city, borough, county, or parish for election purposes.

WARDEN (L, Cor)

A guardian or keeper; the title given to various public officers who perform such functions as part of their official duties.
Most commonly referring to the highest official in a prison.

WARD OF THE COURT (L)

An infant or juvenile under protection of the court, e.g., a juvenile court or a court of equity.
The condition of a person who is a ward (q.v.).

WAREHOUSE (L)

A place for receiving and storing of goods and merchandise for hire.

WARRANT (L)

A written order issued by a magistrate or court directing an officer to make an arrest or conduct searches or seizures. Constitutional restrictions prevent issuance of a search warrant except for good cause, duly certified, and warrant must describe the place to be searched and the person or property to be seized.

WARRANT OF ATTORNEY (L)

In some jurisdictions, written authority to an attorney, by which it is intended that a judgment shall be entered, authorizing the attorney to appear on behalf of the person giving the authority and to confess judgment.

WATCH (SHIFT) (PA)

(1) A time division of the day for purposes of assignment. Shifts may be consecutive eight-hour periods, or they may overlap to meet unusual or peak loads. (2) A body of police officers on duty at night; ward, being chiefly applied to those on duty by day.

WAVE LENGTH (Cr's)

The distance between crests of adjacent waves.

WAY (L)

(1) A passage. (2) Right of passage, public or private; those which are public being usually called highways. A private way, or right of way, may be founded on a grant, license, or prescription, being either an easement or customary right.

WEAPON (L)

Various objects used, or intended to be used, as an instrument for fighting. Often defined by various state statutes.

WEIGHT (Cr's)

A property of matter that depends both on the mass of a substance and the effects of gravity on that mass.

WEIGHT OF EVIDENCE (L)

The balance of the preponderance of evidence; the inclination of the greater amount of credible evidence, offered in a trial, to support one side of the issue rather than the other.

WELFARE OF CHILD (L)

Under statutes requiring, in awarding custody of a minor, that the "welfare of the child" be the guide; parents need only be honest and respectable, with disposition and capacity to maintain and educate the child. The "welfare of a child," is gauged by the father's means and station in life and does not contemplate that the child be taken from the father because another can give the child more in a material way.

WERGILD (L)

Formerly, a fine imposed for homicide or grave injury.

WHEREAS (L)

In view of the following facts; a word which introduces a recital of a fact.

WHITE–COLLAR CRIME (Cr'y)

Violations of criminal law by members of the upper socio-economic classes, perpetrated in connection with their occupations.

WHITE–COLLAR OFFENDER (Cr'y)

One who engages in "sharp" business practices, pricefixing, anti-trust violations and similar activities barely within the criminal law, but occasionally lacking enough discretion that the manipulators are convicted of some offenses.

WHITE SLAVERY (L)

The interstate transportation of females for immoral purposes.

WHORLS, FINGERPRINTS (Cr's)

All patterns with two deltas or too irregular in form to classify.

WIFE (L)

A woman who has a husband.

WILL, CRIMINAL LAW (L)

The power of the mind which directs the action of a man.

WILLFUL, OR WILFUL (L)

Intentional; deliberate.

WINDAGE (Cr's)

The horizontal allowance made in sight alignment for bullet drift.

WINDING UP (L)

The process of liquidation.

WIRETAPPING (L, PA)

Clandestine listening in to telephonic and other communications by wire.

WITHDRAWAL (Cr'y)

A psychological reaction, in which a person attempts to adjust to a frustrating situation by avoiding it. People may withdraw from frustrating social situations by refusing to participate actively in group activities and by exhibiting noncooperative attitudes. Severe withdrawal may include the avoidance of all social interaction, the heavy use of alcohol or drugs, or other radical behavior.

WITHDRAWAL OF CHARGES (L)

Failure to prosecute by the party preferring charges — distinguished from dismissal, which is determination of the invalidity of the charges by the tribunal hearing them.

WITHDRAWAL OF JUROR (L)

Removal of a member of a trial jury from the jury box, to put an end to the proceedings.

WITNESS (L)

One who, being present, personally sees or perceives a thing; a beholder, spectator, or eyewitness. One who testifies to what he has seen, heard, or otherwise observed.

WOBBLE (Cr's)

The unsteady rotation or spin of a bullet; usually caused by insufficient twist in the rifle barrel.

WORK RELEASE (Cor)

A program in which persons go from the institution into the community and work at civilian jobs, returning to the institution at night.

WORK–STUDY (Cor)

A program similar to work release. Here, inmates attend high schools, vocational and technical schools, junior colleges or colleges.

WORLD COURT (L)

An international court, established by the League of Nations, at the Hague in the Netherlands. It opened on December 16, 1920, and closed in October 1945. In April 1946, the United Nations established the International Court of Justice at the Hague.

WRIT (L)

A formal written order, issuing from a court or tribunal having judicial authority, commanding an individual or individuals identified in the order to do, or abstain from doing, some specified act.

See also: Ca'pias.

WRIT IN AID (L)

A court order or process issued after a writ of execution has failed.

WRITING, OR WRITTEN (L)

Any intentional reduction of communications to tangible form; e.g., printing, typewriting.

WRIT OF ERROR (L)

An original writ, directing an inferior court to send the record of proceedings before it to a superior court for review. Analogous to an appeal.

WRIT OF HABEAS CORPUS (L)

The usual remedy for a person deprived of his liberty. Its purpose is to test the legality of the restraints on a person's liberty.

WRIT OF PROHIBITION   (L)
An order, issued by a superior court to a court of inferior grade, demanding that the latter refrain from exercising jurisdiction over some specific suit then before it.

WRONG   (L)
The infringement of a right.

WRONGFUL ACT   (L)
Any act which, in ordinary course, will infringe upon the rights of another to his damage, unless done in the exercise of an equal or superior right.

X CHROMOSOME   (Cr'y)

The female sex chromosome.

X RAY   (Cr's)

A high energy short wave-length form of electromagnetic radiation.

Y CHROMOSOME (Cr'y)

The male sex chromosome.

YEAR (L)

The period during one complete revolution of the earth around the sun; twelve calendar months; three hundred and sixty-five days.

YEARBOOKS (L)

Annual reports of cases in a regular series from the time of King Edward II to Henry VIII.

YOUTH INVOLVEMENT (Cr'y, Cor)

A technique to motivate youth or to neutralize their opposition to program goals.

ZONE IN TRANSITION   (Cr'y)
> An area immediately surrounding the central business district of a large city that is being invaded by business and industrial expansion. This is the area of the slums.

ZONING   (L)
> The division of a city or county into separate areas, and the application to each area of regulations limiting the various purposes to which the land and buildings therein may be devoted.

ZONE SEARCH   (PA)
> A method of searching a crime scene where the area to be searched is divided into sectors and each one is carefully examined.

KEY TO
ABBREVIATIONS

Parenthetical abbreviations following each term denote the area of criminal justice from which the term is derived.

Cor:	Corrections
Cr's:	Criminalistics
Cr'y:	Criminology
L:	Law
PA:	Police Administration